T0367513

THE MOTIVATIONAL SPEAKER

The Game Planner

Tilawan

authorHOUSE®

AuthorHouse™
1663 Liberty Drive
Bloomington, IN 47403
www.authorhouse.com
Phone: 1-800-839-8640

Published by AuthorHouse   07/12/2012

ISBN: 978-1-4685-8595-7 (sc)
ISBN: 978-1-4685-8596-4 (hc)
ISBN: 978-1-4685-8597-1 (e)

Dedication

This book is dedicated to all the people who experienced tremendous changes by imbibing the teachings of the motivational speaker into their lives.

. . . . In Memory

Of my dear mother, Mrs. Alice Tilawan (1938-2010)

About The Author

Suleiman Saidu Tilawan, known to friends by his initials, SST is the writer of the best-selling motivational book on power intriques; *The Laws of the Bosses*.

"... . covet earnestly the best gifts"

Prologue

Beginning of My Story

My name is Sawuntungo Sasukito Talungo. However, my friends find it hard to pronounce and so prefer to call me by my initials, SST. I understand their difficulties, because sometimes I have problems pronouncing it myself. All the same, I have long accepted this convoluted mixture of African and Asian intones and see it as the consequences of a mixed heritage.

This book is not an autobiography rather it is a recollection of several strange and interesting happenings that revolve round me in the city of Lagos in Nigeria when I relocated from Abuja, the nation's capital, to Lagos the commercial city in 2009.

On arrival in Lagos, I moved in with a friend at his home located at the highbrow district of Ikeja in the heartland of Lagos. It is the city that its inhabitants prefer to call the commercial capital of Nigeria ever since it lost its status as the nation's capital. Lagos is a coastal city and was the nation's political administrative capital at independence. It retained the status of being the centre of administration for over 3 decades, before losing it to the city of Abuja that is located in the centre of the country. Unlike Lagos, Abuja was able to align geography with politics.

When Lagos was the nation's capital, it attracted great commercial and economic privileges. In addition, being located at the coast and blessed with a rapidly growing population, it was not hard for it to quickly evolve to a big commercial city.

When the seat of government was moved from Lagos to the city of Abuja, it was however, realised that moving the commercial assets wasn't going to be that easy, and so Lagos was left to retain its commercial status.

Lagos is a bustling and highly congested city. It represents both what is good and bad about Nigeria. It is said that all sections of Nigeria and indeed West Africa, and maybe even a large part of Africa, are fully represented in Lagos; the city that started as a habitat of a few fishermen.

From its humble beginning, the city has indeed grown to quite a big commercial centre, having large industries and shopping outlets straddling its whole length. And being a mega city, the most populous city in Africa after Cairo in Egypt, Lagos is indeed a very interesting place to be.

I promised not go into discussions of my background, and I intend to keep it as such; so as not to bring up unnecessarily details. This is not an autobiography but a comprehensive recollection of the challenges of a young sojourner in a complex city.

Discussing only a little from my early years, I would like to say that after serving in the army for about five years, I decided to take a bow and pick up a civilian job in Abuja, the capital of Nigeria. Many were surprised at my leaving the military in preference to a civilian job. Serving in the army is quite an interesting job in Nigeria. It is a job that is well sought after, maybe for no more reason than Nigerians love for violating laws, and preferring nothing more than being in a profession that guarantees them greater impunity to doing that. It was obviously the reason that made some of my friends to wonder aloud why I abandoned the secured fortress of the military for the vulnerable sections of civilian life.

Well, with glittering medals and shiny boots, I had enough of the army after just being there for five years. And choosing what seemed to be against the good advice of close friends, I left the army to secure a job at a civil security firm in Abuja.

The firm was one out of several that were springing up in every part of the country to fill the vacuum created by corruption and inefficiency in the police force.

After a short stint working at the head office in Abuja, I was transferred to Lagos, where my security firm was opening a new branch to cash on the increasing demand for private security operators in the mega city.

This book is about my experiences in Lagos, and on how I was drawn to its deceitful life style in order to survive. It is said that everybody in Lagos is an 'actor'. You just can't trust anyone, as most were out living a make believe life aimed at deceiving one another. In this book, I took out accounts of different challenging situations that I went through in Lagos, and presented them in interesting contexts.

On coming to Lagos, I found myself overwhelmingly enveloped by the deceitful life of the city, and before I knew it, I was becoming an 'actor' myself. But all these stopped when I had a powerful dream, in which I saw myself being cautioned and empowered by the Almighty to impact my skills positively on the lives of millions of people who were struggling to survive in the city. It was the day I knew, I was imparted with the skills of inspiration. From that day on, my life experienced a complete transformation. I had a rethink on how I went about life. Later, I got another job with Static FM 111. At first, I combined both jobs. I started a radio show known as the Motivation Dance Club, with me posing as DJ SST. The radio programme was a motivational talk show targeted at positively inspiring the people of Lagos to overcoming difficult challenges in their lives. I was able to do that by drawing references from life teaching lessons, and experiences of other people that I read as narratives to encourage my listeners.

This book is really about the power of inspiration through motivational talks on the lives of individuals.

The accounts as contained in this book were compiled from my personal encounters, and lessons taken from other people's experiences. In the arrangement of my presentations on the show, I called on listeners to dance on the floor of the motivation dance club with their problems while waiting for an inspiring response from the DJ SST, who puts on the music (inspiring talks) that suit their dance. In reality, it was just a motivational talk show.

However, it was not too long before strange things started happening to me at Static FM, as my life got entangled in a spectre of treachery, intrigue, and suspense that culminated in murder and high level betrayal. I was overshadowed by events that were far beyond what I would ever have imagined when I decided to feature as a motivational speaker.

COMING TO LAGOS

CHAPTER ONE

Coming To Lagos

My Meeting with Lagos Scammers

The first problem you would encounter as a person coming to the city of Lagos is how to get a suitable accommodation in the overcrowded city. I'm talking of someone like me who belongs to the working class. The only means available to getting an accommodation in Lagos is a craftily woven racketeer operated by the mafias. One can't get a living place to rent except the person goes through any of the several licensed real estate agents who operate under the protection of the powerful mafias that front as a union. In reality, it is just a criminal outfit designed to stop you from getting a house on your own.

Even when you are ready to follow this established means, the mafias, through its agents will ensure that you would be lucky to get a place to rent in a month or two, while all the time pushing you to raise the agent fee. And that is if you are lucky not to fall into one of the traps of a group of these agents that go into fleecing unsuspecting newcomers through ingenious scams. The group is known as the scammers.

A scammer often comes along as the nice looking operator. Sometimes, he could come in a cunning appearance or as an outright crook.

I was unlucky to meet all the three in one. When I relocated to Lagos, I was forced to move in with a friend while looking for a place of mine. And because of the discomfort of this arrangement, I had it in mind not to stay with him for long. I just needed enough time before securing an accommodation for myself. Sharing an accommodation or squatting, as it is popularly called, is not a pleasant experience in Lagos. In the first place, you always find yourself getting in the way of your host, which would be very often because you are most likely to squat with someone trying to make enough space for himself in a one bedroom apartment. I believe you can understand the reason I was so eager to move to a place of my own. If not for anything, at least I needed a place for my privacy. You know what I mean?

The only way to get an accommodation in Lagos, as I said in the beginning, was to go through an estate agent. And there were many of these agents scattered all over the city. Looking for these agents was not hard anymore as we are in the internet age. So I went to check them up on the internet.

While going through several adverts of various estate firms on the internet, I came across an advert with interesting details by a private firm that immediately drew my attention. On the firm's web page was the written advert which reads; Kehind*e Taiwo Estate Agents. We are the most reputable and sought after estate agents in Lagos! For your fastest way to an affordable, comfortable and stress—free accommodation anywhere In Lagos, contact us at Adeniji Jones No6 Ikeja, or on . . .* a personal phone number.

I was particularly elated about this one. It wasn't the name that got me thrilled but rather it was the location of the agent's office. I was excited with its proximity to where I stay. The office was a stone throw from my friend's house, where I was entering my second week of unceremonious squatting. If you have experienced the traffic situation in Lagos, you will understand why proximity often overrides all other considerations in choosing the business to do or where to live.

I quickly took the number and dialled. A voice sprinkled with a tint of British accent answered almost as soon as it rang. It was so fast that one would think the person was standing by for the call!

"Hello, this is Kehinde and associates, reputable estate agents." He was speaking in such a low tone that if I had not taken the precaution of straining the handset to my ears, I won't have heard him.

You would think I called up a cultured receptionist to book a room at the Sheraton! The voice was too sleekly to be for just an estate agent. This guy should be in the hospitality business! Well, anyway, advertising a house for rent in a city, and opening a room for hire in a motel, sounds alike, doesn't it? Is all about hospitality, right?

I quickly replied "Good morning, sir, I am Mr. Ta . . . well, anyway just call me SST, that's my initials. Most people are more comfortable with it!" I gave him my usual introductory pattern that always starts with an attempt to call the full name, and then abruptly stop to end with nothing but my initials.

You will do the same if you have a 'jaw-breaking' name like mine!

"Ok, Mr. SST; I'm alright with that. So, of what service can I be to you?" He inquired.

Wow! Such a nice guy! He said it in the most polite manner I've ever heard, at least since coming to Lagos. Maybe I'm in the right place! La la!

"Yeah, thanks. I just thought about moving to a new place, I'm kind of tired of my old duplex and need a change. We are not in this world to live forever you know, so why don't we move a little?" I tried a little humour to lighten the atmosphere before moving to the issue "I was going through your website and saw that you can help me with a good accommodation." I said it with the assurance of a man not in a hurry for an immediate solution.

You have to learn not to appear too desperate with these people or they will take you for a ride. Just let them think getting a new accommodation is not much of a problem to you, all you needed after all is a change of status and you are not necessarily desperate for a roof over your head. Above all, never say you are squatting, please!

"No problem, Mr. SST, this is my area of speciality. You can come to my office anytime. Do you have the address? When you are around, we can discuss the issue. When will it be okay with you?" He was speaking with the confidence of a professional who is conversant with his job.

When will it be okay with me? Can I get wings and fly now! But as I said, never appear to be in a hurry! I have been warned by my friend, Segun, when you show you are eager, you easily fall for a scam.

"Mmmhh let me see when I would be opportune. I have a tight schedule at my office you know, what about . . . . this evening?" I replied sharply.

I should have put it off a little, maybe a day or two? I shouldn't appear too desperate, as I said. But my brother, I was tired of squatting, the sooner the better, please!

The man took his time to reply, I could hear him chuckling at the other end. *This man was sure not taken in by my act. Surely, I was not the first person he met that gave him that 'I'm not in a hurry line!*

"Ok, Mr. SST, I will be at the office waiting for you, let's say you come by 4?" He offered, seeking my consent for an appointment. I replied that it was all right with me.

I was at the Adeniyi Jones Street address given to me by Kehinde at quarter past four. The Leopard Building where the office was located was conspicuous by the roadside. After inquiring where the Kehinde and Associates office was located in the building from a receptionist, I quickly climbed to the second floor. I could see the name boldly written in gold coloured italics on a metallic plate that was attached to the second door on the right "*Kehinde and Associates Estate Agents*" it reads. I knocked softly and opened the door.

I was expecting to find myself in a cute waiting room and facing a sweet talking secretary, before being ushered to the main office like one of those big business offices. Instead, I saw myself standing in a small stuffy room, looking into the eyes of a medium aged man sitting behind what seemed to be the only item of any good value in the office, a small mahogany table. A small rubber table tag was kept in front of him and on it was boldly written '*Kehinde Taiwo*'.

I shifted my neck around a little, sizing up the little office, Okay! I have seen the '*Kehinde Taiwo*'. But where are the associates? I thought this was supposed to be a firm? The man sitting behind the desk stood up and extended his hand to me across the table "Good day, I believe you are Mr. SST?" He said assuredly.

6

What? Was I the only one he was expecting for the day? No other client? I thought this was supposed to be one of those highly sought after estate agent offices that everyone was crowding over for an appointment! But look what I found for myself; a man in a small office, alone, and expecting only a single visitor!

I looked up and down the small office unable to hide my astonishment. I saw he was looking at me and waiting for me to speak. I quickly got hold of myself and managed a smile back.

I gave him my answer promptly but casually.

"Yes, I am, and I believe you must be, Mr Kehinde. I'm pleased to meet you, sir." I extended my hand to him cautiously. Apparently sensing my discomfort, he added "Oh! Don't mind my office, this is my little branch. My main company is at Victoria Island, but I love seeing my friends here. It is quieter." He said smiling.

Well, that explains some of it, only that I didn't remember reading of any main branch In Victoria Island on the firm's website! Please don't blame me for sounding a little too edgy. In Lagos, one easily gets suspicious when the signal stops fitting in with the information.

He offered me a small seat, facing him. I sat down slowly and carefully not to bend hard on the frail wooden chair. I was not that sure it would withstand any extra pressure. He was looking at me and rubbing his hands together and shaking a little in his seat, like a man that couldn't wait to stick his fingers into a barbecue!

"Well, well, Mr. SST, I'm happy to meet you. What can I get for you?" He asked. I looked round the little shabby office. I don't think I could squeeze anything greater than a bottle of coke here! I declined the offer. He didn't pressed me further, but rather continued with his talk "Mr SST, I should say you really are a lucky man. Something just came in an hour ago since we talked last on the phone. I think it would interest you." He said to me, smiling like a groom before a priest! *I, lucky? You can say that again! Whatever just let me get a place, mister!*

He was going through a small folder in his hands, from where he brought out a little coloured flier "Yes, here is something that might interest you. Elemo Estate has some things that might interest you, there's a three bedroom flat available for rent." He said, his eyes still fixed on the flier in his hands as if he was seeing it for the first time.

Three bedroom apartment? Mine! That will surely be on the high side! I won't need more than a bedroom or two!

I looked at him bending a little against the seat and shaking my head in a comfortable manner "Oh, no I need something smaller. You know how it is. I'm a very reserved person, you know. I like small spaces." I said smoothly, putting up a little bore look of a man not used to not getting his request. He looked at me regretfully "Oh . . ." He said, sounding obviously disappointed at my outright rejection of the offer.

But he wasn't through with the offers yet "Alright, I'm sure you will love this one. It is a two bedroom apartment with a terrace and goes for 500,000 per annum. And of course, you know, we will need a down payment for two years." He said, trying all he could to be convincing.

Yeah, something like that is alright with me.

"I would like that." I said. He looked at my face, finding it hard to hide his excitement. "Yeah, yeah, good, so good! But the house is still occupied; however the occupant will soon pack out. Let me check." He flipped through more pages a little, and looked up with a surprised smile, like an archaeologist that just hit treasure "Yes, that's good. He will leave at the end of the month and then you can move in, my friend." He said happily. I looked up and checked the calendar on the office wall. *End of the month? It's just 3, today! Well, no problem, I can manage till then.*

"It's okay with me." I said, with all the effort I could muster to hide the excitement in me, so as not to expose my desperation for a place to stay.

"That settles it, Mr. SST; you can meet me tomorrow at about this time. We can go to Victoria Island and check the house and also get to talk to the occupant on when he is packing out." He said. I replied that it was fine with me too. I left his office; feeling I needed to have wings, so that I could fly, fly with joy!

Wow! I will soon be an occupant of a two bedroom apartment at Victoria Island, and the money the agent was asking for the house sounded very reasonable to me.

That night I told Segun, my host, my roommate . . . alright. I mean the guy I was squatting with in his one bedroom flat at Ikeja? You don't know him? Well, I guess I didn't introduce him at the beginning. Anyway, I told Segun what transpired between the estate agent and me. Instead of him jumping and giving me a hug as I expected, he stared back hard at me with a cautious look in his eyes and said "SST, a two bedroom flat in Victoria Island for that price? That is a shock. Even in Ikeja, you can't get a house at that amount. You're sure, you are not in the hands of scammers?" He wondered aloud! I stared hard at him.

What gibberish?! Just when I thought Segun should be jumping with joy for me, at least for seeing me off his back, he is here reading out a conspiracy theory! The estate agent, Kehinde, said I was lucky! Was it my fault to carry a badge of luck? . . . but seeing my excitement and determination, Segun quickly threw away his suspicions and started encouraging me on how to go about pursuing the ray of hope. I guess, he realised if he continued like that, he might be seen to be a little envious of my apparent good fortune of getting an accommodation in less than a month of being in Lagos, something that he himself, and many like him, failed to accomplished.

I was at kehinde's office the next day as we arranged. Despite the fact that it was not far from where I stay, I still decided to take a taxi, instead of waiting for the bus. I was too excited to wait.

Kehinde was already there waiting for me. He told me he decided to be earlier than usual to the office so that we could start our journey to Victoria Island in time to check on the new place. We quickly came down from the office floor and moved to the parking lot behind the office.

When I saw Kehinde's glittering, dark red Mercedes Jeep of 2008 Model, my heart skipped. Whatever suspicion I might have had of him, quickly melted on seeing the huge machine! *Wow! This guy must surely be doing good to own a car like that! He must be telling the truth when he said this place was just a small hideout, and that his*

9

main office was somewhere in Victoria. Yeah, and why not? Every man needs a hideout, you know what I mean! I thought excitedly.

I opened the front passenger door and entered, leaping with excitement like a fresh termer in college. I really couldn't hide my excitement when I saw myself sitting inside the huge Jeep that even became bigger when I got inside, feeling like being in the centre of a lecture room!

"Such a beautiful car" I complimented him.

Kehinde immediately accepted my compliment with a huge smile exposing his neatly white glittering teeth that made me think he would have been offended if I had overlooked it!

"Yeah, thanks, I just got this beautiful machine from the boys at the border." He was laughing at what was obviously a good deal, openly enjoying himself about it.

"I really don't want to ride it around town yet. I wanted to wait until I'm able to make the formal papers from the black market boys, everybody does that for these *tokunbo* cars." He said, bringing up the criminal system by which forged import papers are made by a syndicate to pass off smuggled second hand cars, call '*tokunbo*', as legally imported items. It was such an acceptable practice in Lagos, that even the agency in-charge of issuing genuine import papers sometimes goes to the syndicate for help with some receipt papers when their stock runs out.

Kehinde tuned in to the local FM radio station. The car was soon shaking lightly by the sweet filtering reggae music of the legendary Bob Marley as we cruised smoothly on the road.

I was so taken in by everything; the music, the car that I didn't notice when we reached Victoria Island. The sweet fragrance coming out of the perfume container hanging by the air condition vents added an extra comfort which didn't allow me think of anything else as we moved along the road.

We were soon at the entrance gate of Elemo Estate, from where Kehinde drove in and slowly manoeuvred the car along a strip of narrow tarred road that was adorned on the sideways by a cluster of apartments adjacent to each other. We stopped at the frontage of one of the apartments where a man moved forward to meet us.

I noticed the man was standing by the front gate of the house that leads to the compound, and was apparently waiting for us. Kehinde introduced him to me, as Mr. George Oke, the present occupant of the flat he was arranging to rent to me. I introduced myself in a very open way, to let Mr. Oke know I was happy to meet him. After a few exchange of pleasantries on the passageway, he invited us to come in, but Kehinde declined the offer, excusing himself on the grounds that we were in a haste to go back so as to evade the heavy oncoming traffic jam. He added that I came with him purely to acquaint myself with the current occupant of the house, and to let the person know that I will soon be moving in at the end of the month; when he was expected to move out. Mr. George Oke shook my hands warmly, gladly telling me of his eagerness to relocate to the United States before the month runs out.

There wasn't much for me to check on the state of the house anyway. The whole compound round the house looked so clean and well kept, as If no one lived around. The building was all bright and shining as if it was never put to use. I didn't know if Mr. George Oke had a family with him or was even married. All the same, it must have been a heavy task for him to keep the place so clean and neat.

There was no need going about asking questions on the house, it all looked alright. And I didn't want to appear as if I had choices to play with. I should be grateful for the offer of a house in such a site, and at such a price in Lagos. I thought it was important that I avoid seen to be ungrateful by being too nosy or inquisitive. The house was good . . . and judging by my situation, I was not in position to be fastidious about it, period.

On our way back, I brought out a total sum of 100,000 naira in 1000 bills from the bag I came with, and handed it to Kehinde. I was in a haste to pay him the agent fee before another person comes along and he gives the offer to him. Seeing the bundle of notes in my hands, Kehinde quickly looked for a place by the roadside and packed off the road.

With eagerness he collected the money quickly from my hands and tucked it away into his briefcase that was lying on the back seat. He then wrote his bank account number on a piece of paper and passed it across to me. It was for me to deposit the first down payment of 500, 000 naira payment the next day, before I completed in the full amount of one million naira a week to when I was expected to move into the house.

That day when I got back home, I didn't bother to talk to Segun about the progress I was making on my new accommodation. I was sure I would soon be leaving his house to a highbrow district. However, I decided to first have something concrete, to back up my claim, before bringing up the issue with him again.

The next day, I rushed to the bank and deposited in 500,000 naira into Kehinde's account. He called me ten minutes later to tell me he had received the payment. He had seen the deposit I made into his account from the bank alert signal on his handset. And he wants me to come down to his office immediately and collect a receipt for the rent payment. I couldn't wait to get there. My chest was beating fast, now there was something concrete to show Segun on the house . . . . my coming home, bungalow, and villa! Well, whatever!

I met Kehinde at the office and collected a receipt that showed I paid in 500, 000 naira to his firm for a two Year rent of a two bedroom apartment in Victoria Island.

I couldn't wait for Segun to come home that day. I rushed to his office at the Insurance firm where he worked to give him the good news. I met Segun in his office with a hugely built man of a very light complexion, a mulatto, in his office. I quickly guess he must be one of his colleagues.

From the way Segun was deferring to the man, he was his superior.

As soon as Segun saw me entering the office, he burst out with a huge smile. "SST, what's up? What brought you here today? You finally decided to see where I work *abi*? You are welcome. Please meet my departmental head, Charles Nookes. He is not a white man oh! You know Port Harcourt people still carry in their names the traces of what the white men did to them." Segun just couldn't stop! The man burst out laughing and gave me his hand. I shook it firmly and told him I was happy to meet him too.

12

I could feel my stomach twirling as the story of my good fortune struggles to come out. I just couldn't wait to tell Segun the good news, not bothering who was there. "Yes, happy to meet you, sir." I said to Mr. Nookes as I quickly retrieved my hand from his iron grip. I turned my attention to Segun and said "My man, sorry to disturb, but it's worth it! Just thought you should be the first to know." I was beaming with smiles. Segun jumped up from where he was sitting and hugged me.

"Oh yes thank you Jesus, you finally found her, right? When is the marriage?" I couldn't hide my annoyance with him. Must he always embarrass me like this? Telling everyone I was still a bachelor with a bald head? I quickly shook off his sarcasm and went straight to the issue "Segun, it's enough! That's not it and you know it . . . . !" I was putting on a frown of seriousness "Just check this, my friend." I brought out the rent receipt from my left breast pocket, adopting the style and deliberate movement of a suitor handing an engagement ring to his lady. Segun collected the receipt from my hands and stared at it.

"Wow two bedroom apartment in Victoria Island! Congratulations!" He turned to his boss with a huge grin hanging on his face "Charles, my friend just paid for a two bedroom flat at VI and can you believe this is his first month in Lagos!" He shouted wildly, obviously excited for me.

Maybe elated at shaking off a squatter off his back!

The man gave me his hand again. This time to congratulate me. I shook it harder the second time, moving it up and down while bracing my shoulders proudly up a little. He looked at me and said;

"Well done, my brother. I know how it feels. I also squatted in Lagos when I first came to the town. Mmm . . . ! I went through bad experiences before I finally got a place at Yaba after six months of squatting. You're lucky my friend, how much did you get the place?" He asked. I told him the amount. His eyes suddenly hardened suspiciously. "But that amount for a two bedroom apartment at Victoria Island? Which part of the town please?" He asked cautiously. I didn't like the way he was asking about it. It sent a little shiver up my spine. I hope that was not another person trying to discourage me. I told him the name of the estate. He shouted, "A two-bedroom house at Elemo Estate for that amount? My friend there is something fishy!" He said, blurting out like Sherlock Holmes!

Fishy? Oh my God! Why now? Another kill joy? What do these people want from me? To squat forever?

He saw my open discomfort and quickly adjusted "Oh I'm sorry, not that there is anything unusual about that. It's just that I remembered what I went through while looking for a house in Lagos. I lost 2 million to scammers." He was laughing as he remembered it; trying to make light of the experience.

"I hope that won't be my portion." I was trying to put up laughter too. He took his file and quickly bid farewell to Segun and me. But on reaching the door, he turned and looked back at me with a serious frown. 'My friend, if I were you, I would check that house at the Inland Revenue office. Well, nice meeting you." Looking at Segun he added, "See you at the club; please bring a more warming escort this time . . . . maybe two." He laughed again, Segun winked his understanding.

When Charles Nookes left, I thought over what he said and suddenly became worried. What if he was right? What if it was a scam, my goodness where will I hide? That was my whole savings! I turned to Segun; he was going through some papers on his table.

"Segun, does this house scam thing, happens that much in this town?" I asked, trying my best to let it sound perfunctory. But I couldn't hide the fears from my voice. "Mmmmhh" Segun answered, without looking up from what he was doing. That infuriated me! I seized the papers from his hands "Be serious man, talk to me." I said, almost shouting. I was getting edgy! His face hardened a little for a while, and then he burst out laughing.

"Hey man, what's the problem? You are not sure again? Ok, ok, yes, it does happen but not to everyone, some are just unlucky to fall into the hands of these people." He said without attaching much importance to it.

Funny, I was the one so sure before, and Segun doubtful, now we have switched sides. But I have a good reason to be worried now.

14

I had just deposited 500,000 naira into the estate agent's account. I was becoming tensed.

Segun looked up at my face still laughing, but on seeing how serious my expression was, he became serious too "Look SST, Charles was right. It is better to be safe than sorry. Why not check the house at the revenue office? It will take nothing. I will get somebody working there to assist you?" He suggested. I agreed and collected the address of his friend at the state revenue office. The next day I went to the revenue office to inquire about the house.

And there my nightmare started as the truth stared me in the face.

The two-bedroom apartment at Elemo Estate in Victoria Island belonged to a Mr. and Mrs. Mike Olorunyomi and not a Mr George Oke! And that was not all—it was not available for rent!

The Olorunyomi's family are living in the United States and comes to Nigeria occasionally on Christmas holidays, because their two children were married and live abroad. They only had a caretaker who looks after the house. I was taken in by shock. The muscle in my stomach was tightening quickly as I felt like fainting. I managed to get hold of myself and asked the official at the island revenue office, who was helping me with the details to also run a check on Kehinde and Associates Estate Agents. There was no firm registered with such a name! I asked if he was sure, he laughed. Of course he was sure. All registered businesses pay taxes in Lagos, and Kehinde and Associates was not amongst them.

I was sweating profusely as I left the Revenue Office. My muscles were beaming with adrenaline as I thought of going straight to confront Kehinde in his office and demand an explanation.

But then I remembered what my dad once told me when I had misunderstanding with my sibling, he cautions, "Son, when you face a tough situation, your first reaction is anger, the second is thought and your third reaction is wisdom. Never act on your first and second reactions." He said as he admonishes me.

I ran back to Segun's office to tell him of what I found out about the house at Victoria Island and on Kehinde and Associates from the Revenue Office. He was even more shocked than I was!

We went to meet Charles Nookes, his boss, in his office to discuss how he addressed his situation when he was scammed. He listened sympathetically as I narrate my ordeals.

"That's bad, SST, as I told you I faced a similar situation too. These guys are all around the place." Charles said sadly. I stood there dumbfounded, not sure of what to make of the situation I found myself in. I had just moved in to Lagos, and all of the sudden my world was crashing, as I watch my whole savings gone right under my very own eyes!

"What about the police?" My mind was bringing up all possible options. "What about me going to the police and reporting the case?" I could hear myself shouting. Mr. Charles Nookes shook his head sadly. "My friend, that is even worst. The police will be the first to alert him to go underground when you report." He said confidently. I could see he was talking from experience.

"Even if you think you are lucky to have him arrested, it will just be another trick. The police will squeeze money from you, and turn around and accuse you of a frame charge. They can even say you are laying malicious claims, at the end you lose more and the guy gets away free. The police are super corrupt, my brother, and what these guys have there is a large syndicate that has been around for years and has interwoven the police into it." He said. I was now very enlightened on the precarious situation I got myself into. Charles was trying his best to tell me how the syndicates operate in Lagos. His long talk was leading to one conclusion—there was nothing I could do about it!

"It's too late now." He told me. "These guys are often based abroad and before you know it, they are off the hook and out of the country."

I sat there with my mouth wide open praying it was a dream and wishing I would wake up.

"They execute the scams and then run abroad to lie low for years, before returning to fleece more innocent people. They are just con artistes who love living on the fast lane, just anything to hoodwink innocent people into believing they are legitimate hard working people. But my friend, they have nothing like legitimate money in their dictionary." He was telling me what I was feeling I should have known. Yeah! It was now all falling into place! The office, the jeep, the man at the house—all was a set up!

The jeep! An idea quickly jumped to my mind. Yeah, the Jeep!

I thanked Segun and Charles, as I left their office, telling them I would contact Kehinde to see what could still be done. I included some soul lifting talk of being happy not to have paid in the second deposit of 500, 000 naira before realising my mistake.

But I had no intention of going about looking for Kehinde and scaring him and his associates off. I had another idea. I immediately put a call to a friend and requested that we meet in the evening at a restaurant near his house in Ikoyi.

When I returned home that evening from seeing my friend at Ikoyi, I appeared so relieved and looked so different from the last time Segun saw me at his office that he was sure I had found a way of solving my problem with Kehinde. I only told him that all was under control. He didn't push me further.

The next morning, I called Kehinde on the phone. I could detect a little sharp edge in his voice when he picked up my call "Hey, SST, how are you? I was just on line with the occupant of your new apartment, trying to find out his final arrangement on moving out."

He said it rather too fast. I smiled. This guy was still on his game; he was not yet aware of what I found out.

Making arrangements indeed!

I answered him cautiously, trying my best to appear cheerful about the news "Thanks Kehinde, I really appreciate." I said.

He replied in a voice that sounded less worried than the first time "Oh! Please don't mention, we are brothers, right?" He said happily, sounding so relieved at my response as if he expected to hear something different. I guess when he first saw my call he was expecting something else, but my reply had put his mind to rest.

Maybe it was the tone of my voice that put his mind to rest, and let him feel I was still in the dark and it was all well. He must believe I was still not aware of anything about the house. You know what they say, the guilty are afraid, and what's the other one in the Bible? *Yeah, the wicked flee when no man pursueth.*

I said calmly to him "Kehinde, I was thinking, I got some money coming from one of my dealers, I was thinking of paying you up completely, and not to wait till next week as agreed."

He took a little while to speak. I could sense his voice going back to a cautious tone when he spoke again. "There's no need to rush; you can still wait till next week, I'm not in a hurry."

This time I replied quickly and in a voice that was clear and rapturous "Kehinde, my brother, it's not about you. I just want to complete the payment before I waste the money on something else. And come next week, will be unable to give you the balance payment." I said it with a sign of concern.

This time I could detect he had become more relaxed "Ok, SST, I think you are right. It is a smart decision, I'm at the office now, you can come around waiting." He said.

I thanked him, and said I was on my way.

I was at Kehinde's office in less than an hour! He appeared elated to see me and almost went out of his small squeaky seat to hug me as I entered the office "SST, I'm happy to see you, brother." He said.

"Yeah kehinde, thanks. I decided to come here first because I have no car to carry the cash in, and I don't want to carry that amount of money in public transport. Maybe we can use your car to the place and get the money from my dealer? "I was putting on a very congenial approach.

Kehinde quickly agreed, and we got into his heavy dark red Mercedes Jeep and got on our way. I directed kehinde to take a road that lead towards Abeokuta Road on our way to Ota. We were not far on the road when we came upon a police checkpoint. I could see there was a custom patrol vehicle with some custom personnel at the checkpoint too. The police traffic signalled to us to park by the sideway. But, Kehinde, like all typical rich Nigerian men riding big vehicles, impatiently stopped his vehicle a little distance away, and still on the road, expecting this to be a small hold up. Police checkpoints are not set for people driving a car like his.

The Jeep had hardly stopped when I heard one of the policemen shouted "Come out and let me see your papers please." His voice was hoarse and loud. We quickly came out and Kehinde approached the policeman, smiling and exuding confidence.

We all know the system.

He put his hand in his pocket and brought out a 1000 naira note and handed it, in a concealed form to the policeman. The man's palm projected forward quickly and made contact with Kehinde's, snatching the money like a baseball pitcher. He was smiling profusely, and bowing happily like a trained dog as he signals us to proceed. His attention immediately moved to the next oncoming vehicle. But as we were about to enter the Jeep, one of the custom officers that was standing by the patrol van, a little distance away, moved forward and accosted us. "sir, can we see the import papers for that car please?" He asked.

This was a tough one. Everyone knows the bribe for custom personnel is on the high side, unlike the police. On seeing the custom officer coming, Kehinde's countenance changed quickly.

My mind quickly recalled what Kehinde told me, 2 days earlier, that he had no genuine import papers for the Jeep. I could see him shaking a little now.

How easily a man's composure changes when he smells trouble.

"Ah, ah I, I, have no papers for the car, officer but I can explain." Kehinde was stammering now.

The beefy custom officer's face contracted sharply, suddenly becoming hostile "I say show me your papers and you are telling me you can explain, explain *wetin* my friend!" His shout attracted two of his colleagues.

We were soon surrounded by four of them; two holding rifles.

The one in-charge was talking loudly as he ordered us around "Look, if you don't have papers, you will have to come with us. We are on an anti-smuggling patrol" He said.

Kehinde tried to tip them with what he had, but to no avail.

Soon, we were moved away from the checkpoint, riding in Kehide's Jeep, with two of the custom officers coming down in the Jeep with us. The big Jeep doesn't feel that comfortable anymore.

They directed Kehinde to drive to their headquarters, and before long we found ourselves in an office being accused for being in possession of a smuggled vehicle.

I quickly turned to Kehinde, seeing that the situation was getting out of hand and said "don't worry, I have a friend that works here, he will get us off this thing." I brought out my handset and dialled Abdul's number. I informed him of our ordeal, and as we were lucky, he wasn't far from the headquarters. He promised to be with us in twenty minutes. Abdul was with us in ten minutes.

I told him the problem concerning Kehinde's Jeep. And on how we found ourselves at the headquarters, on a charge of being in possession of a smuggled vehicle. He assured us not to worry and climbed upstairs to an office to check what was being done on the case.

He was back in no time "It's not a big problem." He reassured us.

I could see Kehinde letting out a sigh of relief for the first time since we were arrested by the custom officers at the checkpoint.

"Had it been you called me as soon as you were arrested, I would have got you released with no hurdle. But it's too late now as you have been booked." Abdul said, Kehinde suddenly became worried again. Abdul looked at him and smiled. "Don't worry, there is no cause for alarm; you will get your car back. If not for my kind intervention you would have seen the last of your car as it would have been seized and put for auction. But my colleagues agreed to release your car to you." He said it with the authority of a man in charge. I could sense Kehinde getting his spirit back. But Abdul was not done yet! "But my friend, since your arrest has been booked already, you will still have to drop a fraction of what you would have paid had it been I did not intervene on your behalf." He said.

"How much are we talking about?" I asked.

"Just 150 grand!" He said.

I don't know when Abdul started using grand to define a thousand. I guess they see a lot of it where he worked, so they needed to give it a friendlier name.

"Ok, no problem." I replied.

I could see Kehinde starring hard at me. I pulled him aside and said "I think that's the best option. I have 50,000 naira here; I will help you, since I got us into this. "

On hearing I had some money that I was ready to part with made Kehinde to smile broadly.

"Thanks, SST" He said, turning to open the small handbag with him. I gave him 50,000 naira that I removed from my pocket and Kehinde joined it to his 100,000 naira and handed it to Abdul.

Abdul collected the money and left us. He came back after a while and said to us "Please follow me." I stood up first and followed him down the stairs. Kehinde joined us as we reached outside the office.

Abdul took us to a very large open garage filled with different kinds and types of vehicles—Jeeps, trucks, just name it! I have never seen such a large collection of vehicles. "Wow I shouted, what are all these?" I asked Abdul excitedly.

"Oh, that" Abdul answered indifferently, not the least distracted in his action. "These are the cars that we seized over a long period of time that were smuggled into the country." He said.

"So what do you do with them, pack them here to rust?" I asked rhetorically. Abdul laughed and again replied without any show of interest to my question "we auction them." He said.

"To whom?" I put in another question again, by now we have reached where Kehinde's Jeep was packed. I turned around to see if kehinde was following closely behind. He was not there. Kehinde was standing in front of a big black Jeep with heavy tyres with his eyes wide open. I shouted for him to join us to where his Jeep was parked. When he came, Abdul handed him a receipt "Here, take, this is your receipt of payment, you take it to the gate, collect your keys, and come and drive your car out." Abdul instructed as he handed him the piece of paper.

"Thank you, sir." Kehinde said showing his gratitude. I repeated my question "who do you auction these cars to?" I prodded him again.

"Anybody" replied Abdul. He then mockingly looked around to ensure no one was nearby and lowered his head to whisper to my ears "you know this is Nigeria, the auction is supposed to be opened to all, but really we do as we like with it. We sell to whoever we wish and at any price." He said and then burst out with big laughter.

"Wow" I exclaimed "I really need a car" I added.

I pointed to the big car that attracted kehinde's interest "How much is that one?" I asked.

"Which one of them?" Abdul inquired with a sneer, and looking at me he said in voice that sounded like a warning "that one, my friend, is the latest 2010 Cadillac Jeep, we just seized 10 of its type that were brought into the country without paying the required dues, it is completely bullet proof." He was talking so proudly of the cars as if he owned them. I could hear Kehinde whistling behind me. Abdul continued with his advert on the cars "It's a hybrid and an amphibious, in the market is about 20 million naira." He said. But to friends, we let it go for about 2.5 million." He was bracing as if opening a Master secret. I was whistling too. Abdul was talking like a salesman in a car shop.

"Abdul that's beautiful, but it's way off my turf, have you got anything that I can afford?" I inquired eagerly. Abdul nodded his head understandably, as if he was expecting me to run away from that one. He pointed at a Honda 2009 Model that was glittering brightly as if just out of the factory. "That is a good car too, it's 2 million in the market but if I put a word you can get it for 200,000." He said, trying to know if I was interested in the offer.

I can't wait "Abdul, I'm ready, you know I have no car, when can I have something like this?" I asked him. I felt Kehinde's eyes and ears boring at my back, as I discuss with Abdul on getting one of the auction cars. Abdul smiled with his hands in his pockets, pushing his frame forward a little, giving himself the posture of a man of influence. "I can get it for you in two days if you make a down payment today." He said.

"Yes oh! I have my cheque here. I will write down the amount and leave it with you!" I was jumping excitedly like a trained monkey. Abdul nodded happily "It's okay, we can do that when we get back to the office." He turned and looked at Kehinde who was observing us all along. "Alright, if you are ready to pick your keys and drive out your car we can leave now." He said to him. Kehinde just nodded, his mind seemed a far off. He appeared deep in thoughts.

I left Kehinde to go get his keys from the gate while I followed Abdul to his office to write a cheque for the car.

I met Kehinde waiting by his Jeep and we drove out of the custom premises. Throughout our journey back, Kehinde kept bowing and nearly licking my feet. He was flowing with gratitude for my assistance in getting his Jeep out of custom clutches. I knew that was not the only reason he was suddenly paying me so much reverence. It was nothing more than the discovery of my relationship with Abdul that he was most motivated to be obsequious.

We decided we could not continue our journey to the town of Ota, because the car had no authentic papers, so we returned to Lagos. I promised Kehinde to get him the money the next day.

Two days after the incident I called Kehinde, the phone didn't ring twice before he picked it "Yeah, my brother, SST, how are you?" He was sounding very excited. "Your house will soon be ready, brother, Mr Oke will soon leave to Europe." He said excitedly.

I remembered he told me Mr. Oke was relocating to United States. What's this about Europe, now? Well, it doesn't matter anymore, anyway.

"Yes, thanks, bros." I shouted back.

We are on the brother level now.

I then told him why I was calling "I'm just calling to let you know I'm on my way with the remaining part of the money." I said.

"I'm waiting for you, safe journey, brother!" Kehinde replied quickly like a child waiting for a promise of an ice cream cone.

I entered the car that Abdul sent to me and zoomed off to Kehinde's office. As I knocked at the door, he rushed and opened it himself for the first time.

"Please you can come in." he said from the inside.

"Hey! Brother, you are welcome." He said excitedly on seeing me. He was obviously happy to see me. I greeted him and sat down. I quickly opened the suitcase I came with and handed him two bundles of 1000 naira notes. Kehinde almost yanked it from my hand "Good brother, good brother!" He was repeating himself as he count the money. I waited for him to finished expressing his appreciation on the payment of my last instalment before breaking the news to him. "Kehinde I have something to show you" I said in a voice visibly unable to hide my excitement. I signalled to him to follow me downstairs.

When we reached downstairs, we went straight to the car park, and I pointed my new car to him.

"Tan tan!" I shouted excitedly as I ran to open the driver's door. Kehinde reacted more confused than I could have imagined. He ran and hug the car lying flatly with his tummy on top of the car bonnet.

"So, it's true! So it's true!" He was shouting.

I moved to him, "what's true, brother?" I asked.

Kehinde stood up and hugged me. "Oh brother, I have been thinking about this since the last time we saw your friend. I was hoping this auction thing is true." He shouted. I just stood there looking at him running up and down the car. Kehinde pulled me away from the side of the car, dragging me back to his office. Right under the desk he brought out a small bottle of wine and two glasses.

What? *This man had such nice drinks hidden all this while? Anyway, it's better late than never.*

"Brother, you got to help me" he said, his eyes turning misty.

"I could not get that bulletproof Jeep off my mind, oh God!" He was almost talking to himself, "such a car is befitting for someone of my status." He said as he went about expressing his vanity. I sat there quietly staring at him, waiting for him to exhaust his exuberance.

"What are you talking about, Kehinde?" I snoop in when I was sure he has finished. He looked at me sharply as if surprised by my question "the jeep of course, the black bulletproof jeep of course." He said it proudly in a way that sounded as if the car bore his name.

"Oh, the Jeep?" I replied carelessly. "I love it too, but I can't afford the 2.5 million. If I had that kind of cash, I would have been driving that machine by now." I said regrettably.

"Please I want it SST. Help me please! I'm ready to raise that money anytime." kehinde was pleading with me now.

I looked thoughtfully at the ceiling for a while then said "ok, let me call Abdul." I picked my handset and dialled Abdul's number. After discussing the issue with Abdul, with Kehinde listening, I turned to him and said "Abdul said it is not a problem. You can go tomorrow with the money and meet him at the office. He will make sure you get the car in two days time after payment." Before I could finish speaking, Kehinde rushed out of his seat and hugged me, singing and jumping! He was bellowing and bowing before me

"Oh thank you, thank you" he was shouting, obviously overjoyed.

I smiled quietly, and then remembered the words he said to me the last time I inquired of the house from him. I decided to assure him with the same words "oh, don't mention, we are brothers, alright?" I was smiling.

The next day Abdul called and told me Kehinde came to his office and paid 2.5 million for the black bullet proof Cadillac Jeep. He gave him a receipt for it. Kehinde complained on why the receipt contained a clause that stated that once money was paid for a vehicle, it was not refundable if one loses the auction for the car. However, Abdul assured him that it was the normal official terms but he shouldn't bother himself about such possibility, because he will personally hand over the car to him. And if he was interested he could even put in for two cars. Kehinde was overjoyed at hearing that and quickly requested for another Jeep, which he promised to bring another 2.5 million naira for it. I thanked Abdul, and told him he should let me know how their discussion further went. Before hanging up, Abdul called and told me that Kehinde was so insistent that he gets the car in two days time. In fact, he said he won't be interested if it will take more than two days, because he intended to travel out of the country soon, as he claimed.

Kehinde knew in a week's time I should be expecting to move into the accommodation and he wants to get out of the country before then. I laughed within me.

Just as I was about to pack the things on my table into my briefcase and go back home at the end of the day, Abdul called in again.

Kehinde had brought in another 2.5 million for the second jeep. "The man was obviously desperate!" He said.

I immediately put a call to Kehinde. He didn't allow my call to ring more than once like it used to before. "Yeah, SST, thanks, man! You know I am capable man. I have paid to your friend the money for two of those machines." He said with the excitement of an accomplished man as soon as he answered the call. I feigned excitement. "that's beautiful, 5 million for cars that go for 20 million each in the market." I said.

I could hear Kehinde laughing at the other end "SST, you are my brother; I will tell you why I'm after those machines. Some politicians are ready to give me 30 million each for them, wow! Thank you, Lord." He was still shouting in excitement.

I laughed too.

Thirty million each for a car auction for 2.5 million? And you don't wonder why Abdul didn't get one out for himself?

I didn't show that I was not taking in with his talk. I wished him well, promising to call back in few days time when the house should be ready. But as I mentioned the house, I could feel a little tension in our discussion. *Kehinde did not sound boisterous talking about the house, anymore.* Nevertheless, he was still able to put up a brave front and assured me the present occupant will be leaving at the end of the month. And with that he quickly ended our conversation.

Two days later, on the day he was expecting the cars to arrive at his place, Kehinde called me. As soon as I picked the call I heard him shouting "SST, what's wrong with your friend? He told me the cars will be ready today, but when I called he said I should give him two more days, why SST? Why? That was not what he promised!" He sounded like somebody about to burst to tears.

I tried to calm him down "Kehinde don't be upset, if he says that you should give him two more days, it is understandable. These are highly priced cars, not like the one I bought. It will take longer to process them of course." I said to him.

That seemed to soothe his fears a little "Yeah, SST, I guess you are right, hope we can trust him." He was eager to be reassured.

I answered back hotly, showing my annoyance at his doubting my friend's sincerity "of course Kehinde what do you take Abdul for? He is a responsible and high-ranking official in the Customs!" I tried my best to sound angry.

Kehinde quickly reacted with an apology "no, SST, is not that I'm suspecting him, you know Lagos is a dangerous place, there are too many touts around trying to deceive people. Alright, SST, I will wait." It was then I realise that Kehinde's polish British accent had long disappeared without me even noticing. He was now as fluent in the local accent as any street urchin!

It was two days to the day I was expecting to move to the house, so I decided to drive down to Victoria Island, after closing from my work in the evening. I wanted to inspect on my own to see if there was anything I could find out about the real occupants of the house from their neighbours. The last time I was there with Kehinde, we only had chance to meet with the supposed occupant of the apartment, Mr. Oke, at the gate. Kehinde was in such a hurry to go back to the office that day that I couldn't remember noticing anyone from any of the apartments in the area.

As I entered the Estate and drove to the front of the apartment, I saw an elderly man sitting by the open terrace with a lady by his side. I parked the car by the sideway and went to them, introducing myself. The man appeared to be quite a gentleman judging by the way he warmly welcomed me into the house.

I didn't waste time telling him of the issue that brought me to his house. He didn't allowed me to finish before he burst out laughing "young man, look, I have lived in this house for ten years, till all my children left home to abroad. I decided to fix this place, and join them with my wife there. My wife, here, and I only come back occasionally, mostly at Christmas to celebrate with friends. You know we are getting old now. It used to be cold there by Christmas." He said.

My information was correct.

He was looking at me intensely, I could see concern in his eyes "we decided to come back yesterday, because my wife lost her sister and the burial is coming up soon. This house is not for sale and will never be! When I die, I will leave it to my children. If they chose to sell it, that's their decision. But I won't sell or rent it for a day." He then shouted a name and a young man in his twenties suddenly appeared. "This is Okon." He introduced him "He takes care of the place in my absence, he is my houseboy, I'm surprised you didn't meet him when you came here." He turned to Okon, "have you seen this man before?" referring to me, Okon hurriedly replied that he never met me in his life. Mr. Olorunyomi stared at him suspiciously and then asked where he was the day I came to the house with Kehinde when we met the Mr. George Oke. Okon replied that he never left the house except on occasions when he goes to the market.

It is either Okon was telling the truth or Kehinde bribed him to take a walk at the time.

No problem, it was not different from what I knew already. I thanked Mr. Olorunyomi or Chief Olorunyomi as he called himself, and left. Outside, I quickly put in a call to Kehinde. His line was not going. I tried three more times. But there was no reply. I then put a call to Abdul, as soon as he answered I asked him of Kehinde.

"He just called me an hour ago, almost threatening me over the cars. I told him he should give me a day more. He was almost crying on the line. I had to stop the conversation. I told him I was in a meeting and will call him later." Abdul was laughing.

"It was all as we suspected, Abdul, there is no house for rent in Victoria Island." I told him all that I have found out at the Elemo Estate from Mr. Olorunyomi.

"I have been trying Kehinde's number but couldn't get through to him." I said to Abdul.

"Oh! He called me with a new number today. I didn't save it but if he calls again, I will try and get it to you." Abdul said.

I decided to check for Kehinde at his office. It was getting late. When I arrived the complex where his office was located, they were about to close the gates. I tipped the gateman to give me a few minutes while I run upstairs to Kehinde' office. There was no Kehinde and Associates office anymore.

The metallic door sign had been removed!

Abdul was the first to call me the next morning as I was settling in my office. "Your friend Kehinde just called this morning." He said, laughing loudly "I told him the auction has been called off and his money can't be refunded. But I will see what I can do as soon as I come back because I was at the airport on my way to USA for a conference. Boy! The man was crying and begging like a baby. I didn't know how callous I was that I couldn't feel such huge tears." Abdul couldn't control himself; he was laughing and sneezing as he talked.

I told him what I met at Kehinde's now former office. Abdul promised to send through SMS Kehinde's new phone number the next time he calls him. But that was not going to be necessary as Kehinde's call came in the next moment, I quickly answered it. He was crying at the other end.

"Why SST, why? I'm sorry about the house, I know you are aware of it.." He was sobbing loudly. Someone must have called him and told him about my visit to Mr. Olorunyomi.

Was it Okon the houseboy? Well, it doesn't matter anymore.

"What about the house? I thought I'm to move in the day after tomorrow?" I said with clear sarcasm.

"SST, cut that crap!" Kehinde shouted at me "It's all over now, I'm ready to give you back your money. But help me with your friend Abdul. I borrowed the money for the cars from Don Carlos. I told him I will give him back with interest in two weeks. Please, SST, my life is in danger, Don Carlos will kill me!" He shouted. I don't know who Don Carlos was—*I don't belong to the criminal world.*

"What is wrong with the auction? It didn't go through?" I was tormenting him.

"SST, you know everything, please get me the money from your friend, Abdul, my life is in danger, have mercy on me, SST!" He was shouting and sobbing now. I was filled with compassion for him, despite all he had planned against me. But it was too late to get any of the money back now. Abdul had sunk the money in settlement.

After giving me back my one million naira, Abdul told me that the other people that played a part in the drama, his men and the policemen, needed to be rewarded for their role—not to talk of his own compensation.

You see how it goes? Abdul was a Lagos boy too!

I now have the confidence to talk back with the tone of a victor to Kehinde "my friend Kehinde, I'm just an ordinary man that was in need of a roof over my head, but you decided to take advantage of me as you have been doing to many others." There was no need for a long recollection. I decided to cut the sermon short. Long exhortation is for people with a conscience. Kehinde and his kind needed only retribution. I knew their type; they live on fraud. He will be back to his evil ways, maybe more experienced than before. But that will only happen when he is able to recover from this one "ok, I will see what I can do." I said abruptly, and put off!

The last I heard of Kehinde was that he left Lagos, because the local mafias were after his life for the millions of naira he borrowed from them. I only hope Kehinde, has learnt his lessons and turned a new leaf wherever he is now. But that will really be difficult, because bad habit is a comfortable bed, easy to enter but difficult to get out!

How did Abdul get entangled in all this? Well, it all started the day I left Segun's office. I left the office dejected and worried. But after a serious thought, I decided to call Abdul. I asked Abdul that we meet in the evening at an eatery near his house at Ikoyi.

I got to know Abdul when he was working at the Custom Service Headquarters in Abuja, before he was posted to Lagos. Abdul had once offered me a chance to buy one of the vehicles seized at the borders by the customs that were put up for auction. I never gave it a serious thought. Until when I thought of what to do when Kehinde tried to dupe me.

The evening we met, I told Abdul of my problem. I told him how I wanted him to help me recover my money from Kehinde. He readily agreed to do whatever he could to assist me. Abdul was a good friend.

"In Lagos, you must be an actor—play the game or you are knocked out. My friend, never get crossed—get even!" He told me.

Lagos, SST has arrived! It's either you are an actor, or you are played out! That day I became an actor! *Lagos na wa oh!*

Coming To Lagos
Wetin Lagos People Wan Hear Sef?

The first thing I noticed when I came to Lagos was how things were done which is very different from where I was coming from. Really, I didn't know I was having it cool in Abuja until I arrived in Lagos. In Abuja, they just make life easy for one! I'm not talking of taking one along the array of good networks of roads that struggle to fly over one another crisscrossing the city. I mean making things easy when it comes to dealing with people.

You know, Abuja is not only a new, but also a striving modern city that has attracted the high crème la crème of the society. In terms of having the best things of life, Abuja stands out like an oasis located in the middle of a dry land.

In Africa, nothing makes a person feel of a higher status than the recognition that his life was shaped more by a short sojourn abroad than a long livelihood in his nation. It was a habit we thought would die with the end of colonial rule. We were wrong! We were to realised that the impact of British colonial rule had sunk deeper in our mentality than the few colonial houses and administrative staff we were seeing.

It was thus not surprising that most of Abuja's elite residents struggle to be seen able to go in line with how things were done abroad, or even try to go a little higher!

I *am not talking of the big legislator's allowances, abeg!*

I am not also talking of how they live and eat all those uncooked vegetables either!

I am referring to how they talk.

In Abuja, when they ask you a question, they love you go the British way. You know what I mean? The person that asks the question also provides the answers? Seeing you in your glaring uniform, with army written all over you, they will still ask cutely ...

"You say your name *na* SST? Where do you work? In the Army?" ...

Wetin, before nko? Was it not obvious enough?

Anyway, you are only left to nod your head—*please nod the foreign way too, clicking your head to your left cheek.* It was always easy conversing with people in Abuja, as most of the work is done for you anyway. You are only left to nod.

That was not what I met when I moved to Lagos.

Sometimes, I don't know what Lagos people expect you to say. Last weekend I was at the Eko Hospital where my friend's sister gave birth. On my way out of the corridor his phone rang, being with his handset I decided to take the call! It was his aunty calling.

"Oh, my God! Is it true she gave birth to a little baby?" She was obviously excited.

"No, ma'am, it was a huge adult!" I replied.

I could hear the deliberate loud hissing at the other end before the call went off.

Silly question, what does she expect to see, Bill Gate's classmate?

The next day I met her at the hospital, and my friend tried to introduce us "aunty meet my friend, SST, he is new in town, and he answered your call the other day." He said.

The lady was more interested with the wall painting.

Ah Lagos Na Wa!

Coming To Lagos

Lagos Girls Know Better Thing

I liked to call this Lagos experience of mine, *Lagos girls know better thing* because that was what happened at the end of the day.

It all started when I decided to know Lagos a little bit, after moving over to the city. The need to go round and know your way around is always necessary when you are in Lagos. As Lagos, a big cosmopolitan city, has no authentic road map.

Having that in mind, I accepted an invitation on a Saturday, to visit one of my old friends; we were in the army together but he now works in a big oil firm in town. When I reached his office, I met a young lady, a small time contractor, who was there to make a few purchases for the firm. And you know what? One thing led to another.

You know how fast it is with this bachelor, spinster thing!

And before you know it, we exchanged phone numbers, and she promised to call, and she did call. The next few days I was inundated with telephone calls.

But after a few weeks, she all of a sudden stopped calling, and also stopped answering my calls. I decided to check on her and find out what the problem was. When she saw me, she just burst out in anger;

"You lied to me!" She shouted.

I was shocked. "Lied to you?" I asked.

"Yes, you said you work in Shell Corporation, but I later saw you in your uniform." She said it hotly as if announcing a great scientific finding. And was pronouncing the word 'uniform' with much pains as if it was a curse.

"Baby, I never said that!" I blurted hotly, showing my annoyance.

You have to let a lady think you care about your integrity to get her lose hers.

"You said you were there!" she repeated.

She was furiously trying *to make her voice sound in the rich girl 'am used to getting my way with daddy' style!*

"Yeah, baby, when we met at Shell Petroleum, you asked me 'are you here'? And I answered, yes! Of course I was there! Who do you think you were talking to there? A ghost or what?" I said.

Needless to say that ended our relationship, because she sure had no patience with someone below her expectations. As I said earlier, I was still getting to know the city well.

Ha!! Lagos na waooh!

Coming To Lagos

Lagos Girls and Fast Food Joints

When I relocated to Lagos, I found out that there is a business that flourishes in all the nooks and crannies of the bustling city. You just can't miss it. That is the fast food business! And it seemed to have affected the attitude of the people, especially the ladies. Hardly do you meet a lady that doesn't have it on her mind on how to canalize you to one of the several fast food outlets in the city. Really, I don't know what Lagos girls have got with fast food joints. It looks as if they sleep in them.

In the middle of last month, one of my friends said to me "SST, now that you are in Lagos you need to move forward a bit. I mean update your Facebook page a little. This 'in an open relationship' is not the best at your age. Let me get you a friend, anything can happen, you know? You are not growing any younger you." He said curtly.

Do I need to be reminded of that? My head doesn't need a comb in the morning anymore!

At first, I was resisting and being reluctant. But I finally agreed, after six minutes of serious haggling.

It sounded a little too eager to you? I was too fast to give in? You still want me to waste time on an issue of securing a partner, at my age?

So he got me a number of one of the ladies that work in one of the new generation banks in town—*those Hollywood type banks with the more you look the less you see directors! You know them? The banks with CEOs with the mafia film star names . . . . Erastus, Jim, Cecelia, Tony?*

Anyway, I decided to push ahead quickly and call her. My friend had done the spadework. Good help, it would save some credit on my phone. I got her on the first dial.

This girl will be hard to flash!

After some minutes of conversing, I asked which day I could pick her up for a date.

She started with a small pause "mmh" sounding reluctant. *Yeah, I know, lady stuff, trying not to appear too desperate, maybe push it a day or two, no problem, I can wait.*

"What about today?" The reply came back sharply.

I was wrong!

"Today, what time?" I asked back cautiously.

"Let's say by 2."

Wow! That's when people usually go for lunch break in Lagos, what's this girl up to?

"It's all right, where do I pick you?" I asked.

"Mmhh, what about at Opebi road . . . I will be by Sweet Sensation." She said eagerly.

Sweet Sensation! An Eatery! Man, trust your instincts always!

"Am new in town I don't think I can find that place" I replied quickly.

"Ok, what about I wait at Isaac John Street at Ikeja, just in front of Barcelos?" Her voice was suddenly hardening.

I won't fall for that, baby; Barcelos is a popular eatery in town!

"Ikeja? Traffic is hard there, baby, my hands are still weak on the steering wheel, Lagos drivers are rough you know" I was allowing my voice to sound very concerned.

"Ok, what about by Maryland bus stop, to help you see me very well, I will be waiting inside the Mr. Biggs eatery just by the petrol station?" She said with the assurance of one that knew her way around.

This girl is tough! She was still pushing it! Lagos!

"Baby, that's far from my place, it will take some time to get there!" I replied with the concern of one that has a busy schedule.

I stay at Ikeja Estate, a few blocks away from the eatery!

I took over the prodding—*deepening my voice like the popular film star RMD does on telly*!

"Ok, baby let me help, why don't you wait by mama danja's pounded yam food joint. I believe is not too far from where you work? I can pick you from there, ok?" I let my voice to drop smoothly, trying to give it a romantic touch!!

I could clearly pick a deep hissing sound coming from her end "You are not serious!!" She shouted.

That was all I heard before the phone went off!!!

Man, what did I do wrong . . . ? Lagos girls and fast food joints!

Coming To Lagos

Party NA Lagos Get Am

After moving into a friend's house in Lagos, I always tried to keep to myself. I wasn't the type that would go about looking up to know my neighbours. And judging from their airs, there wasn't much in the word neighbours between us anyway!

So I remained within my bounds. You can only be a nobody when you go about looking for a somebody! All I wanted from them was nothing more than peace and quietness. However, I was to find out even that were not forthcoming because it has been hard for me to sleep at night!

Hardly, a day passes without a neighbour holding a party! It was not that the noise bothered me that much, but it looked as if I was being outclassed from all angles by my neighbours! From them blocking the little packing space we share together with their infinity Jeeps, turning it to an infinity time for me to manoeuvre my small 206 Peugeot out, to littering the waste bin near my room with packages of expensive grocery packs, making it hard for me to dispose my empty sachet water packs in daytime! And now, this of all things! Taking away the little time that should have been a season of equality to all mortals—the time to sleep!

I thought of finding ways to measure up a little, however, holding a party in such a competitive atmosphere was something I dared not think about!

But I was to find out later that during the Christmas season, when most of the big boys go to the village or abroad for the long holidays, the coast always appear clear for spare guys like us to hold a house party too!

And so, this year, with Segun away to the village to celebrate the Christmas, I decided to hold one in his apartment; just to feel amongst the big boys for once. No problem, I was sure of getting reasonable number of babes to attend—*without whom of course it would just be a village square meeting.*

Before then it would be a big dream to get any of the required babes to attend a party in my small dinghy apartment. However, now with most big boys away for the Christmas holidays, their options for a free meal were limited. You know, Lagos girls are always ready to update their status anytime, depending on what is on the ground.

So I decided to have one of my parties too; just to feel amongst the big boys.

I got one of the ladies contacts and gave her the details. You know her type? The professional party link ups with names of all lady party goers in town? Anyway, I decided to give her all the necessarily details that she needed in organising my bash. As I talk on the phone she was getting more excited. *I could not figure out what was raising her temperature by the minute.* She promised she will get all her high class girl friends to come.

High class in Lagos means an eye class.

On the day of the party, I suddenly found the small room full.

Wow! Fifty ladies at once, I never even expected to get ten.

They were all happy and giggling and poking each other playfully, *you know now? This 'I'm a young girl'* behaviour! They looked like they were having a great time as they filled the small confinement with their high pitch giggling.

But after some time the place suddenly became quiet as they started appearing irritated.

I *couldn't figure out what the problem was. I made sure everybody had a bottle of coke—50cl! And the fried rice went round too; everybody had a plate and a piece a meat to go with it! Well, maybe a little piece, but when was what is a piece of meat started to be judged by its size?*

"We are not happy!" My lady contact uttered angrily! I looked around at her friends, meeting several hard accusing pairs of eyes. From the hostile looks on their faces, she was speaking their minds.

"What? What did I do wrong?" I shouted back, looking at the empty bottles of coke that cost me a small fortune. Definitely it couldn't be that!

"You said 2face will be here." She blurted out with a sigh of indignation, as if letting out a state secret!

"What? 2face the musician? No, I never said that!" I answered, shocked at the revelation of what was trying to kill my maiden big boy moves!

"Yeah, you did. You said you were with 2face, and that's why everybody agreed to cramp to this your miserable hole, just because they wanted to touch him!" She was so strongly defensive; one would think she was defending a PH.D thesis!

"Touch what, girl? You want to die?! No, girl, I never said that! I only said I'm connected to two phases; I mean my house power connection! You know the light problem in Lagos; I didn't want you to worry about power supply when you are here. I'm connected to power supply on 2—phase! I don't have a generator plant like those people you are used to, you know!" I shouted, trying my best to put a good explanation for her. But the lady raised her face smugly and gave out a well defined hiss.

As if that was the signal they were all waiting for! Before I could further adjust my trousers for a better explanation, I heard the thunderous sounds of more hisses, and the scrambling for handbags as they compete in rushing out of my apartment.

Ladies, not even a goodbye, after all the bottles of coke?

Lagos na wa!

Coming To Lagos
Miriam Na Wa

My experience for Lagos *just de open my eyes!* The other day, my boss at Alliance Security where I work Dr Benjamin Jomoh, decided to be a little bit nice by giving us a gift of some little change from the company purse. It was not that he suddenly developed love for his staff after four years of strained relationship. It was just that his wife gave birth and he was in a celebrative mood.

The next day I was full of excitement, and knowing that nature does not allow such happenings to take place in less than a year or two, I was of course on time to reach the office and collect the promised gift—lest the excitement wanes, and he changes his mind.

After receiving my share from hands that appeared reluctant to let go of the tightly held token, I left his office feeling happy for the first time since I came to know him.

With the small change feeling strange in my pocket, I decided to behave a little strange too! And what more than to do what I was not used to doing?

There was this new eatery that just opened by the corner, and anytime my friends, especially the young ladies that work nearby suggest we visit there; I always have the usual excuses ready at hand. "*Well, you know am watching my weight,*" . . . . or I will just use the old line, "*I don't want to add to my cholesterol level,*" and the rest!

Underneath, I had privilege undercover information about the new comers. Having come to a supposedly highbrow area, they decided to ensure they raise some few eyebrows with their prices too—charging twice what they normally do. Well, I was having no

41

problems with mama sikiru food canteen 100 naira pounded yam, so why carry myself to be fleece with half-baked onions!

But now things were different.

With the little extra cash jingling in my pocket, I decided to move up my lifestyle a little and have a good time at the eatery, even if it was just for the day.

I never know when next my boss will decide to have another baby!

Before going to the eatery, as a seasoned Lagos boy by now, the one we call Lagos actor, I made elaborate plans. I was just one year in Lagos by then. But one year should be good enough for one to understand the ways of Lagos, or you are finished you know!

I have long learned the best time to enter such eateries—avoid 2-3 pm, that's when the banks and insurance houses go on lunch break. And I had many friends working in such places who might not mind emptying my pockets on a plate of pepper soup. Miriam was the most persistent of them.

Miriam was one of the marketers working with one of the new generation banks near my house. Yeah, you heard me alright, marketer! . . . . I'm talking of banks not a supermarket, my friend . . . . you know what they say, some banks do have them.

The lady has been on my neck—*believe me*—*t*o take her out for lunch at the new eatery. *I had been putting it off . . . you know the way it is, of course?* Using the usual excuses men give when they smell a shylock lady . . . . "I'm busy", "we have a meeting the next hour" "I promise next time you are around" bla bla bla—*showing my deep disappointment each time we meet for not being able to take her out. I was always putting on a worried look. It's easy when your face doesn't need much squeezing to appear worried.*

And knowing that such girls love to be at such places, I decided to avoid the place completely. But now that I have made up my mind to visit the place for the first time, I decided to take some precautions. I adopted the reconnaissance tactics I learnt from the army.

I first stopped my car a distance away from the eatery, and then smoothly looked around the immediate surroundings from the car; it all looked deserted—good, just as I suspected it will be at this time of the day. I then confidently drove into the large fenced compound and parked in the designated parking lot.

I smoothly came down from the car and walked briskly to the entrance door pushing the door inwards slightly and started a confident walk across the hall to the sales counter. I was half way across the small hall when I heard the familiar voice behind me.

"'Wow! Oga SST, good morning." Her voice vibrated in the relative silence of the hall!

I froze in my pants . . . sorry, boxers! I turned around, there she was—Miriam! She was sitting with a friend in one of those inner side seats at the corners—the concealed sitting spaces that are found in modern eateries.

I now understood why they have such places in the buildings; it looked like an ideal ambush site for Lagos ladies to wait for their preys!

Remembering I was supposed to be the always-busy SST, having no time to move out of the office to an eatery during office hours, I realised the hole I have fallen into. And so, I quickly put on a disarming smile.

"What a surprise, *oga* SST, I thought you never had chance to go out during office hours?" Miriam was smiling as she watched my reaction. I could see she was leading the question like a lawyer. I was definitely not her first client to be cross-examined on a story like that.

"My dear, how are you? I'm surprise to see you." I avoided her question, keeping the smile fixed on my face.

That's the best way to keep your mind alert while you work on an escape routes.

"It's indeed a surprise." She replied coolly, smiling broadly like one who had rediscovered a long lost brother. I smiled back nicely, swallowing the pain as I take the empty seat near her. I looked at her and smiled ruefully.

Yes, my dear, it was really a surprise!

"So, who is this, your friend?' I quickly shifted my focus to my second area of concern—her friend.

To *meet one girl at an eatery is bad enough . . . . two is fate!*

43

The girl sitting next to her looked up, she had been fiddling with her handset all the while . . . . you know how it is, of course? What ladies do when their phone credit level is at zero? She was a well built, sorry a well endowed lady! I wonder why they call women the weaker vessel. This Amazon could break an iron pot with a sneeze!

"Oh, this is my friend, Catherine; we work in the same place." Miriam introduced her.

I knew such a girl wouldn't be too far from a cat! Cat rain indeed! Well, lady cat, this is not your rainy day!

"Yeah, I am happy to see you *cat rain*." I said. I could see her smilingly sheepishly at me. She didn't notice my misuse of her name! I extended my hand for a shake, at the same time making sure only the tip of my fingers made contact with her iron fist. I didn't prod her further.

You don't ask a girl further question when she says we work together. Lagos is a working town!

"Yeah, happy to meet you, what's your name?' Catherine asked coolly. Smart girl, she detected that I was hiding from an introduction.

A man doesn't go about building an acquaintance so easily in Lagos, it only adds to your unwanted experiences! As the next time you are passing by, someone might shout hey mr . . . . at worst, could be at an eatery!

"Oga, SST, what are you doing here at this time?" It was Miriam asking again. She was quickly building up a conversation, trying to draw me to the team on the table . . . I know the moves, next comes the ball—when you see a menu out.

"Oh, I worked throughout the night, and surprisingly for years, the office is less busy today. So, I decided to come here for something light. It's too early to take anything big you know, just came to take a small snack." I gave her a short talk, emphasizing the word 'small snack' here and there, in case she and her friend had an idea of something more than that when it comes to placing orders from the counter.

. . . yes of course! I was already thinking of placing orders and that was because I knew I was to pay—that's the gentleman tradition. Who started the tradition? Don't ask me. Why do you think I was worried?

I resigned myself to fate. I was in the trap already, these ladies, even if they have had ten pizzas before I came in, will still find space to create in their bellies and fleece me by placing for another order. My small snack talk was just an attempt at reducing the expected burden, by educating them on the need of having a small meal at this time of the day.

"Ladies what do you want to take?" *I asked smoothly and then quickly put on a slight frown of impatience* "Let me have your choices quick please. I have got to be going back to the office, my time is running fast, you know." I was making my voice sound a little hardened. Trying to put up the serious look that I last adopted when a careless bus driver hit my car.

"Oh, *oga* SST, you don't have to, you shouldn't please." Miriam replied quickly with a smile. I smiled back generously too, trying hard to hide my true feelings.

It is you that shouldn't be here in the first place, young lady. I looked at her face, Miriam was still keeping that mocking smile of "I *have got you now, buster.*"

I put my hands on my cheeks, looking down a little to give myself the thoughtful corporate look of a man ready to foot whatever bill. When I looked up, I saw a menu suddenly appeared in Miriam's hands. It must have been hibernating down on her laps under the table, waiting for an opportunity like this.

"Well, well, well," she was rubbing her hands eagerly on the menu and looking at her companion, apparently conspiring on how to coordinate a combine attack.

"I think we will have potato casserole mixed with chicken spice laced onions." She was placing the orders with a deep relish. The type of meals Miriam was calling from the menu sounded strange to me. But that was not the immediate concern; my concern was on the price tag. I quickly peeped at the pricelist on the menu, 5000 naira for a plate. Wow, what a shock!

But of course, trust me, Lagos boy, I did not allow the shock to show on my face. After all, the game has just started. The way she was calling all those continental dishes, with a touch of a foreign accent, you wouldn't believe it was the same Miriam, I saw eating boiled corn near an open canteen just last week.

No problem Miriam.

"Oh ladies that will be just be fine." I said with the *'it's not a big deal' waving of the hand.*

I could see the two of them smiling to a victory—not too soon my dears.

"Yeah, it's my favourite meal too." I added with the smile of a man that has been around such luxury for life.

I wish mama Sikiru could hear me now, she has been begging me for ages to move my taste a little bit upwards; from taking pounded yam always to having fried plantain and chicken occasionally.

"But ladies, to be frank with you, I used to love to it too, but later I had to stop as advised by my doctor, it is very fattening and not good for the heart. I don't think it's the best for such nice shapes like yours." I put on a patronizing smile. I could see even the boxer near Miriam was in agreement with me that they were nice shapes around. I smiled back, fully exposing my teeth. I was trying to make my words as sweet as possible—I knew I would soon be eating them.

"Oh, ok" Miriam said disappointedly, but she was forced to agree with my reasoning. I could still see her friend lapping at the compliment like a dog on an ice cream cone.

Give a lady a compliment on how she looks, and she will buy any crab you sale.

"Ok oh yeah! Another of my favourite, mmmhh, what about Jamaican slice potash in chicken liver soup to go with red wine?" She looked up from the menu with the excitement of a barren woman told she was pregnant. Miriam had a pregnant plan alright.

I could see Miriam was a tough fighter; she wasn't ready to give up on these continental foods with the wonderful prices.

This time I did not bother to peep and check on the price on the menu! I have been properly enlightened on which side of the price tag such a name will fall.

"Are you new to this kind of places?" I asked, turning my head by the side and looking up and down the exquisite environment, adopting the curious countenance of one whose life revolves around such environment.

"I beg your pardon? Why?! Why are you asking me if I'm new here?" She said with a flare. She sounded so annoyed and slighted, as if I was questioning her in her father's house.

Well, new or not new it doesn't matter baby, this can't be your everyday menu.

I quickly put up an apologetic face "No, what I meant was that you should have known how slow these people are, it will take ages to prepare that meal . . . always so annoying!" I pronounced the word 'annoying' with a sting of foreign accent, like all the rich dudes do when disrupted from watching Hollywood movies.

"Ohhh" She lowered the menu disappointedly again, but was forced to agree with me so that she would not look out of place.

I could see looking up the menu and pronouncing such names was not an easy task for Miriam. Such names were surely not her regular everyday meal. Imagine Miriam that I met twice on commercial motorcycle in the hot sun, calling 5000 naira dish her favourite meal, just because she saw a man to cut his pocket. Women! Well, don't worry young ladies; you will see your routine meal soon. No be Lagos we dey?

"Ok, young ladies" I said, stretching my hands to collect the menu from her hands, ostensibly to assist them with making a choice. I emphasised the word young very audibly, to encourage Miriam to release the menu in her hands.

I continued speaking softly, adopting the caring voice of a man sure of his standing.

"Let me go to the sales counter and ask for the best meal they have in stock, you know it's still early for them to have most of what you see on the menu. I will drop some cash at the counter and tell them to get their best dish ready and fast for you, they will serve you soon. I got to be rushing back to the office, I can't wait any longer, and visitors would have filled my officer by now." I blurted everything out with the impatience of an official overshadowed by responsibilities.

I felt the touch of the money in my pocket with a huge regret. There is no eating for me here anymore, hopefully I could salvage something from this unfortunate incident that should see me through the coming week with mama sikiru pounded yam.

I quickly stood up with the speed of one that should be looking for the loo, than one going to the counter to place an order. I almost knocked down the side stool in my haste—don't blame me. I had to move fast before they change their minds and follow me to the counter.

. . . a hungry girl could be unpredictable.

I reached the counter and signalled the young salesgirl standing there.

"Good morning, please can I have two meat pies and two bottles of table water? Please take it to the two ladies sitting there."

I turned, smiling and looking at their direction. I could see them smiling back too, happy with the time I was taking at the counter . . . . presumably, finding out about the best food in stock.

I turned slightly, and remove the bunch of ten 500 notes on a rubber ribbon from my pocket, turning a little for Miriam and her friend to catch a glimpse, before reversing quickly, blocking their views and removing a single 500 naira note from the bunch, which I handed to the girl at the counter, "Please keep the change." I said to the girl with the smile of one used to dropping tips.

You are just lucky to grab my 100 bucks change, my sister! And that is because I had to leave fast. I can't risk waiting and being caught in the middle of my trick because of a 100 naira change.

Before leaving the counter I added softly to the sales girl "and please put the meat pies in the oven for at least 3 minutes, they like it hot." I said.

I kept my eyes on my wristwatch as I walked back to their table, to show how late I was. I quickly took my leave from Miriam and her friend and zoomed off with such a great speed for the first time.

Three hours later my Nokia phone beeped with an annoying noise. I have had enough of this phone. I'm going to change it, six years is the perfect life span for a 6000 naira handset.

It was a text message from Miriam.

The message was brief but long enough to convey her full feelings! Just one word—

Thanks.

This girl should be a confidential secretary.

I quickly replied back "*please don't mention.*"

I wanted to add, "anywhere" but thought better of it. The last time I was insulted with a text message by a Lagos girl, it took me six weeks to recover. Lagos *na wa!*

Coming To Lagos
Small Girls in Lagos with Shakara

Shakara is one word you cannot miss in Lagos. It is a local term the Yorubas of Lagos state use to describe a person who is in the habit of putting airs in carriage, or by the display of possession to impress other people. And when it comes to *shakara*, just give it to Lagos girls.

A friend in Abuja called me the other day, to inform me that he and his family were on their way to Lagos for the Christmas holidays, and I was to receive them at the Murtala Mohmamed Airport. Well, I belong to a profession where we don't travel much. And if you don't travel out, you won't need planes, right? And if you don't need planes you won't have much to do with being around an airport, am I correct? All I'm trying to say is, I was not too familiar with the airport.

I decided to go very early to the new domestic wing of the Muritala Mohammed International Airport, known as Wing 2, to await their expected arrival.

If you happen to be familiar with Lagos, you would know that the new wing of the Muritala Mohammed International Airport is the place where you come across the bourgeoisie in the society. Those whom the only thing we the ordinary people at the other side of the economic shares in common with them is the name Nigeria. And of course the occasional mutual brushes in the busy traffic—provided you happen to find yourself in their neighbourhood.

I decided to make sure I blend a little with the crowd of those making a good living. There was no need to throw myself out of the crowd by letting everyone know how hard my journey to the top was working out.

I chose to wear one of my imported three quarter knickers and leather slippers on that day—The kind of casual wears that is often adorned by rich folks who want to appear to all and sundry that the airport is an extension of their homes.

What's wrong with the deal, if I tried to join them too?

As I entered the airport, I met the place unusually less busy than it used to be; maybe because it was a Monday, or I was just not used to the dynamics of the environment.

There seem only few people in the lobby. However it wasn't long before I got the reason for the low turnout. The public address system announced that flights have been delayed nationwide as a result of the volcanic ash.

Volcanic ash? And all that fuss? The only thing the majority of Lagos residents are concerned with is the ashes of poverty. Well, we can't all live the same way, can we?! It is a big world you know.

There were four people in the lobby, three men, and a woman who was deeply asleep. The woman was yawning so loudly that she shook uncomfortably on the small plastic chair, such that one would wonder why she didn't bother to bring along her mattress.

I searched for a seat near the door and sat down. I love seating near the doors at the airport; not that I expected a stampede, but I have long noticed that it is always a little far from the small cafe always found in such lobbies. You just don't know who would bump into you in such places, and it won't look fine not ordering for a drink or snack for the person, as you will be facing the sales counter directly. It has even become worse these days with the manner girls eat all sorts of junk food.

I stretched myself on the seat for the expected delay. There was no need going to ask the girls at the information counter for the ETA. They love to appear so important about themselves even when they had no details. And they will just end up giving you information that won't pass for a night bus gossip.

It wasn't long before I realised I had also taken off on a sleep flight. I was woken up by the clipping sound of a lady's shoes. I looked up and saw two young ladies .... sorry teenagers.

I was deceived by their excessive use of facial make up.

I straightened myself quickly, and gave them a small friendly smile. But I saw that my smile did not get down well with one of the little girls. She was looking down and frowning at my stretch legs that seemed to limit their access along the entrance. The way she squeezed her nose with a sneer made me to, quickly check to see if someone had poured excrement on my shoes while I was asleep—seeing the way she was squeezing her face at me disdainfully.

"Please do you mind?" She said with annoyance, making it sound as if she was checking a cat out of her way.

Oh my God! A girl whose remaining baby diapers could still be found, talking to an elder like me as if I was her kid brother.

I was taken aback how things have changed from the time when respect for age was the order of the day. What was this girl thinking of? No matter how rotten I could be, I won't have anything to do with a little girl of her age in the first place. I'm not a politician.

I suppressed my anger and smiled, hurriedly shifting back my legs to create enough room for them on the passage. The girl passed without a glance to my direction, shaking her buttocks in the walking steps of what we refer to as *shakara*—something that could pass for a catwalk.

Moreover as she was yet to develop the features of a full grown woman, she sure looked like a walking cat from the behind.

I could see the girls had an idea of the delay, as they immediately went to the counter and ordered for some packets of biscuits and bottles of soft drinks before moving to their seats. They were soon nipping slowly on the wraps of cream biscuits like scared rats, taking it with the reluctance of one forced on bitter pills. You know what women do when eating in public—taking their time? Even those that were adept at swallowing a mouthful of *cooked beans* without chewing in the privacy of their rooms, wants you to believe a small bite of meat pie is too large to smoothly pass through their throats.

Soon, it was clear that the anticipated delay was even going to be longer than we thought. And not long after, many of the people in the hall couldn't withstand it any longer and they started leaving. Before long, I was left alone with the two young girls and a few other people in the waiting room.

I could see that the girls have not only finished the initial stock of snacks and drinks but have added more, judging by the increasing piles of empty bottles and wraps by their side.

Two and half hours later, the plane was yet to arrive, and the whole lobby was now very quiet as many people have gone leaving only the few patient ones behind. I could now see the little girls getting restless. Moving their legs and shaking in their seats. One of them, the one that gave me the sneer as they came in some hours earlier, stood up and went to meet a lady seating by the other side of the lobby. After a few exchange of words, the lady pointed to my direction. I could see the girl was not too happy about what the lady told her as she angrily went back to her seat and sat down.

About 30 minutes later, the girl was on her feet again. This time around, she came hurriedly over to my side. I could see her feverishly clapping her thighs together, no one needed to tell me those bottles of soft drinks and the wraps of meat pies have come home to roost. She looked at me, putting up a broad smile.

Mine! I *never knew her face can bring out a smile.*

"Please sir," she said with the respectable pose of a nun.

Wow, another wonder! So, this girl could pronounce sir.

"Sir, can you please show me to the loo?" She said in a barely audible voice sounding hurt.

Alright? So that was what it was all about, just as I suspected. The other lady must have told her I knew my way around. I could see she was lowering her voice barely enough for me to hear her, sounding even scared like letting out a family secret to a stranger.

I looked around and saw the cause of her discomfort. Three young men have just entered the lobby. The boys were having a problem walking around with their trousers barely able to remain on their waists and dropping down slightly to expose their underwear'.

I don't understand how these boys seem to miss their trouser sizes these days.

I looked at her and smiled knowingly, "oh you mean the toilet?" I asked her loudly.

Unlike her, *I had no concern to lowering my voice.*

I would have expected a less shocking response if I had slapped her. The girl shook as if she had stepped on a snake. From her looks she won't have minded slapping me; only that she had a more urgent need that I alone seemed to have the answer for now.

"Please don't say that here." She said in a voice choking with emotion; anyone passing by would think she was recently bereaved.

"Don't say what, young lady?" I asked a little too loud again.

I could see the normal gossip urge in the human body had drawn the three young men's attention to our side. They were slightly turning their heads to catch what we were discussing.

"Please don't say it here." From the way she was shaking, it wasn't only the words that she was afraid of it coming out.

"Ok, young lady, if you don't want me to say it here, then you can do it here." I uttered the words with a touch of finality.

From the pained expression on her face, it was clear she could not wait any longer.

"Alright, please say it, just show me the loo." She was begging and shaking now. I started shifting back a little. I was afraid it could be my turn to squeeze my nose.

"Say what, lady?" I asked her with the confidence of one that holds the ace in the game.

She could not bear it any longer, "show me the toilet, please." A megaphone won't have carried her cry round the small lobby better. I could hear some giggling from the boys behind us, but the girl didn't bother to even look around to see who was laughing. She clearly no longer cares. I pointed to the small outlet by her right—you need to have seen how cat walk turned to dog rush!

No wonder cats and dogs always have something together.

. . . . Lagos girls and shakara!

Coming To Lagos

Lagos Girls and Christmas Wahala

My brother, Christmas period is not the best time to be caught in Lagos. That is if you are not a smart player. While you are trying to celebrate the birth of our Lord, Jesus Christ, the *ajero* girls will be out to bath you around in the eateries and entertainment joints in town. At the end of the celebrations, you end up giving birth to a load of debts tied by a long umbilical cord to your creditors. This Christmas one of these Lagos girls wanted to play a fast one on me.

But trust your friend, na today?

One of the young ladies that worked in one of the new generation banks near my office decided that this year's Christmas I would be her sacrificial lamb. I started noticing the signs of her impending ambush, much earlier, when out of the blues, the girl started returning my smiles whenever I go to the bank to make one of my small withdrawals. Before then, when I go to the bank and passed across one of my crumpled cheque leaves, she would hand back my small withdrawal of five thousand naira without any natural affection, like handling a piece of smeared toilet tissue. It was always "have your money, oga," she would say, wearing a tired 'it has been a hard day' look.

But since the Christmas season started getting closer, her countenance turned to a beam of smiles and a loaded "ha! Oga SST, *wetin de* for the girls." Of course I was not taken in by her change in behaviour. I knew most of these high-class girls never had time for men like me. Men on salary scales were not their best friends.

They normally hook on to the yahoo boys, and the Sunday, Sunday spare part boys. *Yeah, the Ibo spare parts dealers that you can only get them out of their shops on Sundays. And the yahoo boys?*—They are the ones that live off internet fraud.

Anyway, towards Christmas the yahoo boys that these girls have been scavenging on usually move abroad to corner their victims properly. And the motor spare part dealers would have moved to the village for the annual show up.

So, nothing for these ladies in Lagos at this time of the year.

What about the big contractors—the married men? The ones these girls call baby in their rooms, sugar daddies at their backs and uncle when you are around? My brother, those are even harder for the girls to catch during the long holidays. Their wives cannot be that stupid—no excuses of long meetings at Alausa, or Abuja conferences this time, they were all under lock and key.

So, what do you expect? It's the last cards like us, once in a month happy bank goers, that remain for these professional spinsters.

And so this girl started to patronize me as the season approached. Applying the mode of operation of most Lagos society girls, which is usually to move from the general to the specifics.

Like a military commander giving orders for an attack.

First as the Holiday season gets nearer and nearer it was "ha, Oga SST what's there for the girls?" And before you can think of something cheap, like greeting cards for the girls, they will quickly move to the specifics, giving away their hidden options.

"*Haba*, oga SST, won't you take us to Silverbird Cinema? 2face is having a show there, you know"—Sometimes, I love the great faith of these young ladies. A man that at most cashes a cheque of 5000 naira, you still want him to take you out for a 20,000 naira show, and you work at his bank? You can't even guess his worth? Anyway, Lagos women possess great faith. Always believing men have a hidden source of funds.

My problem with Lagos girls was I never knew how to say, no, to them, like a police officer confronted with a bribe. And since I couldn't learn to say no, I made sure I learn how to survive without a no.

So I agreed to Cindy's request to take her out on Christmas day to the show. And as if that was not enough, she added "Oga SST, my friend just arrived from Paris, she is lonely, and can she come along? Please . . . !" The way she pronounced Paris, you would think she was consulted when the city was named. I quickly answered, as If I could not wait to have her friend added to the team "of course, Cindy why not? She can come along, we can do with more company, it's the festive period, so where can I come and pick you girls?" I said, making it sound as if taking them out was my best Christmas gift.

"Hmmm, maybe we can come and meet you at home, just give me your address" She said with a patronising smile.

Cindy am I just coming to Lagos? I asked myself.

She knows by the time I cross the gutters to her house, I won't price her meal beyond a plate of rice.

Lagos, everybody is an actor . . . EKO NI BAJE!

"Alright, meet me at the Ikeja Estate, that's where I'm staying for now. My accommodation is yet to be processed." I said smiling back.

I needed to make an early excuse to cover up for any shortcoming before they see the deplorable condition of my place. I could see her smiling sheepishly; she was not new to the game too.

So on Christmas morning, I made sure I got a new grape wine bottle and sandwiched it in my refrigerator amongst the packs of sachet water. You know the wine? Made in Ikorodua with the Italy label? And all you need to make it foreign was to exchange the rubber cork with an old wooden one. And since one of my guest was said to be just arriving from abroad—as Cindy claimed, I decided to search for a wooden cork and have a foreign wine.

You can trust girls, Cindy that said it would be a problem locating my place was knocking on my door by 9am. I quickly sprayed the last drops of my body perfume and opened the door for them. I could see Cindy had a friend lagging behind her, the one she told me she was bringing alone.

"Meet my friend . . . . l'asseine." She said as if announcing the queen.

"Oh, l'asseine? It sounds French." I said taking her hand. From the hard touch of her tough palms I won't be surprised if l'assene was not christened at ghettos of Ajegunle. You know what Shakira said hips don't lie? Well, your palms don't lie too; they easily tell how life has treated you.

I still managed to maintain a straight face.

She giggled and smiled "Yes it is; I was born and live in Paris." She said in a very soft voice trying to hide the local accent. Born in Paris? *Oh my God!* Lagos girls, any lie is possible.

I wasn't giving up, so I continue "oh Paris, I love Paris" I said. But hoping I won't be taken on what I know about Paris by my 'born in Paris' friend. From the fear in her eyes, hearing me saying, I love

Paris, I could see my "I live in Paris" friend didn't want to be taken on what she knows about Paris too. So, we left Paris alone.

Time for us to go—I could see the girls have drained half my bottle of wine.

Awuf they run belle . . . anyway, time will tell!

So we went outside to pick my car. My next door neighbour who travelled abroad for the Christmas left his Mercedes Jeep keys with me to be warming the car in his absence. Trust rich men, they always move with rich ideas. The car keys could only start but would not move the car—expensive security system.

No problem! It's in line with my plans.

I could see how their faces lighten up when I approached the sparkling white Mercedes Jeep. They were rusting to catch to the doors of the car!

Not so soon, ladies!

The speed with which Cindy opened the front door and jumped inside the jeep with the agility of a triple jumper as soon as I beeped the security lock, you would think the car was packed at her father's garage. I could see the two of them giggling excitedly as they settled into the leather upholstery of the car seats.

You know, some girls desired nothing more than for a friend to see them in an expensive car, a clear sign that their status has changed.

I started the car ignition, but of course, as expected the car won't move.

"Oh, shit!" I said loudly, banging the steering wheel, but taking care not to use much force.

"What's the problem?" Cindy asked in a worried voice.

"Oh, the car won't move." I replied her.

"Why?" Cindy asked. I could see she was very concerned.

"I was supposed to warm the engine for two hours last night, to get the security system started. But I forgot; now I will need a day to start it, shit!" I exhaled loudly. I could see Cindy and her friend near to shed tears on realising they won't move out to town with the glittering jeep. They looked so ruffled; one would think they were getting a horrible report from a doctor.

"So can we take a taxi drop?" Cindy asked with the determination of 'nothing is going to spoil my day'.

"There's no need for that, we can use my other car. But you have to manage; it's so small, I really hardly used it, except when going to the gym on weekends." I said with a feeling of disappointment. *I felt bad as I was talking so badly of my Peugeot 206 car that had served me faithful in the last four years.*

I hope cars don't have feelings!

I could see their annoyance when we got near to the battered small blue car. The exuberance earlier exhibited by Cindy in entering the Mercedes jeep had since disappeared as she opened the door to the small Peugeot car. As soon as I entered, I started the engine, and took off fast before any of them could suggest anything different.

We didn't go far before Cindy started winding up her side window glass.

"Oh, sorry, I didn't inform you, the air conditioning just packed up, and the car brain box can only be worked on by a computer. The only workshop that has that facility has closed for the holidays. Shit, I never thought I will have to use this car any soon." I said to her.

If I had told Cindy to come down and walked, I would have gotten a less hostile stare.

"There's no AC! Oh, My God! Do you want us to roast here? Are we chicks . . . I mean chicken?" She let out her frustration so loud with the air of one not used to such discomfort.

Just imagine, Cindy that I saw twice on okada commercial motorbike in the hot sun, claiming she can't enter a car without an AC. I almost laughed out loud. But I controlled myself, more so, now that all was going according to plan

"Sorry, girls, I'm so sorry, it's all about that jeep, anyway, I will try and take a shortcut to get there so that we won't take too long in the traffic." I said it in a voice sounding so concerned that even I started to get worried if something was actually going wrong.

Boy, was I falling for my own gimmick? Am I getting so good like that? Wow!

I decided to take the unfamiliar route through Ajasin Adekunle Street that I hoped by then would be choking with traffic. And my brother, I was not disappointed. We soon found ourselves blocked from the front and back by traffic moving at one kilometre in twenty hours. You can trust Lagos; the sun was soon shining like a power exchange station. I could see Cindy and her friend making frantic efforts to fan themselves as they improvised with the Christmas greeting cards I left lying around the car for such purpose.

They were soon getting restless as we pass through the slow moving traffic. I could see L'asseene staring widely at the street sales boys going about in between the traffics holding out bottles of soft drinks and short cake wraps for sale.

"Oh, I feel like taking something." She said loudly, groaning like a young lion in a zoo. I looked out of the window at the boys holding out the soft drinks and smiled.

No way girl, not now!

I shook my head disapprovingly "Oh! No need for all these street stuff. I just can't stand buying food on the street. We will soon get out of this traffic and find a good restaurant." I said it with the authority of one used to good food.

I *was silently praying that none of them would open the glove compartment of the car and discover the empty wraps of galla sausage popularly sold on the streets of Lagos.*

After two hours in the hot traffic, I could see the girls looking very famished and their hands red from fanning themselves. Not only L'aseneine, but also Cindy, was now looking out for what to eat.

I moved along quietly, not taking my eyes off the road, humming silently under my breath as I followed the slow moving traffic. I looked outside the window to check where we had reached. I knew from experience that after passing the shortcake sellers, the next we would come across could be the roadside plantain vendors. I can afford that.

"Oh! Please, I'm so hungry," shouted Cindy; now unable to control herself.

I looked outside the car window. *Good! We have reached the fried plantain and sachet water site. I could see the small girls with the fried plantain chips lying carelessly on small trays placed on their heads, and the boys holding the leather bags containing the sachet water, rushing to the cars, through the slow moving traffic.*

"Sorry ladies, there is nothing good around here to eat, if you can wait till . . . ." before I could finished speaking, I saw the two desperate hands of Cindy and L'asseine flyimg out of the open car windows and almost dragging the badly fried plantain from the small girl's hands! And of course, you don't need to ask if sachet water came along too.

The boy selling the sachet water was right in handy. From experience, he knew after a person finishes rushing down such a hard snack in the hot sun, the next will be the turn of his sachet water, and he wasn't wasting time. Come and see Paris L'asseine rushing the fried plantain with sachet water. Ajegunle style! Yunwa shege!

It didn't take long before the girls started shifting uncontrollable in their seats. The long wait in the traffic, coupled with the afternoon heat—and you know the other one, don't you? Well, after gulping all that wine, and now two packets of sachet water each, what do you expect?

"Please can we go back?" Cindy was almost crying, the pressure building in her bladder seemed to be getting too much on her.

"No, don't worry; we will soon get out of the traffic. We are not too far from Silverbird Cinema from here." I said with the assurance of a man that knew the area. They were not the only ones feeling uncomfortable with a full bladder. I was bottled up too, and of course uncomfortable. But that could wait, I had more pressing needs.

"Please, we want to go back!" Cindy was very loud now, almost yelling at the top of her badly strained voice.

"Why?" I asked softly, feigning surprise.

"Please, I say plaeseee." She was almost sobbing. I looked behind. This time it was the 'Paris born' L'assene talking. The French accent had long disappeared in the present realities.

When a girl talks like that, you don't need to wait anymore, or you would end up creating an unpleasant scene.

I had no problem this time finding a shortcut. We were soon at my apartment in less than 10 minutes. Hardly did I open the doors to my apartment when the two girls rushed at once to my bathroom.

I slowly walked to the bed and lied down, closing my eyes to get a short rest after the hard outing.

Most importantly, I needed to adopt a tired and disappointed look too.

When I opened my eyes, the room was surprisingly quite. I called out, no answer. I checked the bathroom—nobody. My goodness! The girls slipped away without me noticing. Oh my God! These girls can work in the secret service.

I touched my pocket; my last 5000 naira was intact. Phew!

What a break! When I was yet to buy a pack of chicken and make my Christmas stew, these girls are calling for shows at Silverbird. Lagos girls, Silverbird, no face this time!

Na so I escaped. Lagos na wa!

Coming To Lagos

The Wise Prof and His Weird Talks

There was this gentleman that lived in an apartment near Segun's house, where I was squatting in Lagos before moving to my own apartment.

We loved to call him the Whiteman, but he preferred we call him Prof. This Whiteman or prof as he preferred to be called was a really queer old fellow. He kept a bushy hair and an unkempt beard that gave him the appearance that is often associated with the eccentricities of renowned scientists.

Well, maybe, not all scientists, but Albert Einstein was a good example.

Prof possessed a remarkable prowess in the use, or rather twisting of English proverbs. He was as he called himself the "English virtuoso!" He was orphaned at a very early age in life and had a very difficult childhood because he paid his way through school by doing several menial jobs. If you look into the eyes of Prof you would see a thousand stories; none pleasant. The man had a difficult time in his life.

He once told me of the stories of the hardship of his early life.

"Yeah, a lot of us in life started from the scratch." I tried at comforting him after hearing a lot of his sad tales.

"Yes, SST, you are right, most started from the scratch. I started from nothing." he replied sadly!

Despite the hardship of his upbringing, he was still able to complete his primary education. But he was unable to see himself through college. He turned to newspaper vendor at a very early age and out of a natural voraciousness for learning—he easily got himself acquainted with the usage of the English proverbs.

I can remember anytime I bring a word, or a maxim, in English to Prof, or the Whiteman as I love to call him; he had a way of twisting it to his own explanation. And hardly what you could expect from someone in his twilight.

One day, I decided to have a long conversation with him. It was on a New Year's Eve when I returned early from the office.

"Hey, prof, good morning," I said when I saw him sitting in his favourite rocking chair in his patio.

"My son, how are you?" He said to me. To Prof we are all sons to him.

"Prof! I told you, I'm not a son, I'm an old dog too, you know what they say, you can't teach an old dog new tricks." I was teasing him.

" . . . try to slaughter it and it will surprise you of the new tricks it could perform." He replied.

"Yeah, Prof, do you want to start, right? Ok let me see . . . . Rome was not built in a day." I said.

"That's what happens when those in charge want to *eat alone.*" he laughed loudly.

Eat alone, in Nigerian parlance means taking all the slices that come from a deal.

"Good Prof, what about the patient dog eats the fattest bone?" I added another one.

"When the inpatient ones are through with the flesh!" Prof replied gleefully.

"A friend in need is a friend indeed." A difficult one I believe.

"When you do not know how to dodge him, son!" Prof said without batting an eyelid.

"You can take a donkey to the river but you can't force it to drink" I quickly brought another one to throw him off balance.

"You don't need to, just choke its throat with pepper." Prof said without pity.

Wicked man!

"The best always comes to those that wait"

"If those that were there first, didn't know what took them there!" Prof answered with a big grin.

I got the message.

"The chickens are coming home to roost." I said, shaking my armpits to imitate the flapping of a chicken.

"When they are sure they are not coming home to roast." Prof was laughing at this one.

It was the holidays season, remember? Not a good time for chicken to be returning home.

Maybe I should give up; this old guy knows what it takes.

"Ok prof I give up." I said throwing my hands up.

"No way my son, you just started never give up, you can win." he said encouragingly to me.

Well, what do I have to lose?

"Be nice to the people you meet on your way up." I threw a popular one to go with the situation, since he was winning; he should at least show some kindness to the ones he was leaving behind.

"Yea, because you will step on their heads when coming down." He said. Prof was unkind with victory again.

' "A bird in hand is worth two in the bush." I gave it to him again.

" . . . when you don't know how to hunt!" Prof replied smiling again.

You can say that again Prof!

"Is darkest before dawn . . . ." I put it to him again.

"That's the best time to check who is leaving your neighbour's house." Prof's laughter was deliberate.

What! This old crook being spying on us?

"Ok, Prof, you won, old man, hey, how do you make sure your neighbours remember you when you are no more?" I asked.

I hope I didn't make it sound as if he had reached the end of the road.

"Die with some of their debts." He said. Yes, that was thoughtful of him.

"And how do you get your friends to remember you, Prof?"

"...you should have come a hundred years earlier." He said with a sorrowful note. I understood he must have had a hard feeling at how times have changed. An old man getting lonely and forgotten; Sad you know.

"Tough world prof . . . . as they say when the going gets tough" I wanted to lighten his posture as best as I could.

" . . . . sleep starts coming," he said with a yawn. I guess he was tired, it was getting late anyway.

"Yeah, I have got to go, good night prof." I bid him as I leave.

"Thanks, I enjoyed your company, wish you what you wish yourself in the New Year, son." He said to me in a very tired voice.

I stopped and looked back at him with a smile.

He is in my turf now!

"Sorry, I can't wish you the same, prof." I said calmly. He turned immediately towards me and looked at me in surprise.

"What did you say, son? You don't wish me well?" He asked, still sounding surprise.

"I didn't say that prof. I said, I can't also say, I will wish you what you wish yourself" I explained.

"And why if I may ask?" Prof was intuitive. I smiled, and started to give it to him my motivation styles.

"You can only wish for yourself what you know. You don't know enough. You can only wish for yourself what you see. You are not seeing enough. You can only wish what you have heard. You are not hearing enough. So I can't say I wish you what you wish yourself." I can see Prof was more relaxed now and attentive.

"I can only wish you what God has for you because eyes have not seen, and ears have not heard, what the Lord has for those who trust in Him" I said quoting God's promises from the scriptures. Prof burst out laughing and stood from his chair to tap my shoulders.

"Good, son, good, you sure are a great man. You are going far son, you are going far!" He said cheerfully.

"Thanks, prof, thanks!" I said as I walked away.

Coming To Lagos

Shine Your Eyes

It wasn't long before I learned that to survive in Lagos, you would need to *shine your eyes*! Shine your eyes is a popular metaphor used by Lagosians to warn you that when dealing with people, what they say, and what they say they do, are often very far from the reality.

It warns you that you need to be very careful when confronted with situations in life, because seeing or hearing from someone should not always be the basis for judgement.

And so did I found out in Lagos when I studied what a girlfriend tells her suitor when he proposes marriage to her, or the popular excuses boys give their girlfriends when they fail to keep an appointment; and even what you hear from the cocky looking physician when you are admitted in the hospital.

And these were just a few amongst several other things I observe from my interactions, and of course, observations and other instances that I had in the ever intriguing city of Lagos.

I was lucky to collate a little from my observations and put them down to assist my reader's understanding of life in Lagos, the city of mysteries.

Jimmy, Be careful what The Girlfriend Tells You When You Propose Marriage to Her!

Oh Jimmy, you are a nice guy. (*Sorry nice guy. She has no jersey for you in her team, girls prefer rough players.*)

It is not that I do not really care about you. (My friend, *note the word 'love' was craftily avoided!*)

Jimmy, please, I think we should not rush things between us. (*She is eagerly rushing it with someone else somewhere!*)

I like it when a man takes it softly with me. (*She is taking it roughly with that other guy and enjoying it too!*)

We should take our time and consider, please baby? (More time? yea, why not? *Enough time to see if that guy is serious about her!*)

Hope, you do understand my dear. (*Mister, hope you don't mind wasting your time while her guy decides if he wants to make it permanent with her.*)

Girls on the runs are like cars on the run, Jimmy . . . . they both need good spare tyres—you are a spare tyre!

MY DEAR, MR. MIKE PLEASE CONSULT AFTER SEEING THAT CONSULTANT

Mr. Mike, we have run the necessary tests on you. (*Yeah, he is making it clear to you from the start, that we, the hospital, not I, the doctor should be held responsible for any error!*)

The case of your sickness is a little complicated. *(mmhh . . . . complicated in the sense that he does not know what it is all about!)*

We need to run another test Mr. Mike *(Yeah, why not? That would give him enough time to check your case with another physician elsewhere!)*

Meanwhile you can continue taking the drugs we prescribed to you! *(Just telling you that the drugs you are taking now, could be miles away from what might next be prescribed for your illness when you meet again.)*

I'm sure our staff have been taking care of all your needs? *(He wants you to have that in mind when they bring that exaggerated bill when you are leaving the clinic.)*

IT'S BUSINESS ANYWAY!

Mr. Mark Okonkwo, we have gone through your proposal ... *(They said gone through? Not read? Sorry brother!)*

The recommendations contained in your paper are good *(wow! that is the last part in your proposal, looks like they just can't wait to get rid of you!)*

However, we need to wait a little until funds are available for the project, so we keep in touch *sir. (What did they said? Did I heard keep in touch? Just like that? Well, you are lucky; you are dealing with gentlemen, Mr Okonkwo. Such reply In Lagos is synonymous to throwing the paper in your face!)*

A GUY IS FULL OF LIES, WATCH IT MY GIRLS!

Oh baby, I am sorry for not calling you all these days. I have been so busy at the office. (Girl, *why are you wasting time on this fellow? No guy forgets to call a lady he loves for a day!)*

Of course baby, I promise it won't happen again. (Yeah, *why not? He has been breaking promises before and getting away with it!)*

You said we should see on Monday? Alright, please let me check and see if I'm free in the office then. *(Yeah, I heard you Romeo! if the other lady does not require your attention at the time!)*

My Guy, JIM . . . . WHAT THAT GIRL IS TELLING YOU ON THE PHONE IS NOT EXACTEDLY WHAT SHE IS THINKING!

Hello? Who is calling? You said your name is Jim, Jim who? *(Yaaaah! At last! But what took you so long to call me, boy?)*

What are you saying please? You said we met at Basement Club and I gave you my phone number? Mmhh . . . . I don't think I can remember! *(Forget what? how can I forget that? You were in my hard disk all this while, boy!)*

You want us to meet again? Mmhh! *(Oh my God, he is asking me out!)*

No, no please. I said no! Saturday, won't be possible, I will be very busy then. *(I have a mother, buster! I have been taught all the tricks, I have to drag it small, and I can't appear cheap!)*

Ok . . . Yes, I will try and be available on Sunday, but wait! I can't promise anything. *(Sunday, yahuu! I can't wait for the weekend to be over!)*

Talk a little louder please . . . you said we should meet at Mr. Biggs Eatery at Maryland? No! Why don't we see at the Silverbird Gardens? It's not far from my place. *(Don't worry, young man, no need to rush, my boy. When harvest time comes, you will be running debts in all the eateries in Lagos!)*

Alright Jim or whatever you call yourself; I will try and be there on time if I can, please I have other things awaiting my attention now goodbye! *(On time? why mention, boy? of course I will be on time, why won't I? Silverbird Gardens is a dangerous place to leave a guy hanging alone for long, you know? . . . oh my God, your lucky number girl!)*

Coming To Lagos

The Bulldozers

Mr Sani Shittu work in a detergent manufacturing factory that had a security contractual agreement with the security firm I use to work for in Lagos. He was a lively and serious minded person. I got to be acquainted with him on one of my several inspection visits to the factory to check on the security guards that I deployed at the factory. My department was in charge of deploying guards to areas they were needed and it was my duty to check on these guards. On such visits I have to discuss with the staff during which I advise them on ways of ensuring or rather improving on security details in their establishments.

It was during one of such discussions that I got to learn that Mr Shittu had run several jobs in the city of Lagos before finally deciding to settle down for the job of a quality assistant at the Melrose Detergent Factory. He was at one time a personal assistant to a top politician, who was a senator of the Federal Republic. It was during the period of the second attempt at democratic rule that was eventually truncated by the military.

With the return to another experiment at democratic governance, Shittu decided that he has had enough of fooling around with politicians, age was not on his side for such tasks, and so he settled for a steady job at the factory.

During one of our several discussions he said to me "SST, have you registered for the forthcoming elections?" It was the election year, and the National Electoral Commission was updating voters register nationwide.

"No" I replied simply.

He looked at me thoughtfully and said "you see, SST, I used to be reluctant to register like you too. I never had confidence in the electoral system but this time, I believe the nation is ready to chart a new course and have a free and fair elections." He said.

"And what do you mean by free and fair elections, was it not free and fair before?" I asked sarcastically. It was an open secret; everyone knew elections were far from being credible in the last dispensations. It was such knowledge that killed my zeal for participating in elections.

He smiled and looked at me with the kind of pity reserved for someone divulged from the reality. "It was really bad, especially here in Lagos, SST." He said calmly. "I was part of it all and therefore I should know. I once told you I was the personal assistant to Chief Dabros .... it was more than that, I was his chief organizer, the main rigging machine of his landslide victories." He sounded rueful as he recalled the memory.

"Chief, Dr Dabros, as he love to be called, was a medical doctor turned politician. I never really saw any sign of medical knowledge in him, aside from the fact that he seemed to have realized earlier that being a doctor was not his calling as he obviously did not earned the title. Chief Dabros was amongst the politicians known as the bulldozers, the power brokers that break anything that stand between them and their ambitions. I once followed him to visit the resident electoral commissioner that oversees the election in his constituency, at his office after a voting exercise." Shittu leaned further on the leather settee as he started recanting his experience.

"As we entered the office, the resident commissioner, Mr Somas, rushed out of his seat to welcome Chief Dabros, almost tripping down as he tried to cover the little distance to where we were standing. One would think he was welcoming the head of the electoral commission and not one of the contestants of an election he just conducted. Chief stopped at the door as soon as he entered the office, waiting for the man to come forward and meet him; with Chief, every move was to show who was in control."

"Good day, Chief, what a pleasant surprise! I never knew you were coming." Mr. Somas was talking profusely and bowing as he speaks. Chief smiled and extended his hand, leaving Mr. Somas wondering whether to kiss or lick it.

The man decided to shake it with both hands affectionately.

"My friend, I just came around to see how the work is going on after the voting, hope I'm not disturbing you?" He said, looking at the boxes containing the ballot papers of the elections that were conducted barely three hours ago. Mr Somas followed his gaze, staring at the pile of boxes like an unnecessary wastage. It was clear that from the time they were returned from the polling booths to the office none of the electoral officials cared to go near them. What the people were waiting to hear were results from the electoral commission. And Mr. Somas seemed to have that at hand already.

"Oh! Chief! You don't need to worry, we have you in a good lead." He said with a mischievous smile. "My boys just recorded another seventy five percent score for you, another landslide."

It was Chief's second consecutive electoral victory. Four years earlier; he was voted to the senate for the first time, he was now going for a second time. It wasn't Mr. Somas that presided over the first election, but it was all the same as usual. Chief always gets the electoral officers and the results he desired.

Mr. Somas shook his head slightly and said "But the boys were a little immature, they recorded votes for you above the census population in certain areas, so I had to make some amendments. The twenty first amendment of my electoral constitution!" He laughed and quickly added "But no problem, Chief, I was still able to retain you on sixty five percent and give your nearest opponent twenty percent! The rest of whatever vote that remained was to be shared by the other three contestants."he said cheerfully.

But Chief frowned at hearing that Mr. Somas and his electoral staff allotted twenty percent of the vote to his closest rival.

Chief Dabros had been having a very acrimonious relationship with the candidate of the most visible party in the constituency, Mr. Mike Falana. Falana was a very popular politician amongst the huge poor middle class who adore his honesty and selflessness as against Chief's army of thugs and part-time criminals that carry out his biddings. Chief had always seen Falana as his greatest threat and had vowed to humiliate him in the elections. Falana's supporters can only vote. Chief controls the counts. Chief Dabros never bothered about the people that come out to vote, what matters to him was who was to count.

The ordinary voters don't know anything about percentages, all they waited for was to see who emerges the winner. However, Falana, and the party elites know, Chief Dbaros wanted to annoy them with a humiliating defeat. It was not just a question of wining, it was about ego.

There was deep vendetta to settle between the two.

"Twenty percent is a big bonus for that nincompoop!" Chief said angrily. Mr. Somas saw his hard reaction and quickly coiled inwards like a snail sensing danger.

I could easily understand his fright. Chief does not only control people by monetary bribes, those that had sidelined before him had always been **found** missing. As it was well known, you miss a lot by going against a trailer.

Chief Dabros was a bulldozer!

"Sorry Chief, I guess you are right, twenty percent is rather too high." He agreed hurriedly, "we are yet to announce the results so there is still room for another of my amendments!" He laughed loudly in a way to reassure his all important guest. "We will spread around ten percent to the other opponents." Chief didn't seem too relief with that either, so Mr. Somas quickly readjusted to reassure him further, "And maybe add another four percent to you sir, to take you to seventy percent?" He was begging!

Chief seemed to love Mr. Soma's arithmetic as he readjusted the red cap that symbolizes his authority, a habit he does whenever he was happy.

"But let me caution, sir, such high votes could raise suspicion and lead to the other parties taking to litigation on the election results." Mr. Somas was sounding worried. Chief Dabros laughed at his obvious naivety; really, it was Mr. Somas first time of handling an election involving Chief Dabros. He was recommended to Chief by the head of the electoral body to be the resident electoral commissioner. Had he known Chief Dabros better, he would have known that litigation was the least of his worries; more than half of the magistrates live in fear of him. The remaining halves were on his pay roll!

"That would be good, many of you have worked well for my generosity, it would be a good opportunity for the judges to also work for what I'm providing." He said with the confidence of a man that has the system in his pockets. Mr. Somas did not need further explanation. I could see his expression returning to its former cheerful state—he realized he had nothing to fear from the courts. Mr. Somas was smiling with the flavour of a contented man. Working with Chief comes with huge benefits. You get to earn beyond your wildest dreams—and keep your limbs too.

"And what about the rest of your staff?" Chief Dabros always desires that whosoever worked for his interest and in whatever scale was well rewarded.

"Oh Chief! The boys are happy with you, they didn't have much to do for the much you did for them." Mr. Somas was looking with contempt the pile of ballot papers left uncounted as he speaks. His staff would have spent hours shuffling through them, but all they were left to do was to manufacture the results and go home to enjoy their pay and what Chief Dabros had for them.

Mr. Somas eyes suddenly hardened diabolically as he said coolly, "It was good you took care of that stupid boy, John Okoro; he was trying to be difficult. But he later seemed to have come around and gave us no more problems."

John Okoro was an idealistic young man that believed the system could still be salvage with a bit of honesty. After his graduation, he refused to work in the major firms and opted for a government job at the electoral office where he carried his sermon of probity and accountability. It was a wonder how he got posted to Chief's constituency to be a part of the electoral proceedings. By the time Chief Dabros realized his character, it was too late to get him out, so he set out to 'settle' him in.

But Mr. Okoro was going about talking of being an apostle of free and fair elections since his days as a student union leader. He refused all entreaties to be bribed by Chief Dabros. When it became clear he was going to be the weakest link in the chain, Chief decided to strengthen his spine a little. He decided to be free and fair to him in his own way.

Chief sent his gang of thugs to burn Mr. Okoro's home. The thugs brought him and his family out before setting the building on fire. They made him to understand that if he did not display a change of heart towards Chief Dabros they would be back, and the next time they might not have the time to bring him and his family out before going about what brought them.

Mr. Okoro quickly gave up his hard-line stance for a free and fair election after the police failed to come to his rescue. He went on his knees to receive what Chief had to offer and resettled his family in a new house. After that nothing was heard of him as he went about doing his job 'well' like the other staff. Chief even came to love his short-lived rebellion as it helped him to once again send a message of a clear warning of what comes from crossing him.

"Yeah good; well thanks to hear that, I'm on my way." Chief said. Mr. Somas rushed to Chief's side like one trying to help an invalid out of a seat. Before we reached the door, Mr. Somas had already had it open wide making no pretence of his subservience to the bulldozer!" Shittu said with a sigh of one who had carried a big load for a long time.

I was so taken in by this story that I didn't know what to say of it. I knew things were bad with the elections but I had never known the depth of the rut.

"You mean the people didn't follow the laws?" I asked in surprise.

"Laws, SST? We didn't see any law. It's not that there wasn't any, it was just that nobody saw it, maybe, the bulldozers crushed all!" He shrugged. "So, you see, SST, why I was so sceptical about elections? But that was some time ago. I now see that things have changed, people now defend their votes. We no longer have the Chief Dabros of this world and the bulldozers calling the shot. So,

76

I am going to register and vote for the first time." He sounded so hopeful that I was forced to express open agreement with him.

But I left him less confident than I appeared after what I heard, I was left hoping if all had indeed changed, and if we were no more to see the bulldozers.

The Transformation
When SST Met His King

The stories of my experiences in Lagos that I have just related was my life style until I undergo a complete transformation that led to my becoming a motivational speaker and source of inspirations to millions of listeners of radio talk shows in the city of Lagos.

Many of those I later met, especially amongst those that got to know me first in Lagos, use to wonder how and when did I gave up the corny and crafty ways of surviving in Lagos, and turned to the new leaf that led me to becoming the motivational DJ? Most of them wanted to find out how I stopped being one of them and became someone that advises millions across the most populous black city on Earth on how to live their lives in accordance to God's dictates.

I always say that my transformation came to me as much of a surprise as it was to them.

It all started when I had a dream in which I saw myself transmuted in the form of a striving new personality in a different world. I was carried in the form of a prospering young man who suddenly found himself confronted with life threatening challenges.

It all started as a dream.

I saw myself in a trance, living a bustling, carefree and expensive lifestyle. Then all of a sudden, my life was overshadowed by a huge problem that continued growing bigger by the day, like a cancerous growth. I searched through several books, but there was no solution. I called upon friends and relations but none bothered to answer my call. I had a feeling they were all avoiding me. Those that wined and dined with me when all was well were nowhere to be found.

I was advised to go to the old King. I was bewildered; I, SST, The modern theorist and a radical liberalist go to a traditional relic for a solution? The tradition of the ages is the landmark of my parents' teachings but they do not hold water in my modern society. And how can I even present myself before the King after all I have done? I have been amongst those attacking the rule of the King and breaking his laws, all in a bit to build a free society away from the draconian laws of the past.

But when my problems persisted; I knew no peace and so I was forced to swallow my pride. I decided to go to the King's palace.

The Palace was full of people, all loyal subjects of the King waiting to see him. The guards accosted me at the gate and turned me back. They knew me very well. I was one of the prominent ones amongst the bad subjects that were breaking the king's rules, and campaigning for a free society where people will have the right to do all they wanted to, without being told by the King. Then how do I expect to see the king when even loyal subjects have been waiting for years without being able to see him? The guards wondered aloud at my effrontery.

But I had to see the king, my problems were persisting beyond comprehension and nobody was ready to help me. So I decided to place myself in a position near the palace where the king will see me and maybe then I could get a chance to have an audience with him. I was deciding on how to join the workers that clean and take care of the palace, when I heard someone nearby talking to me—saying I shouldn't disgrace myself. What! How could I? A big man like me with men under my command be seen sweeping the palace. What would the people that knew me say when they see me stoop so low to wash the streets? I looked around, but there was nobody around. I realised it was pride talking in me. But my problem had long passed my pride and it was growing to the stage that I can't hide it anymore; even my pride couldn't cover it.

So, I joined the workers at the palace, exchanging my expensive clothes for the rags of the workers. I wasn't there long before what I feared the most started happening to me. My family were scandalised, my friends laughed at my stupidity and mocked at me. The workers at the palace also laughed at me, many of them had worked for years at the palace but had not met the king, how could I just come in a day and believe the king will call me? I realised they were there, many years, at the Palace without meeting the king; because some of them were there working for a pay, others were there so that people would see them at the Palace and accord them recognition, others were there because other people use to come there while others were there because coming to the palace had become a sort of ritual they were used to from childhood. But my case was different. I was there to get an audience with the king. I was there because I had a problem that defied solutions. So I decided to work in a manner that the king must notice me. I was always the first to get to the Palace in the morning and start sweeping, and the last to leave.

I missed meals several times in some days so that I could finish my work while the other workers go for lunch break. I turned those days to fasting. Sometimes, I use to sit down quietly in a corner away from the other workers and go over all my activities in life in my mind begging and hoping that the king would be able to forgive and overlook my transgressions as I regret my actions. After being there for a few weeks, one of the guards called me and told me the king wanted to see me. Wow! He had noticed my service. So, I ran to the court but there were many people on the queue waiting to see the king. I had to wait again.

I refused to go and eat for three days so that I could maintain my place on the queue. Finally, I was ushered into the presence of the king. There were many people in the palace, some that I knew and even helped in the past. I wanted to enter with dignity so as not to embarrass myself in front of them. But my problem was bigger than their opinions, so I went flat on my tummy before the king. I was known to all as a strongman and a seasoned warrior; after all I fought in the wars in Liberia, Sierra Leone, Sudan, just to mention a few.

However, I quickly turned myself to a child before the king and started crying so that he will come to my case.

I saw one of the constant visitors to the palace, a wicked high chief that was banished from a position of prominence in the Palace for plotting to overthrow the king. But he still comes to the palace occasionally to gossip to the king about people that were against his laws and asking to be allowed to deal with them, all in a bid to buy back the king's favour. And I knew he will tell the king of my rebellious attitude to his rule, so before he could speak against me, I helped him out. I quickly started confessing my entire bad attitude, the attacks and campaigns I carried out against the king's laws. I humbly bowed down asking for forgiveness before the king.

The king asked what brought me to his presence. I then had the confidence to move closer to the throne. The throne was high up, the king was not to shift from his throne to hear my request, and it was I that must move nearer to the throne for him to hear me. I was the one with the problem, anyway. So, I shifted closer to the throne and told the king my problem. I had searched for a solution from many quarters and had suffered for long without a solution.

The king smiled, that was a problem that could be solved in one day, even one hour, why did I wait for ten years in agony, he asked. I said to myself it was pride, I was a modern man not a traditionalist like my parents, I was too enlightened and had studied science enough to be going to old palaces, only illiterates still go to an ancient King! But inside me I knew it was more of ignorance. I thought I knew it all while I was just a foolish ignorant man. No matter what I felt about the king if I had known he had the power to solve the big problem afflicting me, no pride would have kept me away to suffer for ten years. The king asked me if I hadn't problem I won't have cared to come and greet an old father in an ancient palace like him. I said no, I agreed that it was the problem that brought me to the Palace. I had always looked down at the old ways that the king presents, and I always thought I was right, but how I wished I had come willingly to see this nice old father than having to have suffered first.

The King told me he had been aware of my situation all the while but as much as He felt for my situation he could not come to me, because I have to come to him first. His palace was free to all, and even to those that committed treason against him, like the wicked high chief that was always coming to lay accusation against other subjects so as to get them banished from the King's favour permanently as he was banished.

The king told me if I refuse to come to his presence, I will always miss a lot and a lot would be said against me. He told me the days I used to sit down quietly in a corner and go over my actions with regrets, he was not far away he was there listening to me. I turned my face away in shame, what I thought was a monologue turned to be a dialogue, what I thought was a quite discussion turned out to be a loud conversation, what I thought was private discussion within me was a prayer to him.

I left the palace elated, my huge problem was over and my burden finally lifted! I promised to always come back to visit the King. I was now back to business. My friends that ran away from me heard the good news and all came back. You see, I forgave them; they were after all my friends afterall.

Later the businesses and good times started coming back big time, and I stopped going to visit the king. Please don't get me wrong. I was not ungrateful and I still loved my king. But it was the tight business schedule and the new and big office work that was keeping me away. Later my friends started drawing me back to the places the king had banned. I had started breaking the King's rules quietly again.

At first I was doing it secretly at night, so that busy bodies will not go and tell the king. But later, I grew more confident. What the hell! I told myself. If the King helped me; and so what? I was not his slave. It was just by chance that he will be the one to help me. I might have gotten help elsewhere anyway, I hissed. But something in me told me I should be ashamed of myself. The king was the only one that came to my assistance when all solutions failed, and all my friends abandoned me.

I started crying.

I ran back to the palace crying and begging for forgiveness. The king smiled and welcomed me back. From that day I decided to stay close to the king always, so that I will not be enticed back to my old ways. And as I stayed and listened more to the wisdom of my king in the Palace, I got more interested and drawn to him, till it reached the stage where I sincerely saw no sense or pleasure in my former ways, and I even started to wonder on whatever led me to rebel against my king in the first place.

My life became so peaceful and fulfilled that I desired nothing outside the Palace anymore. I needed nothing except to be in the presence of my King. And for the first time my eyes opened when a huge light fell across me. And I saw what was written on top of my king's throne—GOD ALMIGHTY, THE CREATOR OF HEAVEN AND EARTH.

And he said "I have touched your tongue with a coal of fire to go and be a source of inspiration to my people. You are to bring them out of the *disappointments and frustrations of the Enemy over their lives and lead them to the blissful realm I have planned for them." The King touched my tongue with a hot iron and ordered me to go and be a good person, to forsake my cunning ways and be a source of inspiration and motivation to all the people, helping them with their problems as I was helped with mine.*

I could feel someone pushing my shoulders, I tried opening my eyes but the rays of the morning sunlight forced me to close them back quickly "SST wake up! Are you *not going to work today?*" I immediately recognised Segun, my roommate's voice.

"*Abeg,* bros, close that window, *what's your problem?*" I said with annoyance—realising I was in a dream—All the same, I felt bad for the way he dragged me back to his miserable flat when I had just arrived paradise. Even if I was to leave my place in Heaven, why should I see myself in *Segun's* dingy room first? What kind of luck was that?

I squeezed my eyes and sat up on the bed, staring around the familiar small stuffy room.

Na wa o! What was that? So, it was all a dream?

What a life!

THE MOTIVATION DANCE CLUB SHOW ON FM RADIO 111 LAGOS

CHAPTER TWO

The Disco Jockey
How I Became the Motivation Dance Club Disco Jockey on Static FM 111

Waking up from the dream, I was filled with trepidation and regrets for my past deeds! I now know what providence had called me to do. The cunning abilities, which I seemed to possess in abundance was now to be redirected solely to the good of the society, and not to use it for wrong motives.

I was in no doubt to what I believe nature had equipped me with great abilities to do, and it was now left for me to find a means of applying the abilities positively to the lives of people around me. I saw my skills as a calling to serve, an instrument of positive motivation and a force for great inspiration!

I first thought of becoming a preacher—however, I did not allow that feeling to go far, for I knew that was not the calling. I later contemplated on writing small tracts and letting my ideas of inspiration go round. But that would need a lot of resources that I obviously did not have. Moreover, such an effort would also require an organisational structure to coordinate—something that was beyond me.

However, haunted by a defined purpose, an idea suddenly came to me. The thought of going to any of the several FM radio stations that were springing up in town, and offering to run a motivation talk show programme came to my mind. I considered offering my services free to a studio that would be interested. I didn't see it interfering with my lifestyle, because it will just be for an hour or two broadcast, preferably in the evenings when I close from work. I really didn't expect anyone to take me on a permanent employment as a presenter.

To further the desire, I started going from one media house to the other, seeking for a producer that would accept my show proposal in any of the radio stations.

Wherever I went, I met a brick wall. They all had their reasons. Some studios felt I was not a trained presenter, so they wouldn't take the risk of putting me on air. Others were of the opinion the show stood no chance of becoming a success, while the rest out rightly didn't want to have anything to do with me.

Nevertheless, I refused to give up or surrender to despair. This is because, deep within me, I knew it was my calling, a task I needed to do. When a man finds his path in life, nothing can move him away from it!

Despite the frustrating setbacks, I continued unrelentingly with my search. It was after three weeks of roaming around the streets of Lagos, and almost at the brink of giving up, that I unexpectedly stumbled on what seemed like a solution to my problem.

It was while riding in the ever crowded and noisy Lagos buses, during one of my seemingly fruitless searches that I heard a conversation that immediately attracted my attention. I was reading a newspaper when I overheard the man sitting next to me discussing with another passenger on how a new media corporation owned by one of the big politicians in town just opened an FM station at Ajegunle, a rough and unruly neighbourhood. The new radio station was aimed at affecting the lives of the large population of the youths in the area that were drawn to crime and lawlessness. The station was however, bogged down; the main problem was finding sponsorship that would bring in the needed funds. The management lacked the funds to hire experience presenters, and the studio was on the brink of closing down, as things were not moving as they expected.

It all bore down to the fact that they seemed to lack a good programme that would attract listeners and bring in corporate sponsorship. I quickly noted the address of the radio station as they were discussing. It was my decision to visit the place and try selling my proposal to a radio station, maybe for the last time.

The next day after leaving the office, I decided to go and check the place. On getting to the address, I saw the big signpost of the radio station in front of a squally looking small building with broken windows.

At first I thought I was at a wrong building, until I saw the transmitters hanging by the side of the house. I immediately recollected what the man in the bus said about the new studio struggling to find its feet.

I knew I was in the right place.

I knocked and entered the first door I met. I saw myself in a small room facing a girl sitting behind a small old table. I guess she was the receptionist, or the counter girl.

"Good day sister." I said. She stretched up lazily from the table she was laying the upper half of her body on, looking up at me nonchalantly.

The office didn't look like a serious place to me. And neither did the girl. I was tempted to turn and leave. But I considered the amount I spent on transportation to get there, and that I needed something to show for it.

I smiled more broadly and said calmly, "I'm here to see if I can talk to someone about something I have with me." I was talking like an immature salesman, not really knowing how to put across what brought me there. The girl was still looking up from the table where she was leaning her small frame. She answered lazily, "mmmhh" and kept mute. I guess it was just her way of letting me know she didn't quite get what I was saying.

Then the door adjacent to where I was standing opened. A middle age man with a slightly bald head, wearing a green T—shirt and holding a blue leather file entered the room and said to the girl "Sasha dear, please, I'm going for break. If there is anything for me; I'm at the food joint outside." He sounded so bored and tired.

He suddenly saw me and smiled, "you are welcome, sir, can we help you?" He said extending his hand to me. I held it immediately.

Good! Here is someone active to talk to.

"I came here to discuss an issue." I said.

The man suddenly burst out laughing. "I hope you brought an advertisement for us, we are really in need of sponsorship." He said. He looked at the girl and added; "people have been advising, maybe we should change our name from static if we want to move forward."

He burst out laughing again. The girl didn't join him in the laughter but managed a smile. I decided to wait for him to finish what he wanted to say before stating what brought me. He stopped laughing and looked at me. He was waiting for me to talk instead.

"I have a programme that I want to present in your station if you would accept me." I said.

The man looked at me thoughtfully for a second, then smiled and said "follow me, we can discuss it at the restaurant, I'm hungry and I don't think we have the time." He turned to the entrance door. I followed him out.

We soon found ourselves at what he called a restaurant. It was an open air eating place. The space was covered with plastic tables and chairs that were crowded under a white coloured canopy that gave insufficient shade to the people sitting under it. A woman was standing behind a wooden table that was directed to the arrangement of the seats. On top of the table were three large aluminium containers from which she served food to her customers sitting under the canopy.

A small girl takes orders from those already seating, and brings back a large heap food on small rubber plates. The whole area made Mama Sikiru's eating joint at my working place looked like a modern eatery. It was the kind of place a person struggling to make ends meet would go for a meal. I didn't need to be told again, on how hard they were finding it at the studio.

He ordered for a plate of rice and beans for himself and requested one for me. I turned down the offer. The little girl soon returned holding a small rubber plate on top of what looked like a careless spray of cooked beans on white rice plastered with red pepper soup.

The two huge pieces of meat made the surrounding space on the plate to look like a valley.

He was soon devouring the meal with relish; he must have been really hungry. "Oh sorry" He said struggling with a mouthful as he tried to speak.

"I'm Mark Charles, and you?" He asked.

"My name is rather long and difficult to pronounce but you can call me, SST." I said.

"No, let me have it, even if I will have to use your initials." He insisted. I told him, he nodded in acceptance. For the first time, I have met someone who was not curious on where I got my name from, someone who didn't ask if I was having relations in Asia.

"So, what can I do for you?" He asked.

I told him again.

"Sorry my friend, at the time we don't need an additional programme. We are finding it hard to even keep the ones we have on air with the constant electric power failure, and is expensive running generator. Without sponsorship, we might soon close down the station." He replied so harshly as if as I was part of their misfortune!

I thanked him and stood to go.

"Hey, Wait!" He shouted, "Can't you even try to convince me to accept you?" He was laughing.

I sat back and told him it was not my style to push anyone. I just wanted to give freely to the community what God had given me. I was not looking for a job or payment for my show, just a platform to air my programme. He became interested when he heard I was there for free.

"Hey SST, you should have said that, let's go back to the office." He was sounding friendlier now. We stood to go; Mark winked at the salesgirl, who winked back. I guess she has a book where she keeps record of a customer's bills or debts, because we left without him paying for the meal.

As we settled down in his office, he said "now tell me what that programme would look like." He sounded interested. I then sat comfortably to talk to him. I started giving him a down load of my plans.

What I had in mind was to present a programme that will motivate and inspire people who are passing through difficult times in the city. It is largely fashioned to attract a large audience, mostly the youths, who form the highest percentage of radio listeners, especially in Lagos.

That was why I decided to name the show the motivation dance club. It would be a programme where a listener with a life touching experience, a story, or a problem, would call the studio and relay his story on air, what I call coming on the dance floor to show your steps. And I being the anchor of the show—I decided to call myself the disco Jockey, popularly called the DJ in dancing clubs—would take him and other listeners on that.

The radio show was designed to simulate the environment of a talking shop club house that listens to and find ways of advising people on solving their problems. I also intended to read out to listeners several story lines on past events or other people's experiences that could have a bearing to their questions or discussions. The story lines or narratives were to pass across the message better. To prepare for that, I had gathered a large sample of such stories in my collection.

Mark listened patiently as I went over my plan for the radio show. I could see he was not very excited—that didn't stop me from downloading the full text of my ideas.

"Well, SST that's good, but I could see that one of our rival stations had something similar to that." He said, tapping the pen in his hands slightly on the table. I told him I was aware of that too, but mine will be unique from theirs.

He scratched his jaws with his two fingers for a little while and then said "Ok, why not? The person anchoring our sports programme has left. We haven't paid him for some time now due to the difficulties we are facing, so he had to go. You can take the time, as we are yet to decide on what to put in there." He gave me a wink and smiled, "moreover you are not asking for any financial inducement which I must confess worked highly in your favour." he continued with the smile.

I nodded my acceptance quickly.

"But let me remind you," he started with a serious expression on his face "if we are able get back on our feet soon, we will collect back the airtime and recalled the sports guy back. What the people are interested in is news and highlights on the premier league and not some novice motivational talk that they can pick on the street." He said with a sneer.

I thought that was quite unkind of him and wanted to tell him so, but I thought it best to swallow my disapproval.

Never give in to your first reaction when you are angry!

That was how I got the chance to start running an hour talk show called the motivational dance club show on Static FM 111.

My show time was fixed in between the hours of the international and local news which made it more difficult for me to make some room for myself, as I had to adhere strictly to the assigned timing. The timing of the news programme cannot be allowed to go late or be shifted, even slightly, that means I run the risk of tempering with the time for the news and running afoul of the producer.

Still, I eagerly took up the challenge. The more the challenges, the more I was motivated because for me to start on a motivation show, I should be able to motivate myself first!

I started the maiden edition of Motivational dance club on FM 111 on a Saturday, exactly two days after meeting the studio producer, Mr. Mark Charles.

First Day at Static FM 111.0
". . . hello good people of Lagos"

'. . . hello good people of Lagos; this is your new show on Static FM 111. The motivation dance club!" I shouted in the microphone. And that was how I started airing my show, on the first day of my broadcast on Static FM 111. The programme that I chose to christened the motivation dance club! My show was squeeze between the time for the twelve o'clock news and the one o'clock morning request show on the first day. Being a Saturday, such days have only one news item at noon.

Mark preferred I start featuring the show on a Saturday, as most people were expected to be indoors at home, so that the new programme would attract a wide publicity on its maiden edition.

That Saturday also coincided with what they call an environmental sanitation day, which was held fortnightly. It was the day when all residents of the city were to remain indoors till 10 a.m and clean their surroundings. Most people remain indoors all right, but few clean their surroundings.

Normally on such days, workers on essential duties, including those with the media, are allowed to move about with a police pass to perform their duties during the curfew period. Mark and his staff had their official passes because they needed to be in the studio 24 hours. I wasn't a staff, right? Just a freelance presenter, isn't it? You can then understand why there was no official police permit for me, and why I had to leave home late on my first day.

I was at the studio some minutes before the start of my programme. I could see how the producer, Mark looked at me disapprovingly. What does this guy wants anyway? I should fly over to the studio before 10 a.m? You can't even find a bus on the road because of the sanitation exercise. Even if I had chosen to brave the police officers on the lookout for defaulters, there was no way I could be at the studio any time earlier.

I quickly settled into the presenter's seat, ready to go on air for the first time. Mark had briefed me on how to use the studio equipment the day he accepted to hire me; sorry, I mean decided to have me on board, as he preferred to call it. There was not much to learn there anyway, as there was not much equipment in the presenter's confine. Just an old table microphone and a desk phone that was connected with large wires to the recording machines in the studio room where radio signals where broadcast in the air.

"Before I start, my good people out there, let me tell you a little about your new show, the motivation dance club." I was feeling nervous!

Thank God I wasn't broadcasting from a television house!

"This is a call-in programme, you can call us on 0123677." I said, giving out the studio phone number. I repeated it twice to ensure they got me. There was no need anyway. New programme or not, it was the same old telephone line the studio had been using in all its other shows, ever since they started broadcasting.

"It is a radio talk show programme, and is geared at giving audience to your life challenging experiences—I mean your problems and giving you a word of encouragement to motivate your spirit back." I yelled the lesson out. That was what my programme was all about of course!

"I would like any listener to come on air, that is on the dance floor, and tell us what you has for us, show us your steps, I mean tell us your problems or needs. And of course, yours in the house DJ SST, is here to handle your problems and receive other listeners' responses on the topic"

Yes, that was it! My nomenclature on the show, DJ SST, was now open to all.

"I want to know who wants to come up first and open the floor on the first day of our show on Motivation Dance Club." I extended the invitation. There was no response. After waiting a minute or so I decided I should move forward. I can't keep on waiting, of course. Hope listeners have not tuned in to another station. But that was most unlikely, I know Lagos people very well. They are highly inquisitive people, if not for anything, they would still want to find out what the new programme was all about!

"This is nothing more than the sharing of love." I added. People love the word love, even if they don't actually care what it takes.

"We love you all, your problems is our problems, your struggles is our struggle, we are all one big happy family!" I kept on repeating the mantra, and praying my frontal advertisement won't turn them off. I was still able to personally excuse myself of any error. It was my first time and I had no prior training on broadcasting. I should be forgiven. I just continued talking, and thinking of what to bring up to draw listeners out of their cocoon.

"Talking about love, there is nowhere love can exist more than in a family? I want you to see the lesson on why we need to share love on the first narrative of our show which I liked to call 'only love can see us through.'"

I was ready to read my first lesson narrative on the show. I cleared my throat to signal to those listening out there that something was coming.

I then started reading.

"In the city of Istanbul, which is the capital of the present day Republic of Turkey, in the time of the rule of the sultanates, the period when men survived on the skills of their hands and the favour of their heritage. Two brothers were left a large estate by their late father. And the produce from the farm was to be shared equally between them. The elder brother had a family of three, a wife and two kids, while the younger brother was a bachelor. Soon there was a war, and things started getting harder in the country, as inflation was rising, and cost of living skyrocketing.

One day, the younger brother thought within himself." I stopped a little to make an effort to introduce a slightly different tone in my voice to signify the thoughts of the brother.

"Times are getting harder, and my elder brother has a family to feed while I am alone. It is not fair that we share the produce equally as he has more mouths to feed. I know he will not agree if I suggest he takes a bigger share, so let me every night secretly take some from my share and place in his barn." And so he started taking from his share and taking to his brother's barn in the night." I stopped a little again to get my breath back before continuing.

"The older brother unknown to the younger one, was also disturbed. He had been having thoughts in his mind that was very disturbing."

I also tried to make a voice for the other brother's thoughts too!

""..He said to himself . . . times will always be getting harder as it is happening now, and this my younger brother has no family, and we share the produce from the estate equally. It's not fair. I have a family, and in my old age they will take care of me, but who will take care of him when he is old? Let me secretly add to his barn from my share, I know he will not agree if I suggest he takes more. So that he has enough to sell in the market and save for his old age." He thought. And so he too started secretly taking from his barn and putting into his younger brother's barn." I stopped.

It is always good to allow a small interlude when you come to the stage where the listeners should be able to pick the pieces themselves.

I have learned that from being a good storyteller for years.

If it has worked for me tremendously, and on several occasions, with friends at home, and at my work place, I saw no reason why it shouldn't achieve the same results now that I'm on radio, with thousands of listeners out there in the city.

"The two brothers started noticing that someone was interfering with the arrangement of their produce. One night, their movements clashed and they met each other holding a quantity of his produce moving to the other side. It was then they realised their actions and what had been happening to their produce, they hugged each other, tears flowing from their eyes. And they remembered what their father said before he died "my children, it not my estate or my property that will protect you in times of difficulties that must come. Only love will see you through it all." I pronounced the last words louder. I had come to the end of the story, my first teaching narrative on radio. And just as I wanted it to always be, I moved on to the last part where I would end up with a short exhortation after a talk to serve as a lesson for my listeners.

"And I want to say to all listeners out there! Whatever difficulties we encounter as friends, or as a family, or in a group, be it in an institution or our nation as a whole, God is saying to us at this moment that it is not our wealth that will see us through. It is not our knowledge that will see us through. It is not our good arguments that will see us through. It is not our understanding that will see us through . . . . *only love will see us through!*"

I had hardly stopped shouting the last words when a call came in. The sharp ringing tone of the desk phone startled me. I quickly calmed myself when I recollected what it was all about, that was my first caller on the show, good.

"Hello is that motiva . . ." I could hear the voice of a lady speaking. I quickly put in to assist her, "yes this is motivation dance club, happy to have you on line, ma'am." I was on my possible best.

"Ha! I never knew this your new programme would shake me up like this." She sounded impressed "I was thinking what this motivation show stuff was all about when you started that brothers story." She said. I had to quickly get the term correct on air, I didn't want people to be calling my narratives a story, I preferred it called a narrative. It was supposed to elicit reactions, comments, and questions to be asked, as life teaching lessons, and not just an entertainment. So, I quickly put in "you mean my narrative, dear?" I said.

"Yes that . . . I was, was, I could not control myself, I was moved to tears." She was incoherent, her voice choking. "I'm not alone. that was so touchy, even some of my friends here at moonside." She said.

Moonside? That's a popular hangout for the rich folks in Lagos; rich young girls are indeed emotional.

"Yeah, thanks my dear, it's all about the lesson, and it's meant to motivate us to show true love to one another." I said, passing the message across to the listeners once again.

As soon as she dropped another call came in.

"Hello Static FM," it was a young man's voice, but sounding more like a teenager.

"Yes good morning sir, you're on motivation dance club on Static FM 110" I quickly replied.

Ops! I jumbled the studio name. But what the heck? It was my first time anyway; I was entitled to some little slips. Right?

"Yeah, thanks, DJ . . ." he couldn't remember the name. I had to come in again, and assist a caller. It was to be expected. The programme was new on air.

"It's, DJ SST, sir!" I said a little proudly.

"Yes, that's what I'm trying to know . . . what is, SST?" He asked coolly. I rather liked that question. If people are trying to know you, it means they are trying to like you. It's ok with me. I told him the meaning of my initials.

"You're sure you are Nigerian and not some, 'imported' fellow with a local accent?" He said it carelessly.

I found this one rather rude, not the words; it was the way he said it! He could be one tiny little kid out there pulling me off. That is why radio is a hard place to be, you just don't know whom you are talking to. I wanted to ignore the question, but this was a new show and I needed friends badly, so I played it cool too.

"No, my friend, I'm a Nigerian. Don't ask me which part I am from, please." I cautioned him politely. I wanted to remain open to all, not to enter all that Nigerian ethnic complications.

"Yes, thanks sir, you are cool. I like your programme." He said. I smiled. I was getting fans so fast. The power of radio talk show!

"Thanks too man, what's your name?" I was beginning to like him too.

"ST" he said laughing. I got it. He was playing initials on me too!

"And what's ST, sir?" I asked.

"Sesun Tolomari" he said.

"Well, Sesun, thanks for calling. It's good having you on the show, have a nice day, bye!" I cut off the conversation before he could give, the 'don't mention' or 'you are welcome' stuff!

"My listeners before I close today's show, I will like to talk to you about preparation. Destiny might earmark you, but you won't have it until you prepare yourself to qualify for it.

Abraham Lincoln once said "I will prepare and my time will come." It might have been your destiny to head that corporation, but when the time was ripe you were found not to have qualified because you failed to acquire the right training. Maybe you believe it would be a waste of time to prepare for that position in your corporation because no woman has ever reached that appointment, but remember Margaret Thatcher once said she never believed she will live long to see a female prime minister in Britain and she ended up being the one!

Maybe you did not qualify because you lack the belief, and when it was time for what God destined for you, you hide yourself because you lack the belief it could be you.

Maybe you did not qualify because you were not focused. It was your destiny to be the CEO of that big corporation but because you were not focused, you moved away to another place when God was about to make things happen for you. Maybe you didn't qualify because you were inpatient. That marriage you were trusting God for was taking too long, so you lose patient and go about with the wrong person and missing what God has for you. Maybe because the child you have been praying to God for is taking too long, so you followed the wrong advice and seek assistance from the devil, and because you were impatient, you missed the great marriage or the great children God destined for you or other great things.

Maybe your destiny was to be the coach of that team, but the requirement was somebody who has no blot in his records and you were found to have ten when it was your time to be considered. It was not that God didn't have a great destiny for you, but when He was about to make things happen for you, you were found not to be qualified.

Qualification is not all about going to school to earn a degree or study a course. It is developing your God given talents so that it takes you to the great heights you are supposed to be and from there your achievements become a source of study to many.

The legendary musician, Fela, once remarked "I didn't go to school to study music but one day, they will study my music in schools." I want to say to you, you might not have gone to school to study poetry but one day they will study your poems in school. You might not have gone to a school to study acting, but one day they will study your style in drama schools, and that would only be possible if you prepare and qualify yourself.

So, my listeners on motivation dance club Static FM 111, please, always prepare yourself so that you will qualify when the time comes. Destiny alone will not carry you there, destiny is a covenant, and covenants are spiritual contracts, you must fulfil your part if you want God to do His part."

I could see from the wall clock hanging above the door, facing where I was sitting, that my time was over. I had to wrap up the show and be on my way or risk annoying my producer and get kicked out on my first day. I preferred the former—so I quickly put in the final touches to the day's show.

"Thanks my listeners for contributing to the first show of the new dance club in town; the Motivation Dance Club! And thanks to all of you that called in. I hope to see you next time, and at same time, for a more interesting dance at the motivation dance club." I repeated the show's name more than it was necessary. It was my first time, and I wanted the listeners to get familiar with the name of the show as soon as possible. So I kept on repeating it!

"So make sure you get your dancing shoes on and be ready to move unto the dance floor next time the floor opens at Motivation Dance Club. Thank you all, and God bless you!"

The Motivation Dance Club
The Fame

It's strange how news travels fast in Lagos. That must be the reason many people call Lagos the entertainment capital of Africa. When a new and exciting thing comes to town, it easily gets around in no time. The city occupies a small landmass but with a large population compacted in overlying layers. I guess that makes news to travel so fast, sometimes even faster than you could imagine. And I was to found out about that, the next day I reported at the studio for the second airing of my show.

As soon as I opened the show there were calls coming in from all parts of the city, even from areas I never expected, congratulating me on the previous show. People were calling to tell me of how my first broadcast had opened their minds to so many other things.

It didn't take more than a single show for callers to start addressing me as DJ SST, or just SST. And they were asking all manner of questions. From those trying to find out on how to open a business, to those looking for ways to losing weight. I didn't even have knowledge on some of the issues they brought, not to talk of searching through my narratives on something related to it. I was so shocked with the fast rising profile of the show that I sat down with apprehension on the presenter's seat, not knowing what to do, as I got ready for the second airing of the motivation dance club show. However, I was able to quickly get hold of myself and get on with the show on time.

I had decided to always start the show with a word of encouragement to stir the interests of my listeners before 'opening the dance floor' to receive calls and watch the dance steps of my listeners; speaking in the parlance of the show.

"My listeners, good morning and welcome to your favourite radio programme, the Motivational Dance Club. You are all enjoined to move forward and enter into our dance club. When Moses entered the presence of Pharaoh, the people that knew him as the runaway prince shouted, it is a lie! When Joseph's father heard that the son he thought was dead was not only alive, but a Prime Minister in Egypt, he shouted, it is a lie! When David returned with the head of Goliath, the soldiers that watched him going to a certain death shouted, it is a lie! And I know in the coming days, weeks, or months to come, when those that knew you, those that you live amongst, those that have been watching your life, your struggles, your disappointments, your seemingly hopeless situation or aware of your humble beginnings, turn and see how far God has lifted you up and how greatly He has blessed you, they will not be able to believe the evidence of their eyes and they will all shout, it is a lie! God has done many great things in your life but the best is yet to come. God's creative power is progressive! He did great things on the first day, on the second day . . . . and the best on the sixth day. My dear listener your sixth day is yet to come.

Whatever people are thinking against you is not what God is thinking for you. Whatever people are saying against you is not what God is saying about you. When God is the one that is doing it for you, you don't need to worry about what is said against it.

I want you to know this morning that God has joined your destiny with greatness, He has joined your destiny with prosperity, He has joined your destiny with success, and whatever God has joined together, let no man put asunder. David started life behind his brothers, Joseph started life behind his siblings, being behind today does not make you to come last tomorrow. Starting late does not mean you are finishing last. Wherever you feel you are being left behind, be it in marriage, in promotion, or in business, please know that God can take you from back to the front, front zero to hero! Do not be discouraged if it looks like some things are being delayed in your life. God's delays are His defining moments! God delayed

Sarah to bring Isaac, God delayed Hannah to bring forth Samuel, and I want you to know today, that whatever God is delaying in your life, will be the defining moment of your destiny!

It does not matter how backward the devil has pushed your life to, when God brings you back, and He will carry you forward. God bought Moses back from the wilderness to establish him as a deliverer. God brought David back from the bush to crown him as a king. God brought Joseph back from prison to make him a prime minister. It does not matter how backward the devil has pushed your marriage, your career, or any area of your life, because when God is ready to bring you back, he will bring you forward. When the devil threw Joseph in prison, Joseph did not despair; he was having a good time. He was having a good time because he knew God was coming to him in good time!

And I want you to know today that whatever problem you are facing, whatever prison the devil has placed you in today, just be having a good time, because God's favour is coming to lift you out in good time.

It does not matter, if you have nothing now, when God's favour comes to you, you will have all you need. Joseph went with nothing before Pharaoh, but came out as a prime minister. David came out of the wilderness with nothing to be crowned a king. As you enter that job with nothing, as you enter your marriage with nothing, God will give you the favour that will bestow on you all that you need. Don't worry about what you are lacking now, when God is ready for you, He will bring you out to splendour! God did not bring Adam out until all was ready. God did not bring Joseph out of prison until all was ready. God will not bring you out to the stage until all is ready for your marriage, for your career and for all aspects of your life!

I don't know the level you are aspiring to climb to; I do not know what great challenge you are facing in life. But I know it is not hard for God to carry you across to the next level. Is your crossing to the next level greater than Moses' crossing of the Red Sea? Is the defeat of the giant in your life greater than David's killing of Goliath? Is the healing of that your sickness, greater than raising Lazarus from the dead? Then why do you doubt if there is a solution to your challenges? I want you all to know today that God will carry you from where you are tolerated to where you are celebrated! I want you to know that God will not only wipe away the tears from your eyes, your cheeks, or your face but God will wipe away the tears from your life!

I do not know what is fighting against your life; whatever it is that is against you, God is going to equip you to stand against it. God is not going to take you to fight against sickness or poverty; He is going to take you to stand against poverty, for whatever God will take you to stand against, it shall not stand against you!

Most of the challenges you are facing today is because of your level, when your level with God changes, your challenges changes! God will take you to a level that you will challenge your challenger, oppress your oppressors, and torment your tormentors! For whatever the devil is using to frustrate you with today, God will give you greater power to overcome it."

I had come to the end of the opening exhortation and it is time to move on to the next segment of my show.

I tune on the receiver on the table phone. I was ready to start receiving listeners call which I suspected would come in faster than the first time. And truly the phone started ringing almost immediately.

My first caller was a lady "SST, I'm happy to be on your show. I'm glad that the station decided to have this show that motivates and entertain us. Mine! You just started yesterday and you are making such a huge impact in town!" Her voice was rising intermittently as she tried hard to force out what was on her mind. "I believed your show will be good for someone like me. I have tried many things in life but with no success, I guess I'm one of those created with less ability than others." She sounded sorrowful for her situation. I was immediately moved to answer her question.

"My sister, you should not think like that." I cautioned her with a notch of concern. I quickly retracted and decide first to commend her, to restore her self-confidence, before moving on to what I had to say.

"I thank you for your views on my show; it could only come from a mind with a great insight. If I had shown any ability as a person it is no different from what God had placed in all of us." I was trying to draw the comment she made on the show to the statement she made about herself.

I continued.

"God created us and placed in us all, the skills we need to achieve our desires. And God has finished with all that has to do with our creation. When God reached the sixth day of creation; He didn't stop because He was tired, nor because He had taken too long, or because He didn't know what to do. He stopped because He was finished. There is nothing more that you need in life more than what God has put in you. No car manufacturer forgets to fix on the steering wheel that a driver needs to drive the car, before releasing the car to the market. God has placed in you the steering wheel you need to drive through life challenges before releasing you to the world. Greatness is in you! Prosperity is in you! Knowledge is in you! You cannot hide it from God like Adam tried to hide from Him, because He created you and He knows you. God knows what is in you, and when you are ready He will call it out for you."

She kept on shouting, "amen SST, amen SST, I received it!" interjecting as I speak the motivating message! I drew her attention to her own words of faith.

"Sister if you believe you have received it then go and live it." I told her.

There was a little pause then she said "Thanks SST, I will try, I will try." She was still shouting.

Another caller came up immediately after she dropped. I was soon to learn that for me to get the time needed to pass across the message for the day on my show, I would need to sometimes cut off calls for a while.

It was a lady calling again. I didn't know why I was getting so many lady callers on my show, maybe as they say; ladies are more emotional and so are more attracted to inspirational messages.

"SST, I want to congratulate on your show. My name is Cynthia." She said. I loved the way she started by introducing herself first,

I didn't even know the name of the last caller because she didn't bother to tell me and I didn't ask her. I noted that in the future I will remember to ask my callers for their names if they didn't tell me.

I gave out a short laughter as I answered this caller, trying to make it look like a conversation with a familiar person.

"Welcome Cynthia, you are welcome to the Motivation Dance Club, can I see your steps? Come and dance on the floor!" I was back to simulating the scenario that I created for the show.

"SST, I want to comment on the last caller." She said. Good! That's how I want my show to go, questions and comments coming from listeners on topics raised by a caller. I was not intending to give all the comments, or my show will lose its flavour.

"The lady that just called should do the little she can do. She should be contented with what she can do, not all people are created to do great things. Some are spectators and some are players. The world is like a football match, SST, not all of us can be in the field. What can you achieve when life gives you a small ball, or a small pot? You can only serve a small meal, you know." Cynthia said as she reviewed over what she just heard from the previous caller.

"Cynthia my dear, thank you for your views, I agree with you that we should not fear to do what we can do in life, no matter how little it is." I chose to comment on an area in which I agreed with her first. It is good to show a person where you both agreed, before moving to where you might disagreed with the person. People do not mind losing a war, if they can win some battles. Always agree with people before disagreeing with them.

"And Cynthia what we create is not determine by what we hold in our hands. It is more determined by what we hold in our hearts." I said it in a way that did not elicit a direct opposition to her opinion.

As I speak, I was checking through my narratives to see if I had something on that.

And luckily I did.

I quickly introduced it into the discussion.

"There was a little poor girl that had nothing. She had no position or any money that one could be ascribed to her. But yet she impacted far greater than many that had all these in abundance and all because she had great love in her heart." I said to her "and It all started on Christmas day."

I quickly started reading through the narrative.

To start the reading of a narrative, I followed a pattern of first introducing it, by giving it a title, before going to the main story.

"I will call this narrative, the 57 Cents Church." I said.

I was reading through the pages "A little girl stood near a small church at Christmas time, as she watched the proceedings inside with tears in her eyes. It was the Church from which she had been turned away, because it was 'too crowded.'

"I'm not allowed to go to Sunday school" she sobbed to the pastor as he walked by. Seeing her shabby, unkempt appearance, the pastor correctly guessed the reason why the ushers turned her away; because she was with poor dirty clothes. It was the period when the rich people in the society come into the Churches in their best attires, and there wasn't enough space for the poor little children.

Some parents might not want their children to share seat with the little poor girl, or allow their kids to play with her. The pastor was overtaken by pity, and taking her by the hand, took her inside and found a place for her in the Sunday school class. The child was so happy that they found room for her in the church. She went to bed that night thinking of the poor little children in her neighbourhood, who have no place to worship God in the Church because it could not accommodate all the children in the neighbourhood." I let my voice dropped to represent the feelings of that poor little child.

"Some two years later, this child who was raised in a homeless, poor neighbourhood contracted a rare ailment, and lacking immediate attention, it deteriorated her body system fast beyond revival. Before long, the child lay dead in one of the poor tenement buildings. Her poor struggling parents called for the kind hearted pastor who was a friend of their daughter to handle the burial arrangements. As her poor little body was being moved, a worn and crumpled red purse was found which seemed to have been rummaged from some trash dump. Inside was found 57 cents and a note scribbled in childish handwriting, which read: 'this is to help build the little Church bigger so more children can go to Sunday school."

I stopped for a while. When a narrative gets to this level, you look for the stop points. These are areas where a story naturally separates into segments from where you continue to the next episodes.

"For two years she had saved for this offering of love. When the pastor tearfully read the note, he knew instantly what he would do. Carrying the note and the cracked, red pocketbook to the pulpit, he told the story of the unselfish love and devotion of the poor little girl. He challenged his deacons to get busy and raise enough money for a larger building. The story did not end there."

I took a short pause to sip from the cup of water on my table. Reading can be exhausting because it is a physical exercise.

"A newspaper learnt of the story and published it and it was read by a wealthy realtor. The realtor was moved with emotions by the story of the poor little girl and offered the Church a parcel of land worth many thousands of dollars. When he was told that the Church could not pay so much, he offered to sell it to the little church for 57 cents. Other Church members were also moved to make large donations more than what they normally would have given. Cheques started coming in. Within five years, the story of the little girl's small gift had attracted up to $250,000.00 .... a huge sum at the time. The unselfish love of the poor little girl had paid large dividends that the little church never dreamt of ever garnering!"

I shouted the last words as I came to the end of the narrative.

"And so my listeners, when you happen to be in the city of Philadelphia, look at the Temple Baptist Church, with a seating capacity of 3,300. And be sure to visit Temple University, where thousands of students are educated today. Have a look, too, at the Good Samaritan Hospital and at a Sunday school building which houses hundreds of beautiful children, built so that no child in the area will ever need to be left outside during Sunday school time. In one of the rooms of this building, you would come across a picture of the sweet face of the little girl whose 57 cents, so sacrificially saved, made such remarkable history. Alongside of it is a portrait of her kind pastor, Dr. Russell H. Conwell, author of the book, 'Acres of

Diamonds' from which this story was recorded." I then moved to my inspirational exhortations.

"This is a story, that goes to show what God can do with the little we have, or with the little we are, when we carry much love in our hearts. It doesn't matter how much is needed, or how little we are having in our hands, we can always make a difference in our community, and in the lives of people around us, like the poor little girl, when we carry much love." I said.

"A lot of us are out there looking for a miracle—but the few great persons amongst us are going about looking to be a miracle. And until we are like the poor little girl, we would not be truly great."

I turned my attention to my caller, "so, Cynthia, and my listeners today, It's not what we are having in our hands that matters but what we have in our hearts that will make the difference in the lives of people around us. As long as we go through life thinking of what we can do for other people and not what other people can do for us, God will always use us for greater things. Because God is looking for those who want to serve not those who want to be served, and he knows them by the love in their hands and not the things in their hands."

I included a little paraphrase from J F Kennedy famous speech in which he asked his countrymen to think of what they can do for their country.

"Thank you, SST, I'm blessed by your speech." Cynthia said.

"Thanks, Cynthia; it was nice having you on the Motivation Dance Club. I loved your steps and hope to see you next time." I turned my attention to soliciting for the next person who has an issue for discussion.

"Listeners, we are still on FM 111.0. I'm waiting for the next person to come out with his or her steps for us to see. It doesn't have to do with Cynthia's steps, you can come forward with your steps too." I said. The phone was ringing and I took the call. It was a man's voice.

Beautiful! A change at least!

"Morning DJ," he said.

"Yeah, good morning, this is DJ SST, on Motivation Dance Club, brother." I tried to remind him.

"Yeah, DJ SST, this is Jack. I love your show, man!" He had a loud and deep masculine voice.

"Thanks, brother" I replied.

"SST, you see, I just want to know how to get back with my life." He was talking a little too fast for me to catch up.

"Brother, please will you slow down so that we can all move along with your steps?" I tried to admonish him a little.

"Yeah thanks. I mean SST, well, I said I did a lot of bad things and I'm not happy with my life any more. I hurt my dad, my mum, my family." He took a deep breath. "SST, I have so messed my life; I don't think God will want me, you know." He was now sounding like a person seeking penance. "I'm a bad man, SST." He uttered with a heave.

"Well I'm sure God won't condemn you, Jack, so I can't condemn you, and you should not condemn yourself either. You can still get your life back and move on." I started to build the foundation that would lead me to a narrative in such areas. I was expecting such things to come up that I collated a lot of narratives on that.

"No matter how life crumpled you, your value remains." I said. "I once read an experiment carried out by a preacher called Gary Smalley. I'm sure it will help you in knowing your true value with God. Please give me a minute to check my collection and bring it out to read to your understanding."

I went through my little folder and saw what I was looking for. "Yeah, here it is! Let me read it to you and to all our listeners out there." I then opened the narrative and started reading from it. "Gary Smalley, a renowned evangelist of the Lord, during one of his lectures brought out a fifty dollar bill and asked the crowd "Who would like this fifty dollars?" Hands started going up everywhere.

"I am going to give this dollar to one of you." He said "But first let me do this." He proceeded to crumple the bill in his hands. Then he asked "who still wants it?" The same hands went up in the air!

"Well" he continued. "What if I do this," He dropped the money on the floor and started to grind it into the floor with his shoes. He picked it up all crumpled and dirty, "now, who still wants it?" Again hands went up into the air.

"You have all learnt a valuable lesson." Gary said "no matter what I do to the money, you still want it, because it has not decreased in value. It is still a fifty dollar bill. And that was how it happened." I dropped the paper I was reading from on the table and turn to my usual exhortation after a narrative to the listening audience.

"Now, Jack, and to many of our listeners out there that might be facing a similar problem. I want to say to you today that many a times in our lives, we are dropped and crumpled into the dirt by the decisions we made, or by the circumstances we found ourselves in. Many a times, the devil made us to take decisions that later went all wrong, leading to shame and disgrace. And we may feel as though we are worthless, and insignificant in the eyes of the people. But no matter what happens to us, we will never lose our values as human beings in the sight of God . . . the value God himself placed on us!" I went on to my now familiar way of shouting the phrases!

" . . . . maybe you were sent out of school, but you should remember that God did not require a Bill Gates to have a degree before taking him to a high position. Maybe you gave birth out of wedlock or you were the product of an illegitimate union, but you should remember the world had world leaders, even a pope that was an illegitimate child.

Maybe you had an accident and lost the use of a limb, but you should remember that Helen Keller was born disabled but ended doing greater things than millions of normal people!

Maybe the journey of your life is a story of failures or near wins. Maybe you are always the one losing at the point of victory. I'm telling you today, it is not over with you.

Abraham Lincoln experienced several electoral defeats in his political career, and ended up becoming the president. Or maybe you are feeling time is not on your side, as all your mates have achieved so, and so, and you are left lagging behind. I want you to know that God is keeping your victory for the period of your highest glory. Everybody thought Churchill had passed his prime in politics, but he later became the most successful Prime Minister at age 66! Ronald

Reagan had a string of losses before becoming the oldest president in United States history at 68!

Maybe you are being discouraged because of the negative things being said about you. But you should remember from history that only people of great destinies attracted great criticism! When your momentum increases, your critics will also increase. It is only a tree that bears good fruits that stones are thrown at!"

The telephone started ringing, abruptly disrupting the flow of my reading. I quickly turned it off.

I was not finished yet!

"I want you all listening to me today, to know that whatever has happened in your life, whatever the devil has created around you, your family, your business or your career, it can't diminish your value! Always remember that your value remains intact in the sight of God! It is always as clean as when you were born. And as long as your value is intact, God is ready to take you to whatever level He desires for you, and use you for whatever task he wants. Whatever the devil has stolen from you, your value remains intact!" It was time to take a deep breath and throw the last punch for this stage.

"So, cheer up, Jack, cheer up all my friends listening out there too, you all have a great value before God, and he can still use you for any task he requires of anyone, because all you need is created in you!

My father used to tell me of the story of the lion. He said when the lion wakes up in the morning, it says just one prayer. The lion always says a prayer in the morning that "please God show me a prey but don't help me and don't help the prey; just let us be!" This is a lion that is aware that whatever that is needed to defeat a prey, God has already created in it and all it needed was to be shown where the prey is! You got to stop asking God to give you this and to give you that! You need to start asking God to show you what is needed to be done to achieve what you desire. Because all you need to achieve that you desire is in you. The power to get that world acclaimed position you desperately need is in you! The money to build that prominent business empire you desire is in you! You just need to ask God to show you the path to follow that will take you to the big position you

113

desire. You only need to ask Him to show you the business that you can turn to a prominent empire!"

Another caller was on the line but I had entertained more than eight callers already and the long narratives have also eaten into my time. I have to close the show for the day. I quickly started preparation to put in the last words. However, I decided to take one caller because he told me his wife just gave birth and he wanted me to give her a word of encouragement.

"Alright what's your wife's name?" I asked him.

"Her name is Grace; she just gave birth to a bouncing baby girl." The man said proudly.

"Good day, Grace, I want to congratulate you on your safe delivery on behalf of Static FM 111 Motivation Dance Club. And I will wish to use you as a point of contact to all young mothers out there. Congratulations, and God bless you all and protect your young babies!

Please don't be carried away with the new fad of feeding your babies with powdered baby milk; keep to the old reliable breast milk. It is the best food for babies. Breast milk is hygienic, contains anti—bodies, has a sweet taste and comes in a nice soft sachet too!" I gave her my candid advice. I looked at the wall clock, I had exhausted the time for the show and it was time to go.

"Thanks sir, I will keep your advice in mind." It was the mother speaking.

"Thank you sister and please call the show when you are back home from the hospital." I told her.

I had now come to the end of the day's show. But I was encouraged to still take one last call.

"SST how are you doing?" It was a man calling; I wish he will get on with his message as my time was almost over.

"Thanks my brother, what's the name and what can I do for you?" I was rushing in all the questions at once.

"SST, I just got a small question here. What would you do as a man when other people unjustifiably attack you?"

"I will do nothing!"

"What!?" He gasped.

114

"Yes I will do nothing, because I want God to come in and take over my battle. If other men come to attack you unjustly, do not move forward to cover the gap by reaching out to them. The gap is where God needs to move in and take over your battle. If you move forward leaving no space for God to move in to take over your battle, you would be left to fight on your own. You are still fighting those enemies; sicknesses, and those setbacks in your life because God is yet to over your battle! When God takes over, it is over! God does not take over to go over; God takes over to finish over" I told him "Thanks my brother, my time is up, thank you for calling Motivation Show."

I ended the conversation.

"My listeners, I would have loved to have more of you on the dancing floor so that I could watch your dancing steps but my time is up. So I will say I love you all. But before I go, I want to leave you with one word.

This programme is not out to mould your life or stop you living your life as you used to.

God is not against us having a good and exciting life. In fact, all the activities we have today were put in place for us by God. The devil has done nothing, he only came to corrupt and destroy what was there. God is not telling us to stop, he is just saying change!" I hope I still have the time to go through the last part. "God is not against us having a good life my friends, He wants to even improve on that, He wants us to have the best of life. He is not against you being on the run sister; He just wants you to apply the right breaks in the right places. He is not against you going on the fast lane brother; he just wants you to be on the safe lane! He never said we should stop, He just said we should change."

"You said you like drinking brother? Good, God is not against that. That was why He made the world three quarters full of water; He even created our body to need water more than anything. Go on and drink brother, He never said stop, He just said changed!

You love going out on Friday nights sister? God is not against that, He made the nights for you to rest and not for him. He does not need rest! But He understands you might need to take a walk

115

out on a night like that and that was why he created the night vigil and worship to keep you happy with Him on Friday nights. He never said stop, he just said change!"

"Sister you love having the men around you always? No problem, God loves being around too. His spirit revolves all around us! He doesn't care if you have men around you, God loves fellowship, let all the men come around you, but he made that only one is to formally come into you! He never said stop, he just said change!"

"You love spending money friend? Beautiful! God created money for you to spend, He knows money answereth all and that was why He made it for you, because he wants you to solve all your problems. But the devil has a lot of counterfeit that goes about spending your soul! God wants you to spend and not for your soul to be spent. So, he puts a sign behind the money, it reads; "legitimate income!" Go on spending, He never said stop, He just said change!"

"You are in love with music? Oh so beautiful! God loves music too; in fact, He lives in an atmosphere of music. He wants you to make a joyful noise to Him, with drums? No problem! Guitar? It does not matter! Computer music? Yes! In fact, with anything! He does not mind what you use or which kind of noise you make, God loves it all! He loves the music, only that He requires you check your lyrics and check his words and ensure there is no conflict and you can continue making the joyful noise!. God never says stop, He only said change!"

God never told us to stop most of what we are doing; He just said we should change our attitude to it!

"You love giving lift to the young ladies in your bright big car, mister? Good, you are doing what is demanded of you. God wants to see his children being assisted. He won't give cars to all His children lest He creates a chaos in the society. He loves to see your types that are always available to help. God will reward, provided your help does not extend to asking for a date or requesting for a phone number when dropping her off that your car, but just restricted to brotherly assistance. God did not say stop, He just said change!

You love having beautiful clothes sister? Oh how nice! God has nothing against beautiful clothing, so continue! God is the creator of all beautiful coverings. He covered the butterflies, the flowers, and even the tiger in His majestic beauty, neither plant nor animal did He left none to suffer the shame of nakedness without giving them a coat and a covering of beauty. In fact, God is the first fashion designer! Having seen that Adam and Eve were not properly covered by the covering of leaves they made for themselves, He killed an animal and made them a coat of animal skin, because He is a God of proper clothing! Cover yourself properly as the Lord did to the flowers and animals, never letting them to suffer the shame of nakedness! God did not say stop, He said change!"

I had to quickly stop on seeing the stage engineer giving me the last warning signal. I seemed to have been carried away that I clearly overshoot my timing.

"I must end today's show here my friends. Thank you for being on the show and see you at the club tomorrow morning and make sure you have your dancing shoes ready for a groovy time at the Motivation Dance Club!"

It was a long day.

Phew! I exclaimed as I stood up from the seat, removing the ear phones, it was time to go home and rest. I could see the engineers getting the stage ready for the next programme.

The Motivation Dance Club

Love Is Blind

It was raining heavily when I arrived at the studio the next morning. It was not easy getting there by the BRT buses and waiting to drop at the nearest bus stop to the studio. Not only was it becoming a problem to get a bus in the heavy rain, but my mind was also getting preoccupied with thoughts of how I would cover the over 2 kilometre journey from the bus stop to the studio without cyclist.

I decided instead to take a cab ride straight to the studio, what Lagosians call a drop, because the cab will take me to the studio, unlike the buses that terminate at the bus stops. But that means I would have to spend a little more than I planned for the week, because taking a drop cost more in Lagos. All the same, it got me to the studio in good time, and dry.

It was not long before it was my turn to be on air for my show.

I quickly took my seat and tune in the microphone. With my callers seeming to be largely females and the heavy downfall in the city that was forcing most people to remain at home, I knew many of them would be indoors at that time.

The growing popularity of my show was sure to put me in a tight spot. I won't be surprised if I was inundated with calls as soon as I come on air. However, I knew what to do to avoid being crowded in. Whoever calls in first, and I start with, will take the story, and before other callers come up; I would almost be through with the show.

I started my opening broadcast with the usual salutations "Good morning, ladies and gentlemen, this is your dance club DJ SST on your favourite motivational dance steps. I know the rain has held many of you good people at home, except of course those of us that have no choice but to drag our skins out in the rain!" I was making a joke of the heavy down pour outside and having my usual good time "So, I do not know who is first to open my dance floor today?" The phone on the table was ringing already. I made it a policy not to allow the phone to ring for long; it disturbs the airwaves and my concentration as well.

"Hello, this is FM 111 motivation dance floor, what steps do you have for me today?" I asked cheerfully as I answer the call.

"Hi, SST, it's Anne, what's up?"

Anne was one of my regular callers. She loves calling to exchange greetings anytime I come on air. It was not that she has any serious issue to discuss, and she normally has nothing much to say. And like most girls, she just ends up exchanging pleasantries across the airwaves.

I was use to her antics by then.

"Yeah, Anne, I'm fine. How are you doing, and how are you coping with the downpour?" I asked, praying that Anne won't take away my little time with idle talk. I had no more than an hour for the show.

"Yeah, SST, I'm at home, and cooling it off with some friends! Great company here, SST! Wow!" She replied cheerful. I was wondering if it was the company of her friends that was keeping her excited or just her usual excitement of being on air. Really, I can't say.

"That's good, male or female?" I asked cynically.

I knew most girls in Lagos, of Anne's age are in the working class and staying in their own accommodation. She had never told me her age really, but from her deep voice and the depth of maturity of her talk, I can guess she would be in her 30s. That is certainly not the age to still be found staying with mama and papa.

She replied my question quickly.

"Both" She answered.

I chuckled.

"Good Anne, you won't do what you shouldn't, my dear." I said. I could hear Anne laughing.

"Of course, SST, we are all legit." She said. She always loved the big mafia don image and talk, legit indeed.

"That's good, Anne," I said. "Give a shout to your friends and have a nice time, thank you" I said to her and continued from where I stop.

"My listeners, this is still Motivational FM 111 on the air, who is next on my dance floor?" I had to move away from Anne, so as to get my show going.

A call was already on, so I picked it up.

"Yeah, who is the next caller on FM 111?" I asked.

"Good morning, my name is John. I just said let me also call you too." It was a man's voice.

"John, what's your surname?" I asked. He took some time before replying—and then he refused to tell me.

"Just call me John, SST," He said.

"Ok, John, you're welcome. You just said you can call us today, too!" I repeated his statement. I wanted to introduce some humour to his awkward introduction. But he didn't seem to get it, or rather he ignored it.

"Thanks SST. I want you to advise me on a small problem I'm having with my fiancée." He was serious now.

"How old are you and your fiancée?" I asked politely. In issues of relationship, I always wanted to know the ages of both partners. It aids my understanding of the problem.

"I am 32 and she is 28." He replied.

I hope his girl won't be mad at him for exposing her age on air!

"So what's the problem John?" I asked.

"Well, SST, I love my girl and want us to get married, but you see; she just had a school certificate and I can't marry a non-graduate. She has tried to get admission to a university for the last two years but to no avail; and time is running out for me, but I can't marry a non graduate." he was emphatically about it.

"You said you love your girl, John?" I asked.

"Of course I do, SST!" He answered back quickly.

I wanted to tell him what I actually felt about his reply. However, I always like my listeners to make out the answer for themselves instead of being told.

"Ok John, I want you to know something about someone like you that was faced with a similar problem of whether to run away from his love or not. He lived long time before now, John."

I then cleared my throat to carry my audience once more on the groovy train of my motivational talk.

"My friend, John, and of course my dear listeners, there was a handsome young man called John Dunns. He was well educated, and had a good job in a reputable law firm. What you can call an every girl's dream. The type of man most women are waiting to whisper to their friends, "oh! He looked at me!"

I was laughing.

"Well, one day John was going through the newspapers and he came across a beautiful poem written by a lady writer, he was so taken in by the beauty of the composition that he decided to write to the composer."

I realised I had to quickly explain why he had to write a letter and not use a telephone. You know, my audience belong to the generation that grew up in the age of the cell phones and the internet.

"It was 1886 in England, not the days of GSM!" I added before continuing with the narrative.

"An acquaintance soon developed between the two. From an exchange of ideas in letters, a romance developed and before they knew it, they started exchanging love letters.

John soon invited Mary whom he had come to develop an intimate relationship with, to visit him in London where he works. She eagerly accepted. Having not seen each other in person aside from exchanging letters, he asked how he was to recognise her when he comes to welcome her at the train station.

She stated that she would be wearing a red rose flower insignia by the right side pocket of her blouse. John replied that he would be in a bright navy blue suit with a matching tie."

I stopped to take a sip from my glass of water, giving myself a small time to rest.

"Sorry for the small pause, I needed to cool my throat, let's continue . . . ?" It's always good to make a small apology no matter how good you are going.

"Where was I? Yeah! John was in his best attire when he rushed to the train station the day he was to meet Mary. He was standing by the arrival lounge when the train arrived. As the passengers alighted, he sight a beautiful well-built lady, dressed in a white gown, one of the most beautiful ladies he had ever seen in his life. She should not be older than 20 years, John was 24. His heart skipped; the lady came by his side, and giving him a nice smile, John's heart skipped the more.

Oh! How he wished she was wearing a red rose on her blouse pocket and he would be Mary and his happiness complete.

As he looked in the other direction, he saw an old lady being wheeled in a wheel chair approaching him. John nearly fainted in shock; his heart was beating so loud that he could hear the sound. The old lady had a red rose flower by the right side pocket of her blouse! John's mind started racing once again, but this time he was thinking of what to do. He thought of hiding in the crowd and disappearing. He looked round and met the eyes of the beautiful woman in the white gown that just passed him, standing some meters off. She was hesitating too, waiting for him to make a move to her direction."

I stopped immediately I reached the point where it is good to allow my listeners to have an overlook of the story before I continue.

"John's mind was telling him to leave old Mary in the wheel chair and pretend he didn't know her, and to quickly accost the young beautiful lady before she leaves. However, his conscience took over. He remembered how he had promised Mary love in those letters and made her to take the long journey to meet him. And now seeing the trouble she took to travel in a wheel chair, and all to see him, filled him with greater love than ever. The fact that she turned out to be an old, ugly and crippled woman in a wheelchair did not changed the feelings he had for her."

I let out a short sign, signifying a hard decision.

"John quickly moved to the old cripple woman in the wheel chair, smiling and said "Mary, I'm John, I know you will be surprised seeing me so young. I now realised why you refused to tell me of your age in your letters, and that you are crippled. But Mary I love you as I always did reading your letters and nothing is going to changed that"

The old woman in the wheelchair looked up at him surprised, and shouted "young man where are your manners! I don't know where you got your ideas from, but I'm not Mary" John was shocked by her utterance, and he started to stammer, "but, but the red rose you said . . . ." the shock was showing on his face. The old woman smiled "oh this red rose? That nice young lady in white I met on the journey said I should wear it and if any man comes and asks me about it, I should tell him to go and meet her." John turned and saw the beautiful young lady in the white gown, tears in her eyes, rushing to hug him!

I stopped for a while as I always do at the end of a story to allow the lesson to sink.

John, my caller, was the first to break the silence "Yeah! Yeah! Yeah!" He was laughing, "I got it, SST, thanks man, I feel you, thanks."

And he quickly put off.

That is a difference between the ladies and the gentlemen. A lady would have been swept off by emotions with the story and start recanting regrets or promising to reconcile everything back with her partner. But a man would be more circumspect, he might have gotten the message in the story, but he would still need to weigh the arguments before committing himself to a course of action.

Ladies have tender hearts, that's why they easily break!

There wasn't much to say to John anyway, so it was good he saved me time as he put off.

I got to continue.

I always make sure that my narratives have didactic lessons not for one person or the one that raises the discussion, but to all my audience listening to the show. I went on to the end of narration exhortation.

"So that's the story of John Dunns whose love was not defeated by his fiancée status! To all my dear listeners out there, the love story of John Dunns applies not only to our dear John that called, but to all of us engage in other activities too.

Believe me it's not all about love and vows, the story goes to show that we should hold on to a bigger picture in life, despite disappointing outlooks." I said it in the normal lesson fashion I have now gotten used to.

"It might not be the issue of a love relationship only." I started on another one.

I love to expand the scope!

"Maybe you had a beautiful discussion with the Lord before going into that marriage, or that your business, or it was a career or whatever that you are involved in! And you kept the faith and discussion with the Lord, and you believe his promises that all will be well with you, and that you shall be the head and not the tail. But whoops! All of a sudden, you are confronted with an ugly picture, your faith sank, and your strength in God disappeared. I'm telling you today that you shouldn't despair; please don't run away from that marriage, that business, that career—despite the frustrations, persecution, or failures! Please do not follow the enticements of the devil and lose focus of what you have agreed with God. Keep the good faith and God will reveal his plan for your life in due course!" I used that last part in concluding the episode.

There were two more calls from listeners, but all were the normal routine calls. Most just wanted to know how I was doing, giving me kudos for a good show and of course exchanging greetings to their loves ones across the airwave, what they call giving a 'shout out'. As young people, mostly students, formed the bulk of my callers, I was never short of such calls. I always try to handle it nicely. It pays to be nice and respectable to whoever was out there.

My radio show was out to uplift the spirit of my listeners who are undergoing tough times in their lives. It would do me no good if I'm bias, aloof or inconsiderate. So, no matter what I feel about a listener's call, I still try to give the person an audience while looking for a more tactful way of getting rid of the discussion, if it looked like derailing my show.

Often when issues are raised by a listener that I had no immediate answer to, or no ready narrative at hand that answers to the problem, I would look for a way to refer the problem to another source or to a book that had a solution that I know of, or I will just postpone it till another day.

Just when I was thinking I might have to fill in the gap with a musical interlude to cover the remaining time left in my show and close the programme on that, a listener brought up a discussion that later appeared very interesting; *or rather an issue that I had an answer at hand!*

I love it the most when it was something I could align with a narrative, and I believe I could with this one.

The caller said his name was Kalu Chukwu; a young man who was thinking of moving into his personal business after serving his master as an apprentice for some years.

"Good morning DJ" He said excitedly.

He sounded quite young.

You see why I took the name motivational DJ when I started my programme on the radio? It excites the youths and makes me more approachable to my listeners, especially the young people.

In my show, young people form the larger part of my audience.

"Yeah, good day, my friend, you've got any dance steps for me this morning?" I asked perfunctorily. From his opening speech, I did not see him being much different from my two of the earlier callers.

"Yeah, DJ SST, I got some reggae moves, wow!" He was laughing. This young man sure was enjoying his day. I just pray he will not waste mine!

"Yeah, thanks brother, let's see what you've got, move to the floor." I could hear my voice hardening a little. I guess he also noticed it too.

He moved quickly to the issue that prompted him to call.

"Yeah, SST, my name is Kalu Chukwu, you see, I have been working as an apprentice with my uncle in Lagos in his electronics business for two years now. He just decided to settle me with some little capital to start my business. But SST, I don't believe the capital is enough to venture into such business, I wanted to stay longer and get more money before I start. My friends' advised me against going into my business now, because there are tough challenges in the business. You know that oppositions and enmity from other businessmen will arise and if I'm not strong enough and experienced I might just lose everything.

Some amongst them even mocked my idea. Others believe I should just go into it like that. They said I should trust in God and move into the business, but I'm still not sure, I believe I need more capital before going in. What do you think I should do?" He was speaking in a clearer voice now, and sounded more serious.

His problem immediately got me moving. I was motivated to take up his story as I believe I have a nice narrative with good teaching lessons to my listeners to go along with it.

"Kalu, that's a hard choice." I said. Of course, I wasn't going to ask him how much he got from his uncle. That was not the issue. The issue was he saw the amount as being small and inadequate. It was an amount he feared to commit his faith to, and that's where I love to move in.

Motivation is all about developing faith, isn't it?

"Kalu, I have never seen anyone that starts something great by doing a great thing at the beginning. It is passion and enthusiasm that would along the line turn a small plan carried with great desire to a great happening. Life is not about what you got at hand, it is about what you got in you! God uses what you have inside you to create what you need at hand. God is not bothered about what you are holding; He is more interesting in what He will bring to your hands to hold. God wants you to do what you can, to let Him know you are ready for him to do what you cannot do!

With God, anything is big enough! Do not be ashamed of what you're or what people say you are, if people don't mock you, God won't make you! If you are afraid of what people would say or afraid if they would mock you, then you can't do new and daring things! And without new and daring things, you can't achieve anything worthwhile.

God always acts from the unforeseen; it takes our bold actions to bring it out in our lives. Samson did not care who was mocking him, he didn't ask for eyes to see his enemies laughing at him. He only asked to be taken to the pillars because he knows when he reaches the pillars he would bring down all his enemies at once. It doesn't matter what disappointment is looking you in the eye, it doesn't matter what failure is taking place in your life, because God will take you to the pillars that end your troubles once and for all!

So take a step to find your pillars. Do not stop on what you know! Knowledge is a just potential that is why it is lying idle in the hands of many people. Action is the real power and that is why it has produced results in the hands of the few that dare to take it. There is nothing new under the sun except one that carries your name, and God is looking for who can do something new!"

I kept on with the message expanding it as I go forward.

"People cared less how Coca Cola is packaged, than for the brand name. Henry Ford might not have made great cars in his lifetime, going by what we are seeing today, but if Ford Motors decides to do away with his name, they will have to start a new battle for customers no matter how great is their product. To get to where it matters, you must be able to do what matters! So be bold enough and come out with something. When Houdini set out to be a magician, his dream was not to be a good or great magician. He set out to be the magician! Don't just be a great worker, be the worker!

There is one area nobody can beat you in this world; when you try to be yourself! Because God made all of us uniquely special and God never made any mistake in His creation and you are one of them. When God reached the sixth day of creation he stopped. He did not stop because He was tired, He did not stop because He ran out of ideas, He stopped because He has finished!

The great furniture you see today have always been around in the trees, the planes and cars you see have always been there in the iron in the ground, and all that was needed was the imagination to bring them out, and God has put that in you, but you are yet to discover! You are running after that job because you are yet to discover what is in you, you are running after that business because you are yet to discover what is in you—you are yet to discover what God has planted in you. And God has given you the imagination to bring out your unique greatness!

You are not coming first maybe because you are allowing the world to compete with you in its own game, let the world compete with you in your own game!

Michael Jordan by adopting his flying jumps led the world to his own game. Charlie Chaplin by adopting a unique style of walk with baggy trousers led the world to his own style! By trying to be like somebody else you would miss what God has created you to be! Whatever a man knows, no matter what a man can do, he can never be greater than the person he is created to be. God has greatness with different styles for different people. Don't worry your style is good enough! When Moses reached the Red Sea God told him to raise the rod in his hands and part the waters. When Joshua reached the Jordan River, God told him to tell the priests to march on the waters and the river parted. God doesn't use the same style twice to carry two different people to greatness—don't worry, your style is good enough to lead to greatness too! There is nothing bad in making small progress in what you are doing provided the small progress takes place every day, so get up and start working on it.

Nothing works except you work on it! Your business won't work, your career won't work, and your relationship won't work except you are working on it! And as long as you are working on your ambition, one day you will wake up and see yourself where you never dreamt! You would arrive and you won't know how you got there. It doesn't matter if you don't know how you get there, because God knows how you got there! He will carry you there! And by the time God puts you there, you would be left to wonder how you got there!

It does not matter if you are down to nothing in your life today. Joseph was down to nothing when he was thrown in prison. David was down to nothing when he was chased away by Saul. When you are down to nothing in your life, it means God is up to something! Don't be sitting there being afraid of what you must do! It was a risk for small David to face the lion. It was a risk for Daniel to dare the lions! But you can't experience God's best if you are not able to take a risk. If you don't take risks, you won't create your chances, and if you don't create the chances, you won't have the choice, and without the choices, there won't be challenges! And what chance of success do you have without challenges? My friend be ready to be ready to take risks!

A ship anchored at the harbour is safe, but that's not what ships are built for. Sitting there and doing nothing would keep you safe from trouble but that's not what God created you for. Go out and help yourself to what God created you to do and do that with all your might. Even God would not help you if "helping you" is not what you have started. No matter how big a task is, do not fear, trust in God and enter it! If you enter a challenge knowing what you can do for yourself, you have not entered correctly—enter knowing what God can do for you. Be ready to take a tough decision when it is the right thing to do. Joseph took a tough decision to do the right thing. David took a tough decision to do the right thing. It is a tough decision that will take you out of a tough situation. And whenever you are prepared to take a tough decision, God will take you out of a tough situation. I know you must have faced some disappointment and think life is not fair to you. Yes, life is never fair. Don't bother about life. Only God is fair—bother only about God."

I had to end the exhortation as I reached the area I love the most. It was time to read from one of my narratives. I could sense already that I had something that appealed to his problem.

"Kalu and my other listeners let me read to you from one of my narratives. It is the story of a soldier who in asking God to save his life thought what God had for him was not sufficient enough!"

And with that introduction I didn't waste time before moving to my narrative.

"During World War 2, Corporal Jack Newton ... Please listeners I have decided to withheld his real name, because that's not the message .... Ok?

Back to my story, Corporal Jack Newton got separated from his patrol unit during intensive fighting. The thick smoke from the very heavy exchange of fire got him disoriented. And he lost contact with his comrades in the patrol. He was left alone in the jungle. As he made efforts to find his way and make contact with his colleagues, he heard the sounds of the movement of the enemy soldiers getting closer and closer to where he was hiding.

Corporal Newton saw a cliff riddled with caves. He ran to it and hid in one of the caves, hoping he would not be found. There he made a silent prayer to God for help and protection. As he was still praying, a giant spider dropped down over the entrance of the cave. Newton laughed ruefully, "God what I needed is a brick wall and you sent me a spider?" He said.

Later, the solder fell asleep a little from the intense stress. When he woke up; he saw that the spider had created a thick web of many layers over the cave entrance. The battlefield was silent. He was still hiding there for hours and hours. Then he heard the steps of enemy soldiers checking the caves near him. He braced himself and his rifle for a last stand! Saying his last prayers and waiting for the inevitable end. But when the soldiers came to the cave, one of the enemy soldiers said to the other, "we don't need to check here, no one could have gone in without disturbing the web." And they left! Newton was later able to find his way and rejoined his group" End of narrative, now the usual lessons learnt for my listeners that I read in the form of exhortations.

"My listeners out there, God does not need any big capital, He does not need any rich man, any big connection or any big degree to save you, to empower you, to raise you up, to promote you or to appoint you. When He is ready to act in your life, the little He has made available around you, the little He has placed in your hands is more than enough! Because God is everything you require! Whatever more that might seem needed, is just to give your empowerment a natural touch. Absalom was camped with his father, King Saul, and the great mighty of Israel against the armies of the Philistines. His father and the soldiers were weary to move forward and decided to remain where they were. They believed they needed more time to prepare enough for their enemies. But one day Absalom rose and took his armour bearer with him to the camp of the enemy! Absalom said to the armour bearer, 'it does not restraint God to save by many or by few' and so he went and wrecked a great slaughter amongst his enemies. Absalom believed God does not require great number to give great victory, and all that He required from us was great faith! When all hope seems lost in your life, they are not actually lost but somewhere being gathered by God to bring out your solution—so have faith!"

I declared sharply in the short exhortation.

"Whatever your problem do not be discouraged if a solution is taking time to come, it could be you are on God's special list! When you are on God's special list, He doesn't come to you when people would say . . . . oh we know you can do it! Oh we know it's possible! Oh we thank God for that man . . . . Rather He comes when everybody will shout . . . . can you believe that?! It must be God! When you are on God's special list, you are His special advertisement! Relax that your problem that seem to defy solution for years is on God's special list! Your problem might be making news now but your breakthrough will make the headlines tomorrow!" I always love finishing my narrative by moving from the specific to the general. It was my style of bringing out a lesson that covers all of my listeners' requirements irrespective of which field they belong to, or in whatever branch of duty they found themselves in! I didn't want it to end just a lesson to one person or a group. As soon as I came to the exhortation in the message, which is normally at the end of my narrative; my table phone was already ringing.

It was always like that now!

There were many listeners out there waiting to call in, and were always in a hurry to beat one another to the call! It is only in rare occasions that the first caller gets a chance to call in back after an answer to his question, because of the heavy traffic. I liked it all the same; my narratives didactic lessons are not intended to be confined to a single person but to a wider audience.

I quickly picked up the phone ringing on the table. My time was going up. I didn't want to have problems with my producer again. However, of recent, I have noticed that the hard man has been lenient towards me. My show rating was rising and the studio was openly happy about that.

It was not Kalu calling back as I suspected. A lady caller was at the end.

131

"Good morning, SST, I just want to tell you I'm blessed by your programme. I have been feeling bad since I received my degree result. I was thinking my life had ended. I felt I had no future with a third class degree, but now I know it means nothing! God is able to raise me high even without a degree, thanks sir." She concluded and put off.

I was not going to ask her for her name as I usually do. It was obvious she wanted some privacy, and not that she actually missed her name in the comment. I can understand with her situation, don't you?

I was still happy with her new found spirit after the discouraging experience, it lifted my spirit too!

Kalu came up later on air to express his gratitude for the lesson he was able to learn from my narrative, and of course what I said in the end of the exhortation. He went on to express a new found resolve and faith in himself too! He was now ready to go along with the little he had at hand, and faced the challenges. I wished him well, and quickly rounded up by leaving a message to my listeners.

My hour was over.

"So, my dear listeners remember Moses came to Egypt with only the stick in his hands but he left with the riches of Egypt and over 600,000 men. Joseph was sold to Egypt as a slave, even the clothes on his body was seized by his brothers. But he ended up controlling the riches of Egypt. Thomas Edison, the renowned scientist and inventor never had a formal education. I didn't say he never started one. He dropped out of school as a toddler after a few months of schooling when the teachers interpreted his impatient behaviour as mental inferiority and called him "addled." Edison went home to be taught by his mother and later engaged in self education by devouring any book that came his way. He ended up employing hundreds of university educated scientist and registering over 1,300 patents in his lifetime! Bill Gates never had a university education. I didn't say he never started one! Bill Gates dropped out of Harvard and by the age of nineteen to have his own business. And went on to becoming a billionaire at age thirty!

It does not matter if you start with nothing! It does not matter if you don't have what other people think you must have to be successful. It does not matter what you came to Lagos with, it does matter if you start that marriage without a house or a car! Because when you have the favour of God, you will one day own more than you can ever imagined! It does not matter if you have no money to build your own house! God has it! It does not matter if you have no wisdom to start that business! God has it! It does not matter if you have nothing, because God has everything, and as long as you can hold on to Him in faith, He will make you have everything, everyday!"

I paused a little. But no calls were coming in! It seems nobody was interested in calling in—they all wanted to sit back and hear me talk. So, I continued talking on a general front as I was getting used to!

"Whatever comes against you as you struggle to start that your business or in an attempt to realise your dream, be it lack of finance or opposition from forces against your progress, please don't relent, don't give up, because God will turn it to a testimony one day!" I was creating hiatus in my speech and allowing time for calls to come in as I was getting exhausted. But even with that nobody called.

I had to find a way to continue.

"The lion came to kill David, it ended a testimony! The bear came to seize the young sheep from his care, it ended a testimony! Goliath stood before David but he ended a testimony, even Saul thought he could banish David forever but he ended a testimony for David! So whatever comes against you, whatever is planning to stop your victory or banished your dreams, God is going to turn it to a testimony! Because God will not allow the lion to kill you, He will not allow the bear to seize you from His care, and He will not allow your enemies to block your victory and nothing can destroy the desire of your heart when you are walking truthfully with Him!"

I took a sip of water from the glass cup on the table while I waited—still no call came in. Either, they are enjoying my exhortation and didn't want to disturb the flow or my listeners have long forgotten about me and have changed to another station!

I checked my small glass cup, the water was almost finished.

I quietly resigned myself to the situation and continued doing what I knew best; motivating in line with God's words.

"God will not allow you to be defeated no matter what you face in life, you can only pass through the situation, but it will not hold you or defeat you! David said "even if I pass through the valley of the shadow of death" please note David didn't say when I'm stuck in the valley of death or when I live in the valley of the shadow of death. Because he knew, whatever wants to kill his destiny will not be able to hold him down, and if it can't hold him then it can't succeed against him as long as he trust in God."

I hope my listeners, if there were still any, were not getting weary on why I was dwelling on David a lot this morning. But really I love the book of Psalms written by King David. It gives me great inspiration whenever I was in difficulties. Inspiration generates practical solutions to life's problems and is the highest point of connection to God's wisdom. And so I always find it easy to relate life's daunting battles by taking up examples from David's triumphant battles as recorded in the book of Psalms. And what more do you need for a talk as a motivational speaker?

I continued on line of David's exhortations!

"David was known for the great thanks he gave to God! Not for the long life he had—it was always a good reason for him to give thanks, yes! Not for the throne he occupied, and houses he built—they were also good reasons to give God thanks! But most of all David gave thanks to God for not allowing his enemies to triumph over him, oh yeah!"

When I shout like that, my listeners know something big is coming.

And I continued with the high note!

"My friends, no one know more than David what it meant to have enemies out to destroy one's dreams! He had enemies in the bush; he had enemies in the field, he had enemies amongst his children, he had enemies from his advisers. He had enemies from his wives, oh yes! David had enemies from all areas of his life, trying to destroy him!" I was loud.

Motivational Dance Show was on a groovy train this morning, and I kept on firing!

"David didn't run away from these challenges! He faced them! He faced the lion and he faced the bear when they came upon him in the bush. He faced Goliath when he came upon him in the field, he faced the challenges of exile when Saul came upon his life, and he faced the attacks of his wife when she came against him while he was praising the Lord. He faced the treachery of his chief adviser, Ahithopel, when he came with treachery during the rebellion of Absalom! Oh yeah!" I shouted in the microphone like a preacher at a crusade!

"David even faced up to the challenge posed by his own son, Absalom, when he came upon him with arms. David was a man always ready to face up to challenges and not to run from them! Because David knew, facing challenges is the key to overcoming them and there is no champion without a challenge! It is the capacity to develop and improve their skills that separates failures from champions!

Do you see how a river is? It is occupied by water just like the ocean, right? But it is not straight and wide like the ocean. That is because the water of the river meanders, avoiding obstacles, but the water of the ocean opens up and faces the obstacles! And that is why the great things that dwell in the water are not found in the rivers, but in the oceans! The great sharks are in the ocean, the great whales are in the ocean! My friends please dare to be an ocean—don't remain a river! Face all your challenges and do not fear adversities! Whenever God is ready to take you to a greater level, he leads you along the path of adversities! Great men are tested greatly, ordinary men are tested ordinarily. The greater your adversity, the more God tests your capability to prove or disappoint His trust! A multitude never reaches its altitude—never move with a multitude. Desire yourself to be special and God will make your gift to manifest!" I was still shouting.

I was carried away in my excitement.

"Don't fear opposition because most times God uses the opposition of opponents and not the love of loved ones, to promote us! David's brothers cared for his safety so much that they didn't want him to risk his life in facing Goliath, but it was in fighting Goliath that David's path to greatness lied. God used the opposition posed by Goliath and not the love of his brothers to promote David. Joseph's father loved him so much that he didn't want him out of his sight for a day, not to talk of him leaving home, but it was in the hatred of his brothers and not the love of his father that Joseph needed to reach his great destiny in Egypt. Moses' mother feared for his life in the hands of the Egyptians that she went to a great length to hide him from them, but it was in the house of an Egyptian that his route to greatness lied.

My friend, that opposition you are facing, that enemy you are running from, they could be holding the seed to your success more than the cautious love of your friends. And most times in life, it is not a desire to make our loved ones happy, but a burning desire to deny our enemies joy, that spurs us on. People of strong characters are more motivated to prove their enemies wrong, than to prove their friends right! It is not destiny that makes men excel. It is the persistence in pursuing their destinies. If you faint in the days of adversity it is not that the adversity was too big or what happened was too much for you to bear. It was just that your strength is weak. Don't waste time dwelling on a situation, spend time more building your strength."

I put a stop to the exhortation and quickly ended the show on that note.

"And before I close today, I want to leave you with one question. What is the greatest expression of love? Gifts, money, time? My answer is time! You can give out anything freely even to those you don't particularly liked. But whom or what you love is determined by the time you commit to the person or activity. The secret to developing a relationship, imparting skills or enhancing knowledge is the time we are prepared to commit to it. Everybody has time but very few invest in it! So always have time for the motivation dance show. Have a nice day all my good people in Lagos! I love you all and see you tomorrow on Motivation dance club Static FM 111, see you next time, bye!"

I noticed the producer didn't come in to check on me to see if I was carried away, as he used to. I checked my wristwatch; wow! He even allowed me to overstay my timing. Maybe, my show was doing well as the boys were saying, and the man is getting impressed!

The Motivation Dance Club
Who Really Loves You?

By the time my show entered the third week on Static FM 111.0 I was already a household name in the city of Lagos. The motivation dance club was not only drawing wave of listeners to FM 111, but above that and of most important to the management, it was attracting heavy income from advertisement fees as well.

Many of the firms that once shunned the studio and took their products to other media houses, where rushing back and begging for airtime on FM 111 because of the increased popularity of the motivation dance club amongst listeners in Lagos. And most, if not all of them, want their products to be advertised during or immediately after the motivation dance club show—when they were sure of a large audience.

The producer, Mark, had now become really friendly and nice to me. The threat of bringing back the sports show to take over my broadcast time was no more an issue. What was of concern was to see how to increase my broadcast time. But that proved to be a problem. I was with the studio on a part time basis; I still had a regular job at my security firm and I had not made up of my mind to go full time in the studio.

As I enter the studio that morning, I met Sasha, the lady receptionist who once treated me like an unwanted object, welcoming me, as she now does, with a huge smile. I had become one of her good and maybe close friends, aside from Mark of course. This morning she met me with a message that Mark wants to see me in his office before I start my show.

The way Static FM 111 was structured was to allow the station function in different departments situated in different locations. The management team that consist of the managers, directors and the rest of the big personalities have their offices at the headquarters of the station located in the business district area of Ikeja. The broadcasting studio where programmes are aired to the public was situated in the suburb of the city, in the ghetto town of Ajegunle.

The popular refrain was that Static FM 111 was established to cater for the teeming low class citizens of Lagos; as a result the studio was at the right place. The argument held no water for me because I know a studio could broadcast round the city from anywhere. I guess Ajegunle was chosen because of the low cost of doing business, where else would Mark had found a place where a plate of rice and beans, his favourite meal, goes for 25 naira?

While at the headquarters there was about 18 staff, the number of people that do the day to day running of the studio are just six, if you don't count the guardsman. There was Mark, the studio director, the four engineers that operate the equipment on shift and Sasha that was there as an office assistant, receptionist, computer operator—and what other menial task you can assign her. I was not counting myself for obvious reasons. I was there not as a staff but as a freelance presenter and there were other freelance presenters like me that anchor other shows too.

I entered the studio producer's office and met Mark waiting for me. My show was to start in 15 minutes time, I was sure he did not intend to delay me.

"SST, you are welcome, please seat down." He said. He was shaking my hands with the new found respect I had started getting used to by then.

"Thank you, sir" I said.

I have been calling Mark, sir, ever since the day I started presenting my show at the studio. He didn't like it and always reminded me not to address him as such, but I just could not stop myself.

"Well, SST, I have something urgent to discuss with you. I know you are supposed to be on air soon." He said.

It must be really serious for him not to have remembered to frown at my calling him, sir!

"Yes?" I inquired.

"Yes, SST, you are well aware that your show has become quite a big blessing to the company, greater than we ever imagined." He said with all seriousness.

That was really a big plus considering the fact that I was almost kicked out of this place three weeks ago. How fast situation changes in life! I was quiet, and kept staring at him. I did not rejoice because I did not know where he was going. That definitely could not be what he called me for.

"Yes, SST, you're a big blessing!" He was openly elated. "I have advertisement contracts here on my table running into hundreds of thousands, something we never saw before." He was shuffling some papers in his front. "Considering where you met us, it was really a giant leap. The management has increased all our salaries and agreed to other incentives. But that's not why I wanted to see you." He said. I knew, of course, he didn't call me to tell me on how much he was earning now!

"SST, the management wants you to increase your shows to cover the avalanche of advertisements coming. I told them that won't be possible as you are a freelance and not a staff, you have your job elsewhere." He said. I could guess where he was going, but I kept quiet. "SST, they want you to work here full time." He was looking squarely in my face. I stared blankly at him, giving away no sign of my feelings. I have learnt never to show resentment or excitement on any preposition that comes my way in Lagos.

He was still talking, almost begging me, seeing that I have kept mute all along "SST, we are ready to pay you double what you are earning where you are working now, and also assign an official car to you." He was sounding desperate. I looked up at him, surprised at how he knew how much I was earning at my working place. He must have read my mind or expected it as a natural thought because he went on to say "We have done some few checks on you, you see? We really want you here my brother." He laughed loudly, relaxing his face a little after a long time.

I looked at my wristwatch; I was supposed to be on air soon.

"Ok sir . . . "I started, but he quickly interjected, "please stop the sir, call me, Mark." He said.

"Ok, Mark, I will sleep over it and see if I have an answer tomorrow" I could see his countenance changing "my show is almost on now, I have to be going." I added for emphasis. He looked at his wristwatch and agreed with me. "Yes, you are right, you better be going. We will meet and discuss when you are ready brother." He held on to my shoulders to the door as he saw me off his office.

Wow! Success is a powerful motivator. I could still remember the time when Mark would have looked at me with high disapproval when I enter his office, reminding me of his threat of seizing my broadcast time if I arrive a minute late. I was the one reminding him of when I needed to go on air now. I quickly ran to the studio room just as the last presenter was getting off. The station engineer was already playing one of the legendary maestro Fuji musician, Fela, songs. I quickly got into the pilot seat and signalled to him to launch me on air. I was ready to go on my dance floor.

"Hey my friends, this is your motivational DJ SST, taking you on the floor of the motivation dance club. Today is not the day for anyhow dance! It is a day to dance to the appreciation of our mothers, because it is mother's day, and I want to give a big round of applause to all mothers out there." I took a small pause to allow it sink in! Many might not even know such a day exist, but it was mother's day and I needed to pass the message across.

I know the way my programme goes. Very soon I should be expecting calls from listeners, to get the discussion forum started, and the only way to get that going, was to stimulate a discussion—so I picked a probing angle on the mother's day, to stir up a conversation.

I moved closer to the microphone and continued talking.

"Mothers are special in our lives. They are the main building block in the lives of all of us, and of course the only trustworthy people we have around." Here it comes! "My friends, it's not hard to know who truly loves you amongst the people around you. Your boss only uses you, your friends accompany you, your employees manage you, your wife tolerates you, but only your mother truly loves you!"

Before I could put down the microphone and adjust my small frame in my seat, a caller came up.

"SST, you have not said anything about the fathers, don't they also love? Are they not worthy of being mentioned, even above the mothers? Is it only your mama that knows how to love you?" He was strongly defensive.

A male chauvinist I was sure. I was expecting that!

"*Brother*" I laughed and continued adopting the confidence of a man that has done his homework. "I'm sure it was because your mother truly loves you that you even know who your father is and that he even knows you as a son." Seeing that the person did not return back my gesture, I added another free explanation. "And that goes for your sister too, *brother.*" I said.

The line went off.

Well, that's that! As I was thinking on how to move on to another topic, to cover up my one hour show, the phone rang again.

"Okay, SST, we heard you about a mother's love, but what about your business partners? I am having a good time with my partners here, we are brothers in this firm, and we are in love, SST." The man said.

This time I didn't waste time trying to build up my decorum

"My friend, you are right your business partners truly love you." I could hear the sigh of relief from the other end, I was sure he was making the call in front of his buddies in the office and wanted to build a stronger bond by an open expression of his love for them.

This was someone definitely wanting to know where he stands with his business colleagues and must be happy with my response. I laughed.

My brother, I have not finished yet!

I then said coolly as if announcing him for a prize said, "and the love of your partners would only be clearly seen when you die with half of your assets undisclosed to your family."

I could hear the gasp of shock at the other end. I hope this man didn't catch a heart attack! If I where him I will start putting my house in order. The call of life has no timetable.

There was no response from him again.

Just when I was satisfied that I have exhausted the limit on this item, and it was time to move onto the main discussion of the day before the studio producer physically uproots me from the seat, another call came in. I guess Lagosians don't have much to do in their offices these days, ha! It was just 9 am and calls were still coming in like wide showers? What happened to the normal going through the early morning files in offices?

The man calling on the line sounded like a gentleman. How did I know? Simple, he started with the normal customary pleasantries.

"SST, good morning, and how are you?" He said in a cool and slow manner.

Yeah, just what I need, a gentleman that is not in a hurry . . . to drag my time off this show.

There was no time remaining for me to go to another topic with 15minutes left on the show. I could see the engineer hardening his gaze at me, it's worse when a programme comes before the 10 o' clock news. You can't postpone news.

"SST, it is Ben." He exclaimed in surprise, as if shocked that I did not recognised him.

Ha! Who is this guy, anyway? Another of those Lagos show offs! How was I supposed to know who Ben was, in a town of 17 million people? I know his type, the ones that were always trying to impress a wide audience with the notion that they are big shots whose names ring bells in the media houses. I decided to help him a little in his attempt to feel big, if not for anything at least to avoid wasting my time.

"Good day, Ben, long time, continue please." I could sense his excitement when he heard the word 'long time' to him it establishes that he was a known name in town.

"SST, I'm listening to your show with my young lovely wife here, we are having a cool honeymoon." He gave a pause expecting some words of congratulations.

My friend, move on!

He decided to move to his question, seeing that no response was coming from me.

Good!

"SST, I just don't buy that." He came up hotly, the gentleman facade slowly fading.

I didn't mind him.

He was still talking, "how could you say only mothers truly love, and the wife only tolerates her husband? I don't agree that that's how it is in a marriage!" He said it with the assurance of one that has gone through the marriage thing long enough. No wonder marriages get old so early these days.

I could imagine the young wife lying there with him, maybe still in bed; I don't blame him for being so defensive.

I didn't want to enter a long argument on the topic with him so I went straight to the point.

"My friend just wait till you are caught pants down with your wife's best friend." He interjected before I could continue

"God forbid!" He shouted defiantly.

I could see he was trying to put up a good show for the young wife. I hope his wife was not suspecting him of having an eye for any of her friends that would be too bad for Ben. Trust women.

I didn't have time for any long explanation to Ben, so I continued from where I stopped.

"When you are caught with her best friend, even without your wife seeing the evidence, she will go about and shout to everyone within earshot."

"I knew I married an idiot! He has been cheating on me even before we were born."

Ben didn't interrupt this time. I could see I have hijacked his attention. He must be hardening his gaze on the poor young wife. "But if it were your mother, even if she was presented with foolproof evidence of your misdeed, she will shout and say *oh no! It can't be, Ben, my son! He has never been like that, oh my God, who has led him to this now!"*

I held on the receiver a little longer to hear what he had to say to that, but no reply came from him. I dropped the phone.

My friend Ben concentrate on finishing what you are doing with your new wife, before the hotel kicks you, why do you think people have short honeymoons? I mused.

I decided to put up a conciliatory remark to other groups as well.

"My listeners don't get me wrong. Mothers, fathers, wives, and true friends all matter greatly to our lives and we must always acknowledge their love in times like this, as we are doing to our mothers on this mother's day. It's always good to always remember the people that matters the most in our lives.

Most a times, we deny those we shouldn't deny, we hurt those we shouldn't hurt and we disappoint those we shouldn't disappoint! And we never know what harm we might have done to them until we are in position not to deny, hurt and disappoint them no more. Because in the moment of our glory, in the period of our restoration we do less to those we take for granted, we remember less those we take for granted. And true companions are always taken for granted. Without a conscious effort our subconscious mind will always blot those that stand by us in periods of our afflictions, removing them from our periscope as we attend great heights.

Life is all about control. It is all about the power we have over ourselves in our season of restoration. It is about having control over what we eat, what we say, where we go, what we do and most of all having control over who we love. Friends that you stand with in periods of their distress will forget you the most when they enter a bliss, but God will never forget you. Julius Caesar said those that matters the most are always attended to last. We give the least attention, love and patronages to people that matter the most in our lives. To activities that matters the most to our lives. To efforts that matters the most to our lives and to those that stood faithfully by us in moment of our trials.

When all is well with us again we go out in pursuit of new acquaintances, in desire to buy over old enemies, in a struggle to get the love of those that deny us, while leaving behind the love of true

145

friends because we always take their love for granted. So let's use the mother's day as a point of contact to reach out to all our loved ones out there, and most of all, let us remember the greatest love of all in our lives which is the love of God."

I decided to end the discussion on Mother's day celebration so as to avoid more contending calls.

I move on to another topic.

"My listeners, I don't know what you have missed in your life or what the devil has denied you that you rightly deserved, but I want to let you know that God has promised in His words that He will restored double to you for your loss." I then lowered my voice to let out a secret. "But you need to file a claim!"

The phone rang and I quickly answered it, it was a lady

"SST, my name is Sarah. I'm curious, what do you mean by saying we need to file a claim to receive back a double of our loss from God?" She asked eagerly. It was just what I wanted to hear.

This caller had made my day!

"Yes, Sarah, we need to file a claim to receive back a double of our loss from God. Whenever we are faced with a situation where we are wronged in our lives, without filing a claim we won't get our entitlements from the courts and so is it with God! When the devil takes away or deny us what is ours, we are entitled to receive a double back from God as He promised—but only when we file a claim!" I brought out the narrative of the day, that I called file a claim against the devil.

I started reading.

"Mr. Jones was laid off after an accident in which he lost a hand at the factory. Without any help, or assistance he was left in the streets hungry, frustrated, and dejected. But someone came along and showed him the law. The firm was supposed to compensate him with a severance allowance. It was his right as written in the law, he had no reason begging or going about in the streets, and waiting for help to come his way. It is in his power in the laws to file a claim at the court. And so, Mr. Jones filed a claim. The firm brought their lawyers to put a defence against his claim, but Jones had a case, and he must be compensated double fold. The firm had no case. The court restored to Mr. Jones what he was supposed to be given as severance allowance, and also added some huge amount for a double of his discomfort over the years!"

That was the Jone's story. Now my talk!

"Many at times, we allow the devil to go off easily after attacking our lives, by demanding back for only what he took from us. God's word says we are to be compensated double fold for all the shame and suffering the devil put us through. But we end up asking for only what the devil took . . . . and that's what we would end up getting from God when He restores us.

The devil made you sick, you are only asking for your health back! He denied you a home for years, and you are only asking for a life partner?! He delayed what is yours, and you only ask for it to be restored in God's time?! It's not wrong to wait for God's time, but God's time should not be a time when you only receive back what the devil denied you alone, but a time when you receive double fold of what the devil took away from you or denied you, because it is your entitlement to be compensated a double of what they devil denied you . . . . but you must first file a claim to receive double what belonged to you!

The devil took away your happiness for years? You need to file a claim! He denied you a husband for years, and you are just praying for marriage? My sister, file a claim for a double of the happiness of what a marriage would have given you if you had married earlier! He denied you a job for years? You need to file a claim not for that job you were asking for but for a double fold of what you would have gotten in the first place! He denied you the fruit of the womb for years, and you are just asking for a baby? My sister, you need to file a claim for a quadruple! He denied you good health for years and you are just asking to get well? You need to file a claim for a double year of good health you are entitled to on earth!

How do you file a claim?—You file a claim by drawing your claim to God's word on His promises for a double portion of your loss! Asking not just for God to restore you, but for Him to double your restoration just as He promised! Tell God you know it is your right and you are not ignorant of your rights for your blessings cannot perish! And by such a prayer you would have brought your case to the court of God!

But know that whenever you file a claim at God's court for a double portion of what the devil has taken or denied you, the devil is not going to let you go easily! The devil is going to put up a defence against your claim! Did you file a claim that he denied you promotion in life? That he denied you that big appointment, or that big position?

My brother, the devil will try to counter your claim before God to deny you a double portion, he will say, he only denied you the appointment, but he was letting you get the small bribes that you were collecting in that small position—so you do not deserve a double compensation!

Maybe you filed a claim that the devil denied you a husband for years, the devil is going to say he only denied you a marriage vow, as you were going about enjoying the pleasures of intercourse more than even a married woman or you were busy sleeping with that woman's husband, you do not deserve a double compensation for the long years of spinsterhood he put you into!

Maybe the devil kept you in frustration for years and you decided to file a claim. The devil is not going to rest, he will put up a defence in God's court, he would claim that you were going about complaining and grumbling against God all the while he was putting you to test and so you don't deserve a double compensation.

You must have a good case to win your claim for a double portion of what God promised for your shame—whenever you come before God's court to file a claim. So, I say to you today, whatever the devil took away from you, file a claim! He took away your happiness? File a claim! He denied you a home for years? File a claim! He took away your entitlements? File a claim! He kept you sick for years? File a claim! He denied you breakthrough in your career, in your business, in your life? I say, file a claim before God for a double portion of your loss!

But please first check if you have a good case!" I ended the narrative.

It was time to close the show. No time to receive more calls.

"My dear listeners as I close the show today, I want you to file a claim for any loss or denial the devil brought to your life. And watch how God restores you a double fold for your loss!

Good day and have a nice day! See you next time on motivation dance show."

The Motivation Dance Club
Mum, am I a Fireman Yet?

The journey to the studio this morning turned out to be a little bit more difficult than usual. The traffic around my area was blocked for hours by a broken down truck. The truck whose huge back carrier was laden with bundles of firewood sticks crashed alongside the street, blocking access to the major road. Not that it was an unusual occurrence in Lagos or should be something to bother about, but it became a big nuisance for what the truck was carrying.

Such road mishaps were normally cleared off in matter of minutes by the array of jobless youths known as *area boys* that roam the streets of Lagos. These boys would move in their droves and surround the truck, practically lifting it from the ground and shoving it away from the road, opening the way for motorists.

However, this broken down truck was carrying dry firewood, and not the usual load of household provision items that most trucks that ply the streets of Lagos carry. There was nothing to attract the youths to it, as there won't be anything worthwhile to pilfer away while assisting in moving away the broken down truck. Therefore, the boys were just not interested as they watched us stranded in the traffic.

The only option left was to contact the Lagos State Transport Authority officials who are responsible for such actions. But they might not also count it a priority as firewood trucks were not the sort of lucrative transport mishap they normally pray for in their morning devotions before leaving for work. There won't be much for them to squeeze from the driver of such a poor commodity as 'official levy' for creating a public nuisance. And so we were left there stranded as the long line of traffic thickens.

But just as I was getting frustrated with the long wait in the traffic, an idea came to me to put a call to the studio, for them to announce the situation on air, and call on the Transport Authority to come to our rescue. Knowing the mentality of a typical civil servant in a system riddled with corruption, the last thing any of these officials would want was a searchlight to be beamed on their area of operation for fear of exposing their ineptitude.

Public officials fear the media poking into their affairs!

I was able to get the message across to Mark, and as soon as he was able to get it announced on air that there was a terrible traffic holdup created by a broken truck, it didn't take an hour for the recovery vehicles of the Transport Authority to arrive at the scene of accident and open up the road for us to pass.

I was able to get to the studio an hour before the start of my programme, which afforded me a good time to get ready.

I could see the studio engineer signalling for me to take over the seat from Aisha, one of my colleagues. Aisha was a freelance presenter like me. She anchors the morning news and weather broadcast daily. I smiled at her as I took the seat, adjusting the microphone to my size. Aisha was a petite young lady so it was normal she brings down the ostrich neck flexible microphone to accommodate her small size whenever she was on the seat.

I started the day's show with my usual patronising introduction "Good morning, good and nice people of Lagos." I said loudly.

I really do not know how much of such people remain in this bustling town, anymore!

"Welcome, to the motivation dance floor Static FM 111. This is your presenter, DJ SST." I allowed a short pause. It doesn't look good always introducing myself like a gladiator entering a coliseum!

"I want to give a shout to all my buddies out there. To the dancers, the seat warmers, the participants and the rest of you in this dance club. I want you to know that there is a lot of good music for my good people to dance out here." I could see the studio crew smiling as they go through their file preparations for the next programme.

151

I continued.

"First let me allow my good people to open up the floor today." I smiled broadly; hoping today's questions and answers session won't drag me off my time, and put me in trouble with my producer. "Of course you know the number to dial to the floor, 00807777, come out and show us your moves." It always takes no time before the phone starts ringing. Lagos is such a big city and the people so love radio discussions that there can never be a time without someone having something to say. It is even more when it comes to motivational talk shows. The hustle of living under the harsh realities of Lagos pushes a lot of people to look for solutions or should I say inspiration to lift their lives. It wasn't that it would directly solve anything really, but it could give them the courage to move on with life and confront their challenges better.

And that is what is needed for success in life!

The desk phone was ringing already. I quickly picked it up and said, "hello, who is the first caller this morning?" It was a young female's voice that answered me.

"SST, good morning, sir." The tone in her voice came out so low and cute that I found it hard getting what she was saying. It must be that of a very young lady.

"Yeah, good morning my dear, welcome to the dance floor, what steps do you have for us this morning?" I asked.

"No, sir, I haven't got no good dance yet." She said laughing "I'm still in school. I am in second year in the university. SST, I am calling to seek your advice. I want to know how to build up my capability. I mean to be able to meet up to my aspirations in life. I want to build my knowledge to meet to challenges so that when I graduate I will move up fast in life!" She sounded a little shy.

No problem, I was use to ambitious young people looking for ways to jump across the ladder of life and be on top before their mates. They are always looking for a magic wand, the right tips that will carry them high. It was good she called the show, that's what motivation is all about anyway.

"Good, my sister, you have the right motives and the right dance steps." I said as I search my memory bank to know how to go about

152

her question. What she needed is a book not a talk. But I must have something for her; after all I was there to help.

"My sister, I love your assertion, but in our entire search for a way towards building our capabilities, let us look for the foundation of what will build us up first." I took a deep breath and exhale.

"It is good for us to increase in capability, but let's not look at our capabilities as the source of our success!"

I allowed a small pause before taking the rest of what I had with me.

"And not only that, it goes to other areas of your lives too." I said softly. It is good for us to be careful, but let us not look at our carefulness as the source of our safety! It is good for us to seek for knowledge to our problems, but let's not look at our knowledge as the source of our solutions! It is good for us to seek a healthy living, but let us not look at our good health as the source of our longevity!

It is good for us to increase in strength, but let us not look at our strength as the source of our power! It is good for us to be vigilant but let us not look at our vigilance as the source of our protection. It is good for us to increase in prayers but let us not look at our prayers as the source of our grace! It is good for us to study but let us not look at our studies as the source of our wisdom! It is good for us to prepare, but let us not look at our preparation as the source of our victory! It is good for us to aspire but let us not look at our aspiration as the source of our elevation! We must always remember God is the source of every good thing we have!"

I stopped there and put forward a question to her.

"My sister, do you understand me?" I said.

Her voice was full of laughter "Yes! Sir," she answered.

I continued "That's good, because the day we forget God is the source of our increase, our pride will block the flow of God's blessings to us and we will dry to our natural form." I said.

"So, how do we remember God as our source, SST?" She was curious.

I loved her line of questioning, she sounded like a person that is teachable and her question was carrying me where I desired to go!

"Good, my sister . . . . Everyday; every morning, as we wake up, and every night as we go to sleep, we must give thanks for all that God has done for us! For what He is about to do! For what we believe He is doing! And for what He has done! And for what he is doing even without our knowledge! At every opportunity, we must run to the sanctuary to give him thanks and tell everyone what He has done for us! It is all good for us to do, as long as it is aimed at glorifying Him, and with that we will not only maintain but increase!" I said.

She did not wait for more; it was clear from the tone in my voice that I have come to the end of the exhortation.

"Thanks, SST, I'm highly blessed by your talk" She said.

My heart skipped at her words of gratitude. I do not know how to get over it yet! I thought it will go with time, but it was always there.

I love seeing my guests happy!

"Thanks my sister, I love your cute dance steps" I said.

I then added to attract her interest "*I feel ya!* See ya next time, luv ya," I said cheerfully.

I have noted that the youths love it when you play it in their fashion, so I spoke a little of the college slang too.

"Thanks SST, luv you too, keep the tempo, ya hear?" She said it so lovingly.

That's it!

"Of course dear, of course!" I replied eagerly. I continued with the show from where I stopped before she called.

"My listeners, it is still your motivational DJ, SST on the air, I want to take another person on the dance floor before our . . ." I was not able to finish what I was saying before the phone started ringing once again.

I stopped talking and picked it up.

"Luv ya programme, SST." It was a lady speaking again!

What's all that love your programme about? Not love me? Well, you can't win them all the time! I was being jovial!

"Yeah, thanks sis, what steps do you have for us this morning?" I replied quickly. I needed to move on with the show; if not, the exchange of pleasantries will take over my programme time.

"This is Suzan, SST. I want to tell you I love your show. It is quite inspiring and entertaining to say the least." She remarked.

That is what I was used to hearing all the time, inspiring, motivating, entertaining, whatever! I have heard them all before.

"Yeah, thanks, Suzan!" I replied quickly. Trying at the same time not to appear inpatient to get on, away from her, with the show.

"SST, I'm here with my 6 year old son. He just had an operation on a broken arm, am so worried, SST, he is all I've got." She was talking with deep grief, almost sobbing. Her situation was not strange to me. When people are in distress, they usually call up the show to receive some words of encouragement and good consolation.

"How is he now?" I was sympathetic.

"The doctors said he will be fine. But he's gone through much pain, SST." She was speaking with the natural concern of a mother.

"Yeah, I know, so sorry, what about the dad?" I regretted it as soon as I uttered the words. But it was too late. I remembered now, she said her son was all she had. I shouldn't bring back any bad memory, if any! Maybe the dad's gone or something, or doesn't even exists! It shouldn't be my business really.

There was a small pause, I guess she was thinking if she should answer that or just let it be. She decided to answer "I'm a single mum, SST." She said in a low tone. Yeah, that explains the initial silence. I can now understand why she took so long to answer. Africa is not Europe or America, single motherhood is not what the society has fully come to accept. I could visualize what is going through Suzan's mind by now, the usual *'hey! What the hell, if I say so on radio, so what?! Who knows about a single mum Suzan in this bustling mega city anyway?'*

I swallowed hard, before replying her. "I can understand how hard it has been, Suzan and I can imagine how dear your lovely boy is to you." It seemed to be the right words, as the consolatory remark immediately softened her.

"Thanks, SST, I appreciate." She replied truthfully, her voice now softening and stronger.

That's real cool!

"Suzan, you are not the only one that face such a problem of seeing an only loved one in distress. In fact, you are luckier than so many people who never got to see their loved ones off from the hospital bed." I let my voice drop down to a sorrowful tip. "A single mum just like you, in Phoenix, Arizona was not that lucky as you are, Suzan." I said. I could see she was getting interested. Often young women facing a situation are interested in knowing how someone in similar situation was coping elsewhere.

"What about her?" She asked eagerly.

"Suzan, I am used to calling this young lady's story, 'mummy am I a fireman yet?"

I was ready to start the reading.

"Well, it all happened in Phoenix, Arizona, in the United States as I earlier told you." I cleared my throat eagerly. I now have a story to close the morning show.

I brought out the narrative for the story and started reading calmly.

"In Phoenix, Arizona, a 26-year-old mother had a 6 year old boy, who was dying of terminal leukemia. Although her heart was filled with sadness, she also had a strong feeling of determination. Like any parent, she wanted her son to grow up and fulfil all his dreams. Now that was no longer possible. The leukaemia would see to that. Nevertheless, she still wanted her son's dream to come true. She decided to help him accomplish the little he wanted to be, in the little time he had left.

Sitting beside her son in the hospital as she watched the life sapping out of his frail young body, the mother took her son's hand and asked, 'Billy, did you ever think about what you wanted to be once you grew up? Did you ever dream and wish what you would do with your life?, the young boy looked at his mother, his eyes suddenly becoming misty and answered 'Mommy, 'I always wanted to be a fireman when I grow up'. The Mom smiled back and said, 'let's see if we can make your wish come true.'

Later that day, the mother went to her local fire department in Phoenix, Arizona, where she met Fireman Bob, who had a heart as big as Phoenix. She explained her son's final wish and asked if it might be possible to give her 6 year-old son a ride around the block on a fire engine. Fireman Bob said, "Look, we can do better than that. If you will have your son ready at seven o'clock Wednesday morning, we will make him an honorary Fireman for the whole day. He can come down to the fire station, eat with us, go out on all the fire calls, the whole nine yards! And if you'll give us his sizes, we'll get a real fire uniform for him, with a real fire hat—not a toy—one-with the emblem of the Phoenix Fire Department on it, a yellow slicker like we wear and rubber boots. They are all manufactured right here in Phoenix, so we can get them fast."

I stopped for a while, allowing a short pause to aid my listeners' comprehension before I continued.

"Three days later, Fireman Bob picked up Billy, and dressed him in his uniform, and then escorted him from his hospital bed to the waiting hook and ladder truck. Billy got to sit on the back of the truck and help steer it back to the fire station . . . . To Bill he was in heaven! There were three fire calls in Phoenix that day and Billy got to go out on all three calls! He rode in the different fire engines, the Paramedic's 'van and even the fire chief's car. He was filmed for the local news program. It was great to Bill to see his dream come true with all the love and attention that was lavished upon him, so deeply touched was Billy that he lived three months longer than any doctor thought possible.

One night when all of his vital signs began to drop dramatically and the head nurse, who believed in the hospice concept—that no one should die alone, began to call the family members to the hospital. Then she remembered the day Billy had spent as a Fireman, so she called the Fire Chief and asked if it would be possible to send a fireman in uniform to the hospital to be with Billy as he made his transition. The chief replied, "we can do better than that. We'll be there in five minutes. Will you please do me a favour? When you hear the sirens screaming and see the lights flashing, will you announce over the PA system that there is not a fire? 'It's the department coming to see one of its finest members one more time. And will you open the window to his room?"

About five minutes later, a hook and ladder truck arrived at the hospital and extended its ladder up to Billy's third floor open window and 16 fire-fighters climbed up the ladder into Billy's room."

I stopped a little again before continuing.

"With his mother's permission, they hugged him, held him, and told him how much they loved him. With his dying breath, Billy looked up at the fire chief and said, "Chief, am I really a fireman now?" The man smiled back and said, "Billy, you are and The Head Chief, Jesus, is holding your hand." The chief said. With those words, Billy smiled and said 'I know, He's Been holding my hands all day, and the angels have been singing . . . ." He closed his eyes one last time.

I finished the story with a big sigh. But I was sure I needed to conclude it with a more befitting eulogy for young Billy.

"6year old Billy was buried a few days after! His mum always remembers his most important last words, "mummy am I fireman yet?"

Today in our lives we always find occasions to look back at our actions in life with regrets, to look back at our losses and setbacks with feelings of sorrow, to check around us for signs of disappointments, but in all we should always find occasion to thank God for all He has done for us. So my listeners, let us be grateful to the Lord for all He has helped us to accomplish in life, just like little Billy, who was happy and grateful for the few years he lived on earth, and how God let him be the fireman he always wanted to be! Whatever we are facing today others have also faced it and God has saved them from it all! If we can't trust God on anything at least we can trust Him to be able to do what He has done before."

I ended the story on that note. I could imagine what Suzan is going through.

"And my friend Suzan, the devil has been making you to shed tears. I want you know that God will not need to stop the tears. He will instead change its name. From tears of sorrow to tears of joy! From tears of disappointment to tears of celebration! God always pays back to you when you hand it back to him!"

It wasn't long before she came up on air again.

"Wow! SST, so awesome! We really need to be grateful to God for whatever situation we find ourselves all the time. It is so easy to stay focused on what is going wrong in our lives and take for granted all the great things God is doing in our lives. I'm just shedding tears here and hugging my son and praising God, thank you SST, thank You Lord, Praise God."

She sounded really grateful.

My heartfelt out to her! Really, sometimes what we see in life as a problem is the blessing other people are praying for! A man on one leg could see his situation as a problem but it is the blessing to be able to put a foot on the ground that a crippled man is praying for! Likewise a single lady with an unwanted pregnancy could see it as a problem but a barren woman is just praying to be pregnant, no state of pregnancy is unwanted to her. Oftentimes, we are all guilty of that too. We love to see the long hours we spent in the office as a problem—we never considered that we have people who are roaming the streets for years just praying for a job. We must all learn to be grateful to God in whatever situation we find ourselves.

"Thank you too, sister, I wish your son a quick recovery." I said to her.

I adjusted the microphone. The phone was ringing again. I picked it.

"Yes, who is coming to the dance floor now?" I was speaking in my best voice.

"Good show, SST, I'm proud of your show. God keep you, man!" The caller replied cheerfully.

"Thanks, sir, and who am I talking to?" I asked politely.

"This is the ultimate crusher, African featherweight champion." He said it in a way that made me feel he was happy that I gave him the opportunity to reel out his position in life.

"Good, champion, I am happy to have you on the show. This is the first time I'm having a boxing champion in my show. It's a dancing floor and not a boxing ring, I hope you know that?" I teased him.

"Of course, man, of course! SST, I have been following your show for a week now. I'm sure impressed with your show man, keep it up."

He gave me a pat on the back; hope it wasn't a punch! I can't see my back surviving a punch from a boxing champion!

"Thanks, champ, I appreciate it." I answered gleefully.

"SST, I got a match coming up, I want you to tell me some good words to carry me to victory. I know I have crushed that midget already anyway." He said it in a way that I detected he was trying hard to make himself sound tough and confident.

"I know you are already a champion, but watch your back closely, don't be like Chuck Wepner." I said.

"Chuck who? Who is the bum?" He was very inquisitive!

"He was once a champion too." I told him.

"I don't know him, SST." He answered nonchalantly.

"But you heard of Muhammad Ali, champion, right?" I asked.

"Of course I know Ali." He answered back quickly.

I expected that.

"Yeah, but you don't know Chuck Wepner because he jumped to celebrate when he shouldn't—before the match ended." I said.

"Yeah?" He asked.

"Yes of course, champion! In boxing matches just as in war, many champions were defeated for taking their opponents for granted! Or celebrating a victory too early! The popular saying "it is not over until it is all over." And so, celebrating a victory too early could be dangerous; just as it was for the once great boxer, Chuck Wepner, as I'm telling you now, champion." I said.

"How did he hit the canvas, SST?" The Champion asked eagerly. I could see he was interested. That was to be expected too. Any fighter going for a match would want to know what brought down great people before him.

"Ok, Champion, give me some few minutes, while I read the narrative out for you and our listeners, of what happened to a once great boxer." I started searching my folder for the Chuck Wepner story. "Yes, here it is, champion, as I said Wepner never knew it is not over until it is all over!"

160

I started it that way as I read the narrative.

"During his boxing career, Chuck Wepner was nicknamed the 'The Bayonne Bleeder' because of the punishment he himself takes in the ring as a boxer! In the boxing world, he was what was called a 'catcher'—that is the term for a fighter who often uses his head, instead of hands, to catch the opponent's punches! Wepner's style of fighting was to continually pressure his opponent regardless of the risk to himself, until he either wins or gets a knock out. Later in his rising career, Wepner got a chance for a shot at the world heavy weight belt title after he knocked out one of the top challengers, Terry Henke, in the eleventh round!

Boxing promoter, Don King, decided it was time he took a shot at the world heavy weight title. He was to take a shot at the then world champion, George Foreman. But before he could have a shot at Foreman, Mohammed Ali defeated the champion and took the belt. Wepner's fight was thus rescheduled to be with Ali. Wepner trained so hard, putting all he had for the fight, to meet Ali, the greatest! He underwent the most gruesome and imposing preparation of his life, at the end he was satisfied with his readiness for the belt. On the morning of the fight, he gave his wife a new pink negligee and told her "you will soon be sleeping with the world champion tonight, dear."

I was reading through the narrative a little slowly now as I approached the climax.

"During the fight, Wepner hooked Ali with a ham like punch to the chest that knocked Ali flat down! He was very excited as the counts were going on Ali and turned to face his trainer at the side ring and shouted, "start the car we are going to the bank, we are millionaires." His trainer, whose eyes were more fixed on watching Ali lying on the canvas, shouted back in shock, "you better turn back! The guy is getting up!" When a man starts to get too confident about him life will give him a shocker punch. Ali came back fully and gave him a humiliating technical knockout, nineteen seconds to the end of the match!"

I halted in my reading as the champ unexpectedly interjected.

"That's terrible!" He said.

"I have not finished champion."

I quickly replied and continued the story.

"After the match Wepner met further humiliation when he entered his bedroom to meet his wife holding the pink negligee, "do I go to Ali's room or he comes to mine?" She asked him. But my listener that is not the reason I'm relaying this story, there are many fighters that Ali had brought down after coming up from the canvas. The fight with Wepner was just one of such footnotes.

And It could have remain so, if not for a struggling film writer cum actor who was at the ring side and saw all that happened and also heard a little about Wepner's preparation and extreme confidence before the fight from his trainers. The young actor had moved to Hollywood not long ago and had been trying his hands on writing and acting with little success. He had been finding it hard getting a role in a good film because producers complained about his incoherent speech, his lack of style, and not to talk of the heavy competition from already established film stars that had kept many struggling young artistes off the stage. He was left broke, and later forced to look for roles in the low budgeted porno sections, that needed not much talent than good physique, and he had much of that! After watching the fight, the young poor struggling actor ran to his dinghy small room and started writing a story on Wepner; he was on his side table writing unstopped for 3 days! His name is Sylvester Stallone!"

I took a small pause as I reached an important point in my story. Just as I always do when reading a narrative.

"Stallone went and offered his story to a big film studio; they were impressed with his submission, and offered to buy the story off! The studio needed one of the popular and established stars to act in such a story. They didn't want to bank on an obscure inexperience actor with no credit to his name. It is well known that viewers are more comfortable with film stars they are familiar with, especially in action filled stories—the producers knew they needed someone renowned if they were to make a good sale. The studio offered Stallone $400,000, a very hefty sum for someone in debt, someone who never made 100 grand before! But Stallone refused and preferred to take only $20,000 if they could give him the chance to act the character ROCKY in the film, if not, he threatened to carry his story elsewhere! Reluctantly they accepted to feature him in the film!"

I allowed a short pause again. This time, I made sure I turn off the phone receiver so as not to be disturbed.

"Since the film was based on Wepner's life story, the producer offered Wepner one per cent of the profit of the film or $70,000 off front payment! Wepner was elated and started celebrating his latest victory! Maybe something good had come out of the fight with Ali after all! Wepner had long quit fighting and was broke, and so you can understand his feelings. The $70,000 looked too enticing to be true, he couldn't see how a film on his life could gross $7 million dollars that could give him 70,000 dollars at the end of the day, it could even end as a flop and that one percent agreement won't be worth the piece of paper it was written on!

He decided to collect the off front payment of $ 70,000 and joyfully forgo the agreement for the one percent take from the gross sales profits. Wepner just couldn't wait to start celebrating a victory once more! Wepner found himself receiving a technical knockout again, as he was once again knocked down while celebrating short of victory! The film ROCKY, THE ITALIAN STALLION went on to be a top office earner and an academy winning film! The one percent Wepner refused was worth $8 million dollars when the film Rocky came out! The film that launched Stallone from an obscure actor picking left over roles to one of the most sought and richest film stars.

Wepner once again lost the battle of his life as he was caught celebrating short of victory! He was last known to be selling liquor. We al know where Sylvester Stallone ended, after passing through Wepner, Champion." I said to him. I turn on the telephone receiver. I knew the champion will call again. I really don't intend to take more than one more call from him, and my time was far spent.

"Thanks, SST. I got the message! I'm proud of you brother! I'm going back to the gym now! But take my word, I'm not celebrating yet but I will still beat that bum!" He said cheerfully.

"I am sure you will, champion, good luck to you." I replied.

As soon as I placed down the phone at my end, it started ringing again.

I took it off!

My eyes were on the wall clock, I had overstayed my time by a few minutes. It was unusual that the studio engineer or Mark had not come in to give me the normal disapprovingly look or even yanked me off the air. I'm really enjoying my new found fame! Seeing my time was off, I quickly put in the last words as I always do.

"And so the dance step comes to an end in today's show my good people. Thank you for entertaining and motivating us all throughout the show with your dance steps! Time to get off the dance floor and loosen our dancing shoes, wish you a good weekend and see you next time, bye."

I raised my left thumb up for the studio crew to put on the music heralding the end of my show for the day. I then removed my headphones and stood up from the presenter's seat.

I had decided to see Mark in his office after presenting my show for the day and discuss with him on the decision I have taken on the management's proposal to hire me. I had made up my mind to leave my job at Alliance Security firm and work with Static FM on full time basis.

The day before, after I made up my mind to leave Alliance Security I went to inform my boss, Dr Benjamin Jomoh of my decision. I usually close from the studio late in the evening and at

such times, he has already closed from office, so I called and told him I would like to meet him at home.

I expected him to be surprised at my words but he wasn't! I have never met him at home before and the only time I visited his house was when he had his son's naming ceremony. He stays at the highbrow district of Lekki Peninsula which is at extreme, an opposite length to where I stay. I had to take a bus going the opposite way. Dr Jomoh lived in a modest house by Lagos elite standard. The security firm was not doing badly but it is not in the league of the oil firms. Moreover, Dr Jomoh was very prudent with funds, and won't want anything that cost him much. He was a lecturer of criminology at the university before he retired and took up employment with Alliance security as the head of the firm's Lagos Branch. Like all lecturers, he learnt to be very prudent with funds while at the low paying teaching job and he seemed to have carried the habit with him when he came to Alliance security. That was the reason, and his fastidious character, that made most of the workers to be uncomfortable with him.

I met Dr Jomoh sitting in his study room when the maid ushered me in.

"Good mor ... sorry, good evening sir" I mumbled.

When you have worked in the army before, you would find yourself tempted to say good morning at anytime of the day!

"Yeah, SST, have a seat." He said, hardly lifting his gaze from the news magazine he was holding.

"How are you feeling now, sir?" I inquired rather awkwardly for the occasion. He had complained of being down with Typhoid fever attack the last time we met. "I'm doing better now, thanks for asking." He took off his gaze from the magazine and looked at me directly for the first time since I entered and said, "I'm sure you didn't come all the way here at this hour of the night to asked how I was feeling."

I didn't know what to say to that so I kept staring at him. He smiled and said, "oh I didn't remember to ask you what you will like to take? My wife travelled with the children. I'm left alone for now." He said.

What! Left alone with a young maid!

I thought maids go home at the closing of their working hours? That was not my business, anyway! I reminded myself. I should avoid getting involved in what might derail my visit. I told him I was okay, and went straight to the issue that brought me to his house.

He was right; it had nothing to do with the state of his health. He looked at me and laughed when I finished speaking.

"I was expecting that when you said you were coming to meet me at home." He said affirmatively.

"You were right as always sir." I said, feigning a surprised expression.

My boss likes it when you behave in a way that shows he was smarter.

"Of course, nothing can pass my eyes around; you know." He said with pride.

I must have said the first right words!

"I know sir," I said again, lowering my head in submission.

"I knew you will soon leave us to that your radio station. I have not listened to any of your broadcast before, I don't have the time really." He said with it a little disdain.

I kept quite.

"But the other day, I was in the church when two youths came up to give a testimony on how their lives changed, from a life of crime to now living a productive life, and they all claimed your show on radio impacted on their lives." He blurted out painfully and then smiled broadly in a way I never knew him.

"I was proud of you really. I believe you are making the right decision. It looks like a calling for you. Anytime you are interested to come back to us the door is open. Is that clear?" He said in an authoritative voice.

That was a signal that there was nothing to discuss anymore. I thanked him and left, not waiting for the maid to show me the way out and even to see her again to say goodbye. She seemed to have disappeared since the time I entered. As I said before, that was not what brought me and not my business really!

I was just happy that my boss had agreed without a fuss to my leaving the security firm and taking full time employment at Static Fm 111.

That was the reason I had to see Mark after the show.

I met Mark in the office with Sasha, the studio receptionist. She left as soon as I entered the room. Our relationship as I said, had improved very considerably since the first time we met, when I first came to the studio and she treated me with disdain.

It was not only my new rising status that influenced Sasha's opinion towards me really. As I found out later; she was naturally a reserved person but quiet a nice girl. It wasn't always easy for her to open up to a person on a first meeting.

Mark offered me a seat. I looked around the office; he had made some new adjustments to his office, and has added some good furniture.

Things are really getting better.

"SST, how was the show today?" He asked.

That question was not necessary; he monitors everything going on in the studio from his office.

"Everything was fine si . . . Mark." I said.

"Good to hear that." He said.

"I'm here to tell you that am ready to take up your offer." I told him straightaway.

Mark rushed out of his seat and hugged me.

"My brother, am happy to have you with us, we really are one good family here!" He was obviously elated with my decision which made me feel greatly at ease.

"Thanks, Mark." I said.

We had a few discussions dominated by what he expects me to be earning from the management, and some other things, after which I took my leave. As I was about going out of the door he called me back

"Oh, SST, I forgot, my wife is having a small celebration at home, she wants you to be there." He said.

Mark took pains to describe to me how I will get to his place at an estate located at the Ajuelegbe District. It was a verbal description replete with torturous descriptions of movement from one point to another, and asking questions from those you come across for the next direction as you move on. I noted all and promised to be there on the Sunday evening.

I had no choice really after the pains he took in laying out the description of his house for me.

The Motivation Dance Club
God Has an Ark

The next day it rained heavily just like the previous morning. I noticed that many people, as I was coming down the road, were scrambling for the few available places under the roof of the bus stop terminals and corridors of offices to hide from the rain. And just like the rest of them, I was also looking for a place to hide out from the rain as the cab driver dropped me some meters short of the studio. I had told myself the day before that I will make sure I get an umbrella so that the rain won't meet me in the open again. But like the people I met hiding under the available sheds, I was once again caught unprepared.

The annual downpour was not an emergency or an unusual occurrence. It was something we were all expecting, even eagerly waiting to arrive at this time of the year! Then, why, were we, always caught unawares? I mean as regards to our personal preparations?

I guess we all have a tendency to forget or to be less serious and prepared on some issues. We aren't better than people that were left out of Noah's Ark! No! We are worst, they never believed the floods were coming, but we knew the rainy season was coming.

I could not remove the thought of Noah's Ark from my mind as I entered the studio, appearing partially drenched in my usual attire of T-shirt and jeans. I know I had written something on that story before, and what better time to talk of it than now?

I could see the set engineer, who anchors my show on the engines, looking at me worriedly. It's not that I have been late for my show before, but I'm always coming at the nick of time, and that was putting him on the edge!

My almost late attitude could be late one day!

I went to his side and pat him lightly on the back to reassure him of my preparedness to go on air, and quickly went against the big side fan to dry up, as I waited my turn to take the presenters' seat, which was not more than five minutes away when I arrived.

I could see the last presenter leaving.

I went to the seat and quickly sat down, adjusting the microphone to my size and waiting for the thumbs up signal, from the engineer for me to know the music interlude was over, and it was time for me to be on air.

I saw him giving the signal.

I adjusted myself once again and started speaking rapidly as I open the floor of the motivation dance club show.

"Hello, good people of Lagos State, you are once again welcome to your favourite programme, the Motivation Dance Club! It's your man on the steering wheel, DJ SST, waiting for the first dancer to come on the floor."

I inhaled some air deeply before continuing.

"Hey! Wait a minute! Please don't wet my dance floor! I can see the rain drenching Lagosians so badly these days! It's not only raining cat and dog, it is also raining boys and girls, as the heavy downpour had led to a search for a 'hiding together from the rain' amongst our youth. Don't get me wrong, we all are hiding from the rain." I said loudly as I stopped to take breathe in before continuing.

"You know what? Every year the rain wins! It wins because we are always caught unawares! We start looking for umbrellas when the rain starts saying goodbye, chuckling behind the clouds at us, after a long period of getting us drenched. We should not be like the people that missed Noah's Ark and drenched to death."

I was now approaching my motivational topic for the day! "Talking of Noah's Ark, what lessons of life can we draw from it?" I asked my listeners.

I then removed the telephone receiver from the hook. I did not want any disturbance from incoming calls when I start my talk.

"It was raining heavily when Noah went into his Ark! In life, we need an ark, a place of refuge, because one day, life will rain heavily on us! It could be the loss of a business opportunity, death of a loved one, loss of promotion, bad investment, whatever! As they say, it does not rain, it pours! When misfortune comes, it will come pouring on us like the downpour of Noah's day, and we need to have an ark! Each and every one of us needs to have ark!

Your ark could be the word of God! When all your plans go wrong and the waves of failure are threatening to overwhelm you, run to the ark that says, it shall be well with you! When you find yourself in financial difficulties not knowing where to go and with debts threatening to swallow you, run to the ark that says, the Lord is my shepherd I shall not want! When enemies gather against you, run to the ark that says, they shall fight you but will not overcome you! Yes! Because enemies would surely come and gather against you! Your enemies can only see your front, but only God sees to your future! If only they could see to your future they would have known that what they are busy putting on the way to block your front is useless because it has no effect on your future, because God cares for your future!"

I smiled and pause for a while to allow the audience get the message before I continued.

"Or you can run to the ark that says, a thousand will fall by your side, ten thousand by your right but it will not touch you! My friend, it is good to see your enemies falling before your eyes, and for that, you need an ark to run to! Noah saw all those taunting and ganging to destroy him falling all around as he sailed safely in the Ark! The first lesson about Noah's Ark is that you must make sure you have an ark in life that you can run to when life's challenges attempt to overshadow you! And the ark you need is the word of God in your life."

I paused for the next lesson from Noah's Ark.

"The second lesson about Noah's Ark is the need to plan ahead. That is the reason why many of us were drenched in the rain today. We failed to plan ahead. Lack of planning could be the best planning if you are planning to fail! You want to start a business? Start planning ahead! You want to start a family? Start planning ahead! Plan ahead for the kind of home you want to live in and the kind of schools you want your children to go to, and not to wait till when the family arrives and then you start running for help.

Another lesson is that you should not listen to criticism. Whenever you want to start something great, there will always be people out there ready to discourage you, forget them and stay focus on your aim. Another lesson from Noah's Ark is that we should not regard speed as the only indication that we will get there. The cheetah was there in the Ark first, but the snail also left with the Ark! Your friends might all have gotten to the altar before you, but that does not mean you will miss the marriage train. Your friends might have achieved their career ambitions, secure a great status in life before you, but that does not mean you will not one day find yourself in the realm of success with them. Your colleagues might be in the houses they build for themselves, driving cars they bought with their money while you are still jumping buses and living in rented accommodation. But that does not mean you will not one day be a successful landlord and car owner! As long as the door of the Ark of life is still open, you will one day enter too!

Another lesson from that Ark is that the Ark was built on a high ground, and as soon as the flood started, it easily floated on the rising waters. Because Noah was planning for the future and not the present, he ensured his Ark was raised on a high ground. Always plan your future on a high ground. Do not plan on the low ground, because a low ground is a ground of fear, of self-doubt, and a ground of half-heartedness! Rather, plan on the high ground because a higher ground is a ground of self-confidence, faith in God, courage, and a ground of knowledge.

Noah was 600 years old when God commissioned him to build the Ark. God has many assignments for us all, but we need to be found ready when He comes to call us. Noah was found ready when the time came because in the days of waiting, he ensured he was physically and mentally fit for any task. We need to get ourselves physically and mentally fit for any task that the Lord might have for us. Another lesson from the Ark was that it was not built by engineers like the great Titanic that sunk in 1912; the Ark was built by amateurs!

So my listeners, please, never look down on yourself because you feel you do not have great qualifications, God can use you, when you make yourself available and prepared. You only need to have the right ideas to achieve the right results remember!

The first idea you need to overcome any task is called passion! Along the line when you start your journey, you will meet another idea called competence! With the last idea that you need on your way, called determination, you will always win! Noah worked hard on building the Ark for forty years, and from the day the Ark started floating, he rested! Your body is meant to take a rest after a hard day's work, make sure when you are stressed, you allow your body to take a rest by floating a little.

In the Ark, you will find both animals and human beings travelling together! Whatever you are in life, whatever God has given or allowed you to achieve, if you are not ready to move along with those lower than you, then you are not fit for the Ark. And lastly, the lesson about the Ark which covers all other lessons is that no matter the storm that comes around, no matter the degree of destruction and commotion around, no matter what arises, always know that God is with you."

I pause as always to let the audience get the message.

"And as the rain continues to fall, Noah was enjoying the cruise from the safety of his Ark. He was just looking peacefully, because God was watching! God was watching as the sky gathered storm, God was watching as the thunderstorm started, God was watching as the Ark shook and floated on top of the waters, and Noah was only cruising! I remember when I use to travel along the narrow road between the towns of Warri and Port Harcourt. As we pass along the narrow road my companion looked in fear at the approaching vehicles all struggling to share the narrow strip of road with us and exclaimed in fear as I manoeuvred the small car along the narrow dangerous road 'I hope you are watching your front sir.' She asked. I turned to her and said 'lady, I am not watching." She looked up at me with fright and exclaimed 'what did you say? She asked in a choke by fear. I smiled at her and said, "yes, Lady, I am not watching. I'm only looking, because God is watching!"

And I want to say to all my listeners today, as you go about your life, I want you to know that, in your studies, you will only be looking! In your marriage, you will only be looking! In your business, you will only be looking! You will only be looking because God is watching everything! And when God watches over your studies, your marriage, your business, and when God watches over any part of your life, success is what you will be seeing! Greatness is what you will be seeing! Breakthrough is what you will be seeing! Because when God watches, disappointment disappears! Frustration fizzles out! Setback goes back, because He is watching! And I pray for you, that God watches over all aspects of your life so that you can have a good time looking!" I said as I concluded the lessons from Noah' Ark. I then moved to the second part of my message.

"But it's not to all rain that we are to run and hide in the ark; we need to get drenched in some" I said the last part in a loud way because I knew my listeners would be wondering what has gotten over me! Everybody was complaining of the heavy downpour and here I am telling them to get drenched.

"I am talking of the latter rain, God's latter rain of blessings that has been pouring all over us." I know my listeners would be laughing by the way I played on their curiosity. "God does not have love. He is love. He does not have blessings, He is the blessing! And He has sent the latter rain of blessings around us, but we are not feeling it. It is raining but we are dry and hot!" I observed the normal small pause.

It was time to start receiving listeners call.

My first caller for the day introduced herself as Sarah and that she was a member of the National Youth Service Corps that was a compulsory one year programme for graduates from the university. Her place of assignment was at the Lagos State Ministry of Finance.

"Sarah, you are welcome to the dance floor, so what steps do you have for DJ SST?" I asked in my normal fashion.

"SST, I just want to congratulate you on the huge success recorded by your show within a short time and to tell you that today you were the talk of everybody in the office. I wish you well and greater success! You are really entertaining and motivating." She said with great excitement.

"Thanks, Sarah, I appreciate it, best dancing steps I have seen here in for a long time, thanks sis." I said.

The next callers after Sarah were virtually saying the same thing.

It was as if that was what everybody out there was waiting for! I was soon receiving an avalanche of congratulatory and appreciative messages, and was getting scared that the show will end on that note until a listener with an issue for discussion came up. It wasn't that I was not grateful for their kind words, but where will the show be if I concentrate on gathering laurels from past achievements? It's either I continue moving ahead with new achievements or the future is not for me, and no one will call to say hello, when that happens!

"SST, I'm happy to be on your show today. My name is Chukwudi Amadi." The man said.

"Happy to have you on the show, Chukwudi!" I welcomed him.

"SST, I have been monitoring your programme and I can authoritatively tell you it is number one now in Lagos." He said it with so much confidence that one would think he ran a poll on it!

"Thanks, man!" I shouted, praying that will be enough to convince him to end the conversation.

Oh no! I hope this is not another well-wisher! I need to get on with my show.

"Yes, SST, I'm serious about that, but that's not what brought me to the show." His tone was changing.

A real discussant for a change, good!

"SST, I need help about how things are happening to me. I have tried to improve things in my life but they always end up badly. When one thing fails and I try to move to another, I will find out before long that problem will come out of that too! It was so painful and I have now become very scared! I have now decided to keep to the little things am doing, and not to try anything new or big anymore, so as to guard myself from the pains of failure." He said in a very difficult voice.

"They did not end up in failure, you stopped them in failure." I said to him.

"What do you mean, SST?" He asked with a soft and innocent voice.

"'Yes, life will always hit hard against you in whatever you do, ask all great achievers nobody has ever had it smooth to success! In business, in career, in relationship whatever, name it!"

I started expanding the scope of our discussion in a way to encompass other listeners in different situations but with a similar problem.

"Whatever you start doing in life, you will at first meet with failure, and with disappointments. Instead of giving up, or running away, or hiding yourself from it so as to guard yourself from further pains, you should instead hit back! If you don't mind the pains that keep on coming your way as you struggle along, one day life will give way for you to march to success."

I quickly brought out a narrative that I felt would answer his question and also helped other listeners having similar experience.

"I believed I must have said it in this show before, but if I have not, I want to tell you today that I once served in the army, for five years, before I retired from service. I was trained at the military academy where I learnt the lesson that hitting back against pain and frustrations is what will carry you to success."

I brought out the narrative and placed it on the table before me.

"I have made a narrative on that and I always call it, "SST you are not hitting back." I said.

I was preparing my listeners to another of my narratives.

"This narrative is my personal story and not an offload of someone's account. It started the day I was told by my trainer that *you can't win, if you are not hitting back.*" I said.

I started reading the narrative quietly.

"When I entered the Defence Academy as a fresher cadet known as a first termer, I was told I had to fight in a novice boxing bout. It was a boxing bout that was organised for all fresh cadets. I said to myself, me? Fight? No way! But it was a requirement; a requirement to be an army officer. In life, you would always have requirements, if you want to reach your goals or you want to be a successful person, there will always be a requirement, if you want to have a great life, there is a requirement! Therefore, because it was a requirement and I wanted to be an army officer, I had to submit to a boxing training exercise to prepare for the bout along with other freshers. We were all grouped into various teams.

Our team trainer was a senior cadet, a fourth termer, holding the appointment of a Cadet Sergeant. We really needed his assistance to help us win, and he was eager to train us because helping us to win will also assist him to move to a higher appointment in the Academy. In life, my friends, you are going to meet people along the way that would need your assistance to succeed! The more you are eager in helping people to succeed, the more God pushes you higher the ladder so that you can be in a greater position to help more people.

The Cadet Sergeant told us, we must first learn how to protect ourselves from blows from our opponents, because blows must come in the ring! We must learn how to cover our faces with our hand gloves—what in boxing terminology is called "guard up"! In life, as we set out to achieve our goals, there would be need for us to ensure we protect ourselves against the hard challenges that must come! So we have to guard up. We must guard up by praying all along the way, and getting inspiration from the word of God, and that of His servants; we must learn to guard up against the blows of life that would meet us along the way!

During the training session, I entered the ring to spar with the Cadet Sergeant. He was an experience fighter and my first fear was to protect myself, so I just stayed, guard up! As he was hitting at me, I just kept my hands to covering my face and guarding up! But the more I guard up, the more the blows kept coming! After sometimes, he stopped throwing blows at me and said, "you can't win a fight. If you are not hitting back! If you don't hit back you will only end up a punching bag for your opponent." He told me. My dear listeners, life is going to throw blows at you, you might see yourself busy covering yourself in sadness, disappointment, or sorrow and just guarding up as you hide yourself from the public, sulking in private, or remaining in self—pity! You will become depressed, and try shielding your mind from the reality. But the more you draw inward, the more the blows of life keep hitting you down and you become a punching bag for the devil, who will be hitting you more freely with the blows of frustrations, disappointments, and the blows of failures!

The Cadet Sergeant further said to me, "your hands can't hold for long against the blows if you keep on absorbing it. They will get tired, as the blows will keep on coming the more, and then the blows will get you down and your hands will break down exposing you to your fall." Likewise in your life's battles as you keep on guarding up your mind, the whole of your life cannot hold onto sadness, disappointment, grief, frustration and whatever you are facing now, if you just keep on absorbing it inside! It could be the loss of a loved one, loss of promotion, marriage crisis, job loss, or whatever! The more you continue to suppress them, the more the affairs of your life deteriorate, until your life finally breaks down. From then I decided to listen attentively to the Cadet Sergeant's advice, and stopped "guarding up" and from that time I started hitting back. I then realised the more I hit back, the more the powerful Cadet Sergeant draws back, and the least blows he could get at me! And the least I feared him too! When you hit back at that problem, that loss, and that disappointment by not allowing it to take over the affairs of your life, the more it would become smaller and smaller in your sight, as it starts to retreat from your life, and the least other problems could come out of it to compound the situation! And the least it looks frightful to you too!

As I continued hitting back, I became more relaxed, confident, and happy, jumping, shaking, and raising my shoulders like a real fighter!

The Cadet Sergeant was also happy and said to me, "you have come back!" And that was how I overcame my fears!

And to my listeners on motivation dance club FM111, I say to you today; the day you come back from that business problem, from that setback, from that loss of a loved one, from that disappointment, it will be the day you would know you have overcome the test God has designed for your destiny, as your confidence in yourself and in

God will be restored, and you will be able to raise your shoulders high." I said.

"So on the day of the real fight, I faced my opponent confidently in the ring as I continued to hit back at him! I did not even look to see if the blows were effective, I just continued hitting back. At the end of each round, I will go to the ringside and hear the Cadet Sergeant say to me "well done, SST, you are fighting well," because he saw me hitting back, and he knows as long as I was hitting back I will achieve result against my opponent!

I want you know that whatever is confronting you in life, as long as you are hitting back, you might not know if you are making great impact. But please know today that you are making progress—you are achieving results against that marriage break up that is getting you down, you are achieving results against that loss of a loved one that is keeping you sad for so long, against that your big job lost that is threatening to destroy your life! And as I continued hitting back against my opponent and avoid hiding behind guarding up I was able to win the fight!

That was just a novice fight for beginners, which was a requirement for all. And not the real boxing tournament that is for those that dare to go further. To go further to join a boxing team in the Academy was not a requirement, but a matter of choice.

The Cadet Sergeant tried to encourage me after my novice victory to go further and fight in the tournaments, "you have great abilities to be a good boxer, you can make a champion, come join my boxing team." He told me. I said to myself, what? I, fight in the great tournaments? That was not what I intended from the beginning. I never intended to compete for laurels or to be a champion! I fought in the novice fight because it was a requirement!

Many of us do things in life because it is a requirement and not because we intended to rise to be champions! We write an exam because it is a requirement to earn a degree; we do a business because it is a requirement to earn a living! We might have the talent to be champions in what we do, but because we entered casually and took it only as a requirement and not as a challenge to establish our place in destiny, we dare not to go further! We stopped short of becoming what God created us to be!

And that was how I didn't join the boxing team.

I didn't fight in the big tournaments because I dare not to go further. And gradually all my friends, even the Cadet Sergeant forgot I had the talent to be a great boxer. Likewise, in your life journey, because you gave up short of advancing into the great tournament of life, because you dare not go further and achieve great things in the area God has blessed you with a great talent for great success, the world would leave you and gradually forgot you had the talent to be a champion in that business, in that profession, or in that career—because you had not dared to go further. The world would instead concentrate to develop and elevate those that made themselves available, even those of lesser talent than yours!

Because I dare not to go further, my boxing experience ended, till I gradually lost the knowledge of even knowing how to guard up! And later in life, I saw some of my colleagues that we featured in the novice boxing together becoming champions. I had more boxing talent than some of them at the beginning, but it did not matter now! They had become champions and I was left at the stand applauding instead of standing to collect laurels with them! Because when I came back and started hitting back, I stopped when I got my requirement. I just did not dare to go further and fight in the tournaments after winning the novice fight. I never had the idea to be a champion. If only I came back, keep hitting back, and dare to go further I would have been a champion too!

Life might have hit you hard once and you decided to hit back and you were successfully to come back to your feet! But if you don't continue hitting back, you will remain at the stage of your success and many of your colleagues will pass you by, and you won't be the champion God intended you to be!

And because I never had champion mentality, I never developed champion attitude. You need the mentality of a champion to be a champion in whatever you are doing in life. I now remember, years after, what the Cadet Sergeant said to me, "SST, if you don't hit back the blows will continue hitting at you, and you can't win!"

God has created many of us with the capabilities to be champions, but fear, inferiority complex, lack of a deep desire to seek opportunities or just plain indecisiveness has made some to "guard up" throughout our lives without hitting back at whatever was holding them back!

With some, it was because they lack the awareness of the great capabilities God placed in them, and so they didn't dare to come out! With some other people, it was the feelings of disappointment that was formed from failed trials that forced them to "guard up" throughout life, and even when they hit back, they lacked the ambition, the drive, or the energy to continue hitting back with the energy and vigour required of someone daring to go further to become a champion.

We sometimes set limit on our abilities by regarding our vocations in life only as a requirement to earning a living and not the path to being the great people God has created us to be! We often love stopping short of what God had set for us. So my dear listeners on FM 111, whatever you are facing, whatever you are about to do, or doing right now, just continue hitting back at anything that is stopping you from moving forward, and keep moving forward, as the cadet sergeant said; one day you will be the champion that God wants you to be, and not the punching bag for the devil attacks of disappointments, and frustrations. It does not matter who is trying to stop you, it does not matter how many kicks you might have gotten from your enemies, or what disappointments they might have brought to you! Just know that things will work out for you, when you walk out with God. One day you will send gifts to your enemies because it was their big hatred that enabled you see God's big love for you! It was the hard kick they gave you that made God give you the high life you are having now, because while they lay ambush for you on your way, God diverts them to His garden! So don't give up, hit back!" I said.

A call came in as I finished reading the narrative, it was someone else and not Chukwudi that called earlier.

"SST, thanks for your words of encouragement, and I think Chukwudi should even count himself lucky to have something to do that was giving him pains. I don't even have anything to hit back at!

My situation in life is so bad that I don't even have the gloves to hit back with either!" The person said as he made fun of his situation.

It is not easy talking to a blank face so I always liked asking after a caller's name. I politely ask him for his name.

"Yes, SST, my name is George Aku, I'm an applicant, so don't ask what I do in life, please." He said.

"George, God has given us all what we can hit back at! We don't need any government or factory to give us what to hit back with, because God has given us a natural glove and a natural target to hit back." I told him.

"Yeah, then where is mine?" He asked incredulously.

"Yes, George, you are not the only person I have seen in such self doubt before, Danny Cookan had the same experience too." I said craftily, introducing a new narrative.

I just hope I had enough time to go through another one.

"Who is Danny Cookan?" He asked.

I expected that response.

"Danny Cookan lived in Dallas Texas. He was out of jobs for years, living on social security and staying in the homeless travellers' caravan. He gave up hitting back at life after watching several of his businesses go bad. He thought he had no skill, no capital, no training, and no luck! But he later realised it can't be like that, because God couldn't have created an empty shell. He remembered an incident when he bought a can of peanuts only to open the tin and find only preservative inside without the peanuts. When he returned it to the factory, they told him, it was fake, that it can't be theirs, because they were too advanced to cover empty tins. So, Danny told himself, if the company was too good not to cover an empty tin. Surely then, God couldn't have created an empty person. He knew he only needed to open the can and find what God had put inside him!" I told him.

"That's a good observation." George said.

"Yes, George but wait it's not over yet." I cautioned him softly, he seemed to be one of those listeners who are always eager to jump in when they believe you are through with your talk.

"So, Danny Cookan searched himself, and found that from an early age he had tried at mastering the voices of great presenters on radio, and he had developed what he believed was a good voice for a radio presenter. He didn't know where to go or who to hire him, so he wrote a small poster on a piece of paper and pasted it on his caravan. The poster reads; 'I am blessed with the gift of a radio presenter, am open for hire'. Just as simple as that!

For everyman that dares to hit back at his failures, it will give way to success for him.

One day a big producer of a popular TV documentary was passing by and saw it. And it happens that his studio needed a new presenter for sports stories. He decided to try Danny on the TV documentary. And from that day, my dear George, Danny became a celebrity with more job offers on his hands than he could handle! Don't ask me where went his travelling caravan when he decided to hit back at failure, it all gave way to a new home in Beverly Hills!" I said.

George replied excitedly, "SST, that message is for me! Just today, I was considering my natural gift in creating campaign slogans that I use to do in my days in school, and was dragging my feet if I should go to any of the political parties, I don't know if anyone will want me." He was shouting!

"George this is the election year! Don't seat back wallowing in self pity! Hit back at any failure on your path! Take your gift to a political party, if you meet a brick wall, hit back! Hit back at the political parties, at the politicians when it look they won't want you! When you meet failure, hit back! When they said they don't need it, hit back! When you are turned away, hit back! And before long life will make a way for you and they will start looking for you, because all things will work for your good! Frustration will turn to fruition, disappointments will turn to distinctions, failures will turn to fame, trials will turn to triumph, but that is only when you hit back! Don't mind the pain, wait for the gain! As they say, no pain no gain . . . my friend, all things will work for your good says the Lord." I was doing my best to encourage George.

He sure needed motivation. I was giving him some dancing steps!

"Thanks, SST, I'm going on with life now! I'm hitting back hard at my situation." He shouted excitedly.

"And George, I want you to always remember the prayers of the lion my father once told me! The lion wakes up every morning with a prayer to God, saying, "God, please just show me a prey, but don't help me, don't help the prey, just let us be!" The lion knows that God has placed all the power it needed to succeed and it does not need anything else! And as long as God does not alter anything in His creation, no opponent can defeat it! So George, pray that God shows you, your opportunity and you make it your responsibility. You can dodge your responsibility . . . but my friend; you can't dodge the consequences of your responsibility! Good luck George, pray about it! And thanks for calling." I came out sincerely as I close the discussion.

But George has not finished!

"SST, that is the problem, I have been praying to God but to no avail, of recent I have been asking myself, if really there is a God! Maybe the Big Bang theory of creation s right after all!" He blurted it out forcefully.

"George, I don't know about that, I use to doubt it too until I saw a hurricane that passed with great force through a window across a big hall and at the end when it was coming out of the door it made a big bang and brought out a brand new 747 Boeing plane!" I said.

"No, SST, I don't believe that, you must be joking! Someone must have kept the plane there! No great wind passes through a house with a big bang and produces a new plane!" He was laughing at what he saw as my obvious stupidity.

"Then George why do you think the planets, the earth with the orderly form of the oceans, land animals and the perfect atmosphere for life to survive, just appeared by chance or was created by an accidental big bang without anybody being behind the whole creation? George, take it from me, there is a God that created all." I said it with a touch of finality in my voice.

Two other callers called to criticize a few things I said and another tried to pick an argument with them on that! I tried not to push the arguments, and struggled to cut the conversations short too.

It is good to give room to people to criticize, but it is not good to allow people to become critics in your life; lest they become a demoralising force. It is not every wrong that should be corrected and it is not every right that should be brought out. It is good to always look at a situation carefully; delving on what the final outcome would be before acting against or coming in support of it!

Time to close my show, the phone was ringing but I ignored it. My time was off!

"My good listeners, we have come to the end of today's dance steps, it's time to close the club and let all of us go home in one piece. kidnapping is now the new business in town, I don't have the ransom to bail out any of my dancers, so let's go home dry and safe, see you tomorrow on the dance floor of Motivation dance club, bye." And with that I closed the show for the day.

I removed my head phones and stood from the seat.

"Great SST, I was highly motivated by your talks today." Someone was talking to me as I walked away from the presenter's arena.

It was Elias, one of the studio engineers. Elias was a young man in his early twenties; he and Sasha were the kids around as I used to say, because the rest of us were on the wrong side of thirties or in a friendly distance from forty.

"Yeah, Elias thanks." I said profoundly.

All my life I find myself at a loss when it comes to responding to compliments. It always leaves me wondering how to respond. The popularity of my show was not helping issues as I was getting them far more than ever before in my life!

"Mark says you should see him in his office." Elias said as he turned to set the equipment for the next programme.

I don't know what Mark wants with me now, going to the studio manager's office after my presentation is now becoming a routine. I entered the office after knocking just once. I and Mark have now become friends and are so familiar to each other that I don't have to wait for an answer to enter his office.

He was openly excitement to see me!

"SST, see this! "He was pushing into my hands a copy of the Daily Reporter; the most circulated newspaper in Lagos. I looked at it; in the front page was a large caption:

THE HUB!

I looked at Mark with a cursory glance.

"Read it!" He snapped.

The story was about my show, the newspaper described it as the new hub; what it called the centre of attraction in the whole large city of Lagos. It was coined the centre of attraction, apparently taking a cue from the city slogan of Lagos, which is the centre of excellence. The story line talked about how Static FM 111 that was a virtually unknown radio station, coming far behind the raving Star FM and the long popular Ray Power FM, had suddenly and within a very short period leaped above all the stations to the number one spot by waving a magic wand called the motivation dance club. It ascribed the success recorded by the show to the unique understanding of the producers of the needs and challenges facing the teeming population of Lagos citizens in such dire times.

There was also a talk of how the radio station is smiling to the bank due to the increasing patronage it is reaping from advertisements coming in from big firms that include lucrative contracts from the oil companies. I looked up, Mark was smiling broadly. There was a sense of self-accomplishment in the way he was looking.

"But Mark, don't you think the story was a little exaggerated." I said, and slyly looked at his direction, and added in a low suspicious voice, "I hope it was not sponsored."

"What are you saying my friend?" Mark snapped. "If you were in the advertisement department, you won't be talking like that! You would have known what the company is raking from the show! We run your programme three, sorry, four times a day now, and it is still not enough to cover our advertisement demands. I'm even thinking of doing away with the news time and adding it to your show time." He was tapping his table with his pen, what he does when he is thinking seriously about an issue.

I was surprised, he was sounding serious on the news time issue.

"Well, we thank God. I never expected such a huge response really. I only know I was doing what I was called to do." I was less responsive than Mark would have expected. He stared hard at me, looking a little disappointed, maybe he expected me to jump and hit the ceiling with joy when I saw the newspaper story!

Sorry, I wasn't that kind of person.

"Well, that's not the only thing I called you for." He said, trying to change the topic.

"Have I done anything wrong?" I asked trying to sound worried—*could I really do anything wrong here anymore?*

"Oh cut that crap, SST!" He said with a wave of his left hand. "I want you to know that the Chairman of Static FM 111 Chief Charles Dukubo wants to meet you in person. In fact, he wants you to be at the senior board management meeting taking place at the headquarters this afternoon." He handed me a copy of the invitation letter with all seriousness as if it was a gold medal! "We got to be going man, the boss will be waiting, I mean he will be around by now." He said as he hurriedly picked his bag. I followed him out of the office.

We travelled by the only vehicle at the studio, a kombi bus. Before then, the bus was driven only when the need arise by one of the engineers or Mark himself. But just a day earlier, the studio was able to employ a full time driver.

The Headquarters of Static FM 111 was a large compound with nice coated tiles and a flurry of staff moving around. It never actually reflected the status of the station as the radio station was hardly raking profits until the commencement of the motivation dance club that attracted adverts from several companies and businesses bringing in huge funds. The whole structure was part of the business conglomerate of Chief Charles Dokubo a renowned businessman with interests in shipping and oil. The Chief was running the radio station just as a past time to give him the public status he desired. He hardly comes to the station headquarters except on the few occasions when the senior board management meetings were held, which was often on Saturdays when the Chief was less busy. It seemed this was one of such Saturdays.

When we arrived at the headquarters, I saw the whole area full and busy, with people and cars moving in and out of the compound. The flurry of activity was not all about FM 111. That was just the facade. Chief Dokubo also runs other of his business activities from the compound. Though the office complex was known as the FM Static building, it hasn't actually had much to do with the radio station. Mark took me round the Complex to meet some of the directors, and management staff. They all were very happy to meet me and were graciously making commendations on my show. They all knew of my show, of course, but most of them have not met me in person until then. I was moved from one office to another and from one commendation to another.

I felt like a movie star!

Mark was moving ahead of me as we were ushered into a large waiting room where we met other staff already sitting and waiting for the Chief to arrive so that the meeting would start. Chief Dokubo had not even left his residence to the complex! And all the while I thought the breakneck speed applied on the dying bus to get us here in time was because the Chief was waiting, sorry, was around, as Mark told me! I didn't know I was taught some good lessons on how protocol works at such high levels.

The Chief was not even informed of our gathering yet!

It is after all of us were seated that the Chief will be contacted and be informed that all are seated. It is then that he will start coming; that is if he has taken his shower. If not, we'll wait longer!

The long wait was not too comfortable for me as the small radio set in the waiting room was playing one of my shows. I was turned to a subject of friendly discussion and poking jabs from the other staff in the waiting room.

It was soon announced that the Chief was on his way, so we had to quickly abandon the waiting room and take our seats in the adjoining large palatial conference hall. It wasn't long before the door to the conference hall opened and a large middle height and dark complexion man wearing a navy blue safari jacket on an immaculate white shirt entered. Another man closely followed him, coming slightly behind, and holding a black leather suitcase. Everybody immediately stood up as he entered.

It was Chief Charles Dokubo!

The Chief went about greeting everybody by name; it seemed he was very familiar with all of them. When he came to me, he held my hands with both hands and exclaimed loudly, "nobody needs to tell me who you are! The only new face here I'm expecting must be the new presenter at my radio station." He was being very friendly, even though he didn't know or couldn't remember my name, he actually knew or guessed who I was. I didn't know what to say so I nodded quickly.

"Good, good, am happy to meet you! My children used to taunt me at home with their preference to Brilla and Ray Power FMs, when their dad has a radio station! But now every time I come home the only thing I hear is; daddy do you know what was on motivation dance club? Thanks man, you restored my joy!" He was patting me lightly on the back! I wouldn't have been more encouraged if he had given me a thousand dollars! Figuratively speaking of course!

I won't mind a grand you know!

"Thank you sir." I said.

"Thank you too my boy." He answered.

The Chief went back and sat on his seat. He hardly comes for a management meeting except if there was an important issue he wants to discuss. Chief was a busy man. He always goes straight to the point.

"Gentlemen good afternoon, I'm sorry I will have to leave early, I have an important meeting waiting for me, so I will not take your time." Nobody could recall when Chief had ever come to a meeting without first apologising for having to leave early to another meeting. It was his way of life. Just like all other big businessmen in Lagos, politics is the major part of their businesses, so there was always a political meeting to go to. And with the nation bracing for another election, there were strong rumours that Chief was dreaming of a senatorial seat.

"The reason I assembled you all here today, taking away the beautiful time you would have loved to do something else, was to discuss what everybody is discussing in Lagos. I am talking of the rising profile of our darling radio station, Static FM 111!" He shouted, and as if that was the signal everybody was waiting for, the hall erupted with wild applauding, I joined too.

The Chief gave a few seconds for all to calm down before he continued with his speech.

"You all know the radio station had become more like a hobby to us, because it was never able to stand on its feet without drawing funds from my other businesses. But now it has been accruing so much that it will not only stand on its feet but get others to their feet as well, and I say congratulations to the staff." Another round of applause followed.

I was afraid we would soon turn the meeting to a worship centre with the way we keep on clapping with vigour.

I was enjoying it anyway!

' "I must confess, there was a time I thought about changing the name of the station because we just stopped at one point without progressing! I thought the reason why everything remained static, was because we were jinxed by our name." *He stopped and looked around at us then burst out.* "Now I won't mind we remain static, static on success." Everybody started laughing. This man is truly a politician.

"Please my friend mr . . . Mmhh?" He was pointing at me, I quickly helped him, emphasising on the use of my initials of course.

"Yes, SST, please stand up." He said. I quickly stood up.

"I want to express the appreciation of the management of FM Static to the good work you have been doing with us, in front of all of us and we hope you continue to remain in our big happy family." *The Chief was looking directly into my eyes. I lowered down my head and held my hands behind my back.*

The way I stood in front of the table reminded me of the days when I used to stand before a superior in the military when brought forward for disciplinary action. The men in the room turned their eyes on me. I was shaking frantically in my shoes feeling like a man about to be guillotine! Chief called for his briefcase. He opened it and brought out all what everyone saw to be a cheque. He stood from his seat and called me to step forward and stand beside him.

"On behalf of the management of FM Static, I want to extend our gratitude for the good work you have shown with a token bonus of 500,000 naira." Another round of applause followed! I nearly collapsed!

A bonus of 500,000 naira, after being here for just a few months, and my old security firm was enticing me with an open job offer if I decide to return? I won't get a bonus of a free meal from my old boss in a decade! Mine! Have I arrived too?

It appeared Chief was not through with the good news yet!

"I have acceded to the long demand of the studio for an official car. And I have even gone further to approve two. One of the cars would be for the studio producer and the other for our newest presenter, SST!" He said it as if calling on an award winner to get on the stage. I thanked him by profusely nodding my head like a happy lizard.

It was clear he was not going to allow me to make a thank you speech. Chief Dokubo saw all that was happening as nothing big but a small way of rewarding his boys, and there was nothing special about it! He let me go back to my seat and we all sat back.

"With that I must take my leave, I wish I could stay longer but you remember I have earlier told you, I have a meeting waiting for me. Thank you all and see you another time." And with that he stood to go. The management meeting has ended, everybody stood to go too.

As I was leaving, I saw the man that entered with Chief, his personal assistant, coming towards us. He reached to me and said "Chief wants to see you by his car."

I left Mark standing, and followed him.

We got to Chief as he was discussing with one of the directors by the car door. As soon as he saw me, he held out his hands.

"Yes, SST, come here, I have something for you." He said, bending to reach at something inside his car. He reappeared with a card in his hands.

"SST, I have been invited to a symposium as a guest speaker at the Covenant University Ota, I don't think I will have the time to attend, so I would like if you can present me." He said, thrusting the invitation card into my hands.

He was not waiting for my response.

"It would be on Monday . . . . I believe the details are on the card. I would have send one of my drivers to pick you to the place, but now that you have your official car, I hope it won't be a problem to find your way." He said as a matter of fact.

I told him it won't be and that I am highly honoured to represent him.

"Good, let me know how it all went, when you are through." *He said turning to the director who had been standing there all the while watching us. He was through with me.*

I met Mark where he was waiting. I could see two new Peugeot 307 saloon cars, with the big inscription STATIC FM boldly written on them, being driven to where we were standing. I stood there waiting! Yes, I think I should be static too; remaining till they reached to where I was standing. Mark and I drove away together in one of the new saloon cars while the other car and the Kombi bus followed us behind.

There was a mini party at the studio to celebrate the new additions, with Sasha sharing the drinks in Mark's office. The studio now has enough vehicles for its functions. The engineers will be in control of the Kombi bus while the two saloon cars were to cater for the need of the rest of us. The other presenters that anchor the news and other entertainment programmes were freelance reporters who had steady jobs elsewhere and only take out some hours with the studio; understandably the vehicle planning did not include them.

At the end of the day, I took my leave from Mark in whose office I was throughout, from the time we returned. I had nothing more to do at the studio anyway. The recordings of my show were usually repeated from the previous episode twice, or sometimes even thrice daily to get the message across and cover the broadcasting time, and of more importance to Mark, was to cover the avalanche of advertisement requests. Mark reminded me of the invitation to his wife's small house party the next day being Sunday. I bid him farewell, rolling my new car keys in my hands as I walked away. My days of rushing for the early morning buses are over. Feeling of the cheque resting in my pocket, I also knew the days of squatting in Segun's apartment was also over, because from my little savings and what I have now, I could get a suitable accommodation of a room or two, in Victoria Island, where I had always wanted to live.

I met Sasha writing on her table on my way out. I stopped to exchange a few words with her. The two of us have become very close friends now and were behaving like familiar friends. I told her of the cheque Chief had given me which I did not mention to the rest during the small celebration in Mark's office, or rather I didn't see any reason why I should bring it up. It was a personal gift not an addition to the studio's purse. Actually, I wanted Sasha to know that since I'm now financially buoyant, I might choose an offer for an accommodation at Victoria Island that I had been considering for some time. And as she lives in the area, her days of dropping from buses will soon be over, because I will be able to always give her a ride.

When I got home, I also had a small celebration with Segun before I went to sleep. I had to leave for the early church service the next day, and of course, I will have to go for Mark's wife's celebration after, celebration of what? Mark did not tell me and I did not remember to ask him! But that was not even the issue. The issue was to be able to locate the house from his description in the confusing street locations in Lagos.

The next morning, I decided to attend the first morning service at my church. The church runs three services on Sundays. I usually prefer the last one. The struggle of climbing and coming down from buses made me to prefer the afternoon service. But now, with a new car with me, I have joined Segun and other car owner's in the neighbourhood in deciding when I chose to leave for work. I remember that I had to create enough time to locate Mark's house.

However, getting to Mark's house was not as difficult as I envisaged. It was Just as I thought; get to one of the places he described and ask the next man for description, and you are there. That's Lagos for you! You can never be short of someone ready to assist you with directions in the city. The people of Lagos are aware of how difficult it is to move around the city and are always ready to assist.

Mark's house was located in one of the normal large housing compounds protected with heavy gates at the street entrance. The type of houses where the owners safeguard their homes by erecting iron gates at a location on the street, making it an entrance to their neighbourhood. By the time I reached his house along the small street, nobody needed to tell me I was in the right place. There were two canopies erected in the small pavement with several plastic chairs that afforded the large number of colourfully dressed people that gathered there a good seating place. I could hear the usual loud music blasting from huge standing speakers. It was a typical Lagos social gathering—large, noisy and colourful!

I met Mark in the inner sitting room in the midst of people that were eating and drinking, it was a sort of a big merriment. He smartly stood up when I entered and held my hands, carrying me around the room and introducing me to his guests. He told them I was God's greatest gift to him and the studio for the New Year. After going round and shaking the people seated in the sitting room I was finally taken to the inner room to meet his wife. The woman had a young baby of about a year old in her hands and a small boy was holding on to her on the seat. She is a lovely looking, nice and well cultured lady. She welcomed me warmly, asking after my family, I didn't know what to say to that, so I just keep nodding and saying, "thank you madam." Hoping she moves to a more friendly topic.

The lady ensured I was well taken care of, in terms of getting a good portion of what was being served around. It did not take long before I learnt the reason for the celebration; actually nobody told me. It came out when it was time to offer the normal prayers in such gatherings. Mark's wife had been ordained that Sunday morning in her church as a minister of God, a pastor, and the members of her church have trooped to their home after the ordination to rejoice with the family. I was also surprised to learn that Mark was a deacon in the church. He never cut out to me as a religious person since I knew him. However, that was not strange; some people love to keep issues of their faith personal.

I was not the crowd type so it wasn't long before I took permission to leave, giving the usual excuse of avoiding the Lagos traffic. All the same, it was a very interesting outing as Mark and his wife made sure I was properly welcomed at their home. They both came out warmly with their two kids to see me off to the car. It was a great thing seeing this family side of Mark. I loved the way he handled things at the office, and now seeing him at home, I admired him as a loving family man the more. Despite enjoying the warm reception, I still had to leave their happy home and move back to my co-bachelor, Segun.

The Motivation Dance Club
The Garden of Eden

The next morning, Monday, I was in the studio earlier than ever. It was my first time of coming to the office in my new car. I felt great. There was no more bustling for buses with all its inconveniences and risks. I don't even need an umbrella to hide from the rain anymore. I now have my own my ark!

The studio was running the early morning news. The newscaster was on a story of kidnapping in one of the neighbouring states when I arrived. Kidnapping has now become the new phenomenon in the country, and it is increasing especially with the rise in election violence. The menace of kidnapping started with the indigenous tribal gangs in the coastal areas of the country. The gangs were going about kidnapping foreign workers and demanding a larger share from the proceeds of crude oil exploited from their land. Before long, criminal gangs in other parts of the country saw the benefits in such enterprise and started kidnapping highly placed persons for ransom. But sometimes the reasons were more political than financial.

Now hardly a day passes without receiving a report of kidnapping in one part of the country. The early morning news was about a kidnapping involving a school bus carrying 23 children that was waylaid on its way to school to a hideout. It occurred in a state located in the eastern part of the country. The kidnappers, as usual were asking for ransom in millions of naira. Aisha was at the point of finishing the news item on the latest kidnapping incident when I arrived at the studio. Lagos has been spared the scorch of this social malaise since the crime reared its head in the country. I'm yet to hear a report of any kidnapping since I came to Lagos. In fact, since

I started monitoring the stories of kidnapping in the country, and that was before I came to Lagos, I was yet to hear a case involving a kidnapping incident in Lagos. I was not surprised to find out why Lagos was spared from the spates of kidnapping. A lot of things about Lagos made kidnapping not a common criminal activity. The chaotic traffic situation in the city renders it hard to secure a quick getaway with a victim, and the large congestion of the city denies a secure hiding place for kidnappers.

The news broadcast was almost over as I entered the studio. Aisha was already reading back the major highlights in the news. The first person to greet me as I entered was Sasha.

"Why? Oga SST, you are early today." She said with a mischievous grin. It never mattered to her if I was late or early! I knew what Sasha was trying to get at! When a man has a new addition in life, he faces such poking jabs from his friends.

"I'm as early as I have always been, Sasha, maybe you want to refer to my new mode of transport. If that's what you are trying to get at; then baby, you had better know I am having a great time with it." I gave her a wink and tapped her shoulders. I left her still laughing.

Aisha was coming down from the presenter's seat. The engineers had already placed in a musical programme to cover the short interlude before my show comes up.

"Hey, SST, I have been looking for you. I need someone to give me a ride back home today." She hollered.

It was now Aisha poking me over my new car. She was laughing too. *Oh! Can't these ladies let me be with my new car? Was the change in my status so unexpected and shocking to them or what?* But I knew why they were taunting me, it was their turn. I was the one always leading the jokes when it comes to jesting someone, now it was their turn to have a good laugh on me!

"Anytime, Aisha, anytime you want, I'm at your service! You are my best babe, remember?" I smiled at her as I hurried in to see Mark in his office. I still have about five minutes before I go on air with my show.

"Good day, Mark." I said as I entered his office after a perfunctory knock on the door. Mark and I had become so close now; the sir was long gone and buried between us.

"Morning, SST, my wife sends her gratitude for your presence yesterday." He said as I sat down on the new settee by the wall that was recently added to the office.

"No it's my pleasure. I had a great time and your family is really nice. I didn't know I was working with a bishop." I said with all seriousness. Mark laughed and stood up to refit a wall photo. I knew he was just avoiding my eyes. There is something about the eyes, people don't want theirs to meet that of another person if they are feeling shy about something, unsure of themselves or maybe lying!

"It's my wife that is the prayer warrior, I'm just co-opted in the whole thing and trying my best." He turned to face me. "SST, I never told you about my wife's spiritual work, right? My wife has a growing congregation and with the ordination, she might soon be on the way of opening her own ministry. She is a great woman, SST, I don't feel I deserved her." He sounded sorry about something.

I wasn't going to be drawn into any topic on someone's marriage, moreover, I'm yet to show any sign of seriousness in having a family of my own. I quickly moved away to another discussion.

"Mark, I'm here to run my show before dashing to Covenant University for that lecture am to represent Chief." I digressed from the discussion.

"I have not forgotten, SST. What did you said the lecture is about?" He asked.

"I only have the theme 'Living in an ever changing world." I told him.

He looked at me with great admiration in his eyes and said "You are doing very well, SST, just a few months here and first time meeting Chief Dokubo and already he is sending you to represent him at major functions. I told my wife you came as a result of her fervent prayers for the studio. I'm very happy to have you man." He raised his left thumb at me. I quickly seized an excuse to run away from his office. I was never comfortable when found in the midst of compliments.

My time was up anyway!

I took my seat in front of the microphone in the studio, waiting for the signal from the studio engineer to signal me to go on air. Elias gave me the thumbs up and I started the show in my usual way of introducing the morning show.

"Good morning, good people of Lagos State! I hope the busy weekend has not given you a hangover! It is funny how we look at weekends as a time for us to rest. These days, weekends are when we do all our real work. Oh, forgive my manners; I forgot to tell you who is intruding in the peace of your day! This is DJ SST. You are all welcome to motivation dance club!

And who is coming first on our dance floor this morning?" I asked in my normal fashion of soliciting callers. But by this time I don't even need to; they were all out there, bending over each other to be the one to make the first call! I had hardly finished speaking when calls started coming in from listeners, just as I expected. The first three calls that came in were the normal well wishers and those congratulating me on the continuing success of my show. The next caller after that was that of a young lady.

"SST, good morning and how is your day? This is Mrs Olaitan from Maryland! Really, I'm not the one that wants to shake on the dance floor this morning, it's my small daughter that has a question for you." She said, handing over the telephone to her daughter.

"Good morning sir," I heard the voice of a young girl on the line.

"Good morning, my dear, who am I speaking to? Please." I said.

"It is Esther, sir, my mother said I should take my question to you, sir." The little girl said.

"Ok, my dear, let me see your dancing steps." I said as cheerful as I always do when I have someone coming in with a topic for discussion.

"We were told in school that God created the Garden of Eden with good fruits and I asked my mama, where the Garden of Eden is? And she said I should ask you instead." Her voice was so innocent in asking. One would think I was hiding the Garden with me! What do this people take me for; a living encyclopaedia? I quickly removed the entire jumble up items in my brain to get what to come up with.

"My dear, how can we know what God himself has hidden from us?" I started quickly as I searched for more information.

"My daughter, the Garden of Eden cannot be located by any man, because God has hidden it from us! But we can have an idea of the general area it can be found when we look at the positions today of the four rivers that fed into the garden as recorded in the first book of Moses, the Genesis." I quickly brought out my scriptures.

"When we look at the Book of Genesis, Chapter Number 2 from verses 11 to 14, the second river, Gihon, is said to encompass the whole of Ethiopia, and we know Ethiopia is located in the horn of Africa. The third river is called, Hiddekel, and is said to go towards the east of Assyria, which is in present day Syria, and the fourth river is Euphrates, which is found in the Republic of Iraq. These rivers are all found in the Middle East, and the horn of Africa. So, by looking at the rivers, we will know that the Garden of Eden is located within that area of the Middle East.

Furthermore when you consider that history has recorded the early settlements and civilizations to be found within these areas, you will see that when Adam and Eve were thrown out of the Garden, they did not really travel very far, by today's standard, from where they were!"

I inhaled a big breath at the end of the small explanation.

"Thank you sir." The girl said kindly.

"Thank you too my dear, but why are you interested in finding the Garden of Eden? I don't think Eve left enough apples there for anyone when they were leaving." I made a little joke, using Eve's love for the forbidden fruit.

"Sir, we were told there is a tree of life there, and I just want to eat from the tree of life, so that I will live forever. I don't want to be gone someday like Jack." She said almost crying.

I quickly felt for her, it is always terrible losing a loved one. "Sorry my dear, accept my sympathy, and who is Jack?" I asked in the voice reserved for showing respect to the bereaved.

"Jack was my puppy." she said with nostalgia!

A puppy? What the heck! I felt a little angry at the use of my show to hold a wake-keeping for some puppy! But Esther was a guest; it was she that has the respect of coming on my show, and not her dead puppy.

"Sorry to hear that, Esther, I hope Jack arrives safely wherever puppies go when they die." I offered a short prayer and moved on to her question.

"My dear, the tree of life is all what God was protecting when he hid the Garden of Eden." I started back on my talk by drawing reference again to the Book of Moses, the Genesis, which recorded the early history of God's creations.

"Go back to Genesis and look at Chapter Number 3 and verse 22, you will see Adam and Eve where still left in the Garden of Eden, even after they were punished for eating from the forbidden fruit. It was later when God decided that they might eat from the tree of life, and live forever, and because they have the knowledge of good and bad when they ate from the forbidden tree, they would be turned to gods. Then He decided to send them away from the Garden of Eden. My dear Esther, there is nothing so special about the Garden of Eden that God would deny us than for the tree of life and death. And for that He set an angel with a blazing sword to protect the Garden from us."

It was Esther's mother that came back after I finished the second question from her daughter.

"Oh! My God! SST! You have not only answered my daughter but uplifted me too! I thought it was all a joke my daughter was throwing at you but you came out so strong that I now understand motivation dance club is greater than I thought. SST, you are my man." She was obviously overwhelmed with admiration. And can you imagine that I was afraid at the beginning of her question that I might act short of her expectations!

So much for our fears!

The next two callers brought up several comments and references on the Garden of Eden, some interesting, some cynical, and one out rightly vulgar on the issue of what was actually referred to as the forbidden fruit, so much such that I had to cut off his call. The next caller gave me what I was longing for, just when I was almost about to shout for it—a new topic!

"SST, my name is Chukwudi; please I need your advice on what to do. I work as an apprentice in my Master's shop; we are about three of us with him. The problem is; whatever I do the rest of my co-workers see no good in it. They make jest of me, they condemn me even in front of visitors. I think it's because the boss is always praising me in front of them and they hate me for that! They call me names; I was so dejected that I tried to enter my shell by doing nothing! But SST, it is in my character to always do my best. But anything I do, they all rush to pour dirt on it, I'm tired. I want to leave the work; I can't withstand their mudslinging any longer!" He poured out his problems in a very painful voice. Surely, it was an issue that grieved his heart deeply.

"Chukwudi, next time they condemn you, shrug it off and step on it like Caesar did, and you will grow higher." I told him.

"SST, who is Caesar? The one in Shakespeare's story?" He offered!

If he had not said that, I would have been disappointed, anybody should think of Julius Caesar when he hears the name Caesar!

"I mean, Caesar, the mule. I am sure many of us might not have heard of Caesar the mule. But Caesar had an important lesson not only for Chukwudi but for all our listeners that are facing unjust attacks in different areas of their lives, be it in a marriage, career, business or whatever" I said getting ready with the next narrative. I started the narrative.

"A farmer had a mule called Caesar. One day, Caesar fell into an abandoned well fifteen feet deep. Jacob really loved his old mule. But when he surveyed the situation, he realised there was no way to save old Caesar. The well was very narrow and Caesar was crammed at the bottom. The mule had not move or make a sound as he shouted at it. Jacob figured Caesar died in the fall. As much as it bothered him to give up on the mule, he was a practical farmer. He decided to leave Caesar at the bottom of the well and fill it with dirt. The farmer called some friends to help him shovel down dirt down the well. The first shovel of dirt woke up Caesar, who it seemed was just knocked out. When the mule felt the next load of dirt on his back, it realised what was going on. But instead of letting itself get buried, the mule shook it off. Every time a load of dirt hit its back, the mule shook its body, tossing the dirt to its hooves. Then he would step on it. After an hour of shoving dirt into the dark well, the farmer and his friends were surprised to see the mule's ears appear at the top of the well. They realised the mule was not dead. So they increased shovelling until the mule stepped out of the well and walked out to freedom. They had poured dirt to bury Caesar in the well, but they raised him up instead!" I said as I conclude the story on the mule called Caesar.

"You may be in a deep hole now. You may be facing disappointments, and failures. People may be pouring the dirt of lies, the dirt of failures, or the dirt of disappointments on you; I say step on it and rise to your victory! Your friends might be ganging against you, step on it! That bad examination result, step on it, that betrayal from your lover, step on it! That third class degree, step on it! That family frustrations, step on it!

It does not matter what is being used or who is being used to pour dirt on you, or who is used to bury your ambition, to bury your relationship, to bury your career, or to bury your life with shovels of dirt! I say don't mind them, just step on it! As long as you can step on the dirt of failures, on the dirt of disappointment, and on the dirt of betrayal being poured on you, it can never bury you! And when you step on it, it would lift you out of the deep hole the devil wants to use to bury your marriage, your relationship, your career, your ambition or your life!

The farmer and his friends came to bury Caesar the mule, but lifted it to freedom instead . . . . disappointments will come to bury you, but it will lift you instead! Frustration will come to bury you, but it will lift you instead! Failure will attempt to bury you, but it will lift you instead . . . . because when the devil came and shove the dirt of disappointments on you, you stepped on it! He came and poured the dirt of failure on you, and you stepped on it! He came and poured the dirt of slanders on you and you step on it! And you keep on stepping on all the devil has against you, till you took the last step that took you to your victory!

It didn't matter to Caesar the mule if it was a stranger, or its owner that was pouring dirt to bury it, the mule was just concern on stepping on it and moving out! It should not bother you if it was a spouse, a colleague, an opponent, or a friend that the devil is using to pour dirt on you, just step on it and move out! It didn't bother Caesar the mule how many people the farmer was able to gather to pour dirt on it, the more they come, the more the dirt they poured and the more steps he was able to take to victory! The more they will gather against you, the more dirt they will pour on you and the more you should step on it, carrying you faster to your victory! It didn't matter to Caesar, the mule, what their motive of pouring dirt on it was; whether it was to bury it or save it, whether it was out of love or hatred, the mule didn't care; it just concentrated on steeping on it! It should not bother you of what anybody's motive of pouring dirt on you is, whether to discourage or kill your plan, whether out of hatred, jealousy, envy, or unfounded animosity! It doesn't matter, just step on it!

Caesar had no time to get angry over the dirt they were pouring on it, because Caesar knows it isn't bitterness or anger that was needed to carry it to victory but to keep on stepping on it! I want you to know that you don't need to be bitter or angry about what is being said or done against you, you need to just keep on stepping on it as it comes! And I say to you today, when disappointments comes your way—step on it! When failure, Victimisation, hateful attacks come, step on them, and step to your victory!

I remember when we use to go on long endurance race in the army. Anytime we start getting fatigued from the long running and falling behind, the trainers will introduce a song, shouting on us to step on it, step on it! And you see yourself moving till you will reach the finishing line! So, no matter how far you have gone into frustrations and disappointments, I say just step on it, and it will take you to the finishing line! They will try to bury you as they pour dirt on you. But when you keep on stepping on it, it will turn to victory instead!" I shouted the last words that carry the lesson of my talk.

Chukwudi quickly came back on air with a loud exclamation.

"*Chineke* (my God), what a way of life! I never knew I could learn from a mule's attitude until today. Thanks SST, may God continue to anoint you with greater knowledge. I wish you the best in your work, in your business, with your wife and kids. In fact, everything SST, God bless you." Chukwudi was breathlessly showering me with praises and prayers! Some I received, others I don't know where to place them.

"SST you do a lot of good and may God bless you really big."

"Thanks Chukwudi!" I accepted.

But he was not through.

"SST, I have a question for you." He sounded shy.

"Yes, go on Chukwudi." I encouraged him.

"Yes, SST, it's a kind of silly, but I can see you are doing a good work here ... mmhm and I know God will reward. But SST, how will you feel if after all these efforts in people's lives God didn't reward you; I mean you end up old and poor, you know what I mean?" He asked.

What a boy!

' "No I won't Chukwudi."

He was just trying to gorge his feelings out.

"Yeah, SST just that I remembered my dad was a good man who did a lot of good SST. But he died poor and uncared for, leaving us to struggle through life on our own." He sounded sorry and bitter.

"Chukwudi I'm sorry about your dad." I tried to comfort him as best as I could "But you see, for me it's too late for me to be disappointed in God."

"It's too late?" He was curious.

"Yes Chukwudi too late for me to be disappointed in God!" I then faced my listeners on the show. "My friends, it's too late for me to be disappointed in God! Looking back at my history, I always remember when the enemy afflicted me with measles at age two. I was turned a piece of rag in my mother's hands and moved from one doctor to another.

Doctors usually don't agree a lot, but they agreed very well in my case! I wasn't going to live, just another baby waiting for a small coffin, not too great lost to no family member, no one really knew him anyway, they said! But God said no! And today I'm still around and many people including you know me.

So, even if God adds nothing more to my life today, it's too late for me to be disappointed in God! Even if He takes away all that He gave me today, it's too late for me to be disappointed in God! Because what you are seeing as a disappointment in my status can become a blessing. It's God's grace that carried me here, on my own I won't have even reached the disappointment you are seeing! I have already collected what I don't deserve. I have already used up what I don't deserve. I can't return what I have used up! So, do you understand why it would be too late for me to be disappointed in God?" I directed the question to my listeners. "And if you are listening to me on this show and you have a reason why you feel you would be disappointed in God, I want let you to know' it's too late! I don't know what the devil is using to make you feel incomplete, I don't know what desire he has put in your mind that is making you to question God's love for you, but I believe if you look back and see what God has done in your life, whatever might come your way; failure, sickness, loss of loved ones, loss of promotion, family crisis, financial crisis, unfair treatment, betrayal from friends, it would not cause you unnecessarily worries. It won't deny you the comfort of your bed this night, because it is too late for you to be disappointment in God!"

"Gee! SST, thanks a lot! You have uplifted my spirit more than anything else since I lost my dad. Thanks and sorry for taking much of your time sir." It seemed Chukwudi was finally through; quite an interesting fellow.

"Thanks Chukwudi and I wish you the best." I concluded.

The phone was ringing once gain as soon as Chukwudi was through.

I pressed the button for the next caller.

"SST, good day, how are you my dear? It's Christy." She said, I could detect her voice was not particularly sounding happy.

"Yeah, Christy, my sister, I can see you are not in the mood for a happy dance steps today." I said.

"No, SST, everything in my life is just not moving right! I'm failing everywhere! My business is going bad; my relationship is terrible, my . . ." I cut her off before she could continue the long narration of woes!

"My sister, the scripture says let the weak say I'm strong, not that let the weak discuss its weakness; your words have power you know, speak faith into your situation, that's what motivation FM is all about." I was in my usual style of trying to lift up a broken spirit. But I could see she was still not quite lifted!

"Yeah, SST, I know you are trying to encourage me. But my situation is far gone, my problems are overwhelming, I can't even pay for my . . ." I cut in again. "Oh no my sister, motivational FM is there not only to encourage you but to show you your strength, the scripture says let God arise and let his enemies be scattered."

She came back again quickly.

I could hear her voice vibrating hotly on the speakers!

"That's it SST, I'm waiting for the Lord to arise for me too, and pursue all the occult people after my life. It is my family . . ." I entered in quickly again before she change the discussion again from the subject at hand, and introduce a new dimension to it. Family squabbles, from my experience with counselling people, are never ending, and easily get intertwined in confusing details.

"My sister, (*I started softly and in a patronising voice*) it is you that will have to let God to arise, God can't arise in your life if you don't let him." I tried to counsel her. She came back sounding genuinely surprised.

"SST, really?" She said.

I now have her full attention.

Good!

"Yes my sister, failure is an enemy of God, disappointment is an enemy of God, poverty and misery are enemies of God because they are all from the devil! But God won't arise to scatter them away from our lives if we keep on speaking negative words! Negative words won't attract God to arise, discouraging words won't allow God to arise, and pessimistic words won't allow God to arise, because God cannot arise in such an environment. He is a Holy God."

I stopped momentarily, waiting to see if any of my listeners had something to say to that, but nobody called in either. Not she or any other listener was ready to interject, so I continued.

"To get God to arise, we must speak His words in the midst of our difficulties. When there are disappointments, you should say it shall be well with me! When attacks come your way, shout God's promise that sadness may last for a night but joy comes in the morning! Continue to speak God's promises in the face of any problem in your life and God will arise and scatter all your enemies, all disappointments, all frustrations, and all negativity will be scattered from your life if you allow God to arise!" I finished on a usual high note.

She came back on the air again.

"Oh, SST, thank you very much. Thank you, I'm now ready to do as you've said and allow God to arise against my enemies." She said.

I was elated with such comments as usual. Why can't I get rid of this excitement whenever I feel I have impacted on someone positively? The phone on the table was ringing again; another caller was on the line.

"Hello, Static FM 111, DJ SST here." I put up an unusually long introduction, normally with me it was to just mention the name of the station and urge the caller to move on.

"Yes, SST, it's Julian." He said.

I recognised the name.

I had a long discussion with him some time ago. Julian had a problem with an uncle he was staying with in Lagos, and the man sent him away from his house. With nowhere to go, he later pitched his tent at one of the various construction sites with one of the contractors working on upgrading school buildings by the State Government. He was given not only shelter but also daily sustenance by the contractor whom he assisted with basic clerical work of checking the labourers input and use of materials at the building site. Julian was just seventeen years and attends a day secondary school. He would have finished secondary school like most of his age mates; but for the fact that he missed some years of schooling when his father passed away, and before the uncle agreed to take him in. His mother had also passed away when he was just a toddler. He had no visibly knowledge of her.

"Good day Julian, how are you doing with life now?" I asked.

"Fine sir!" He answered quickly.

Julian is one of my success stories. He was on his way to self—destruction when he called the show. His uncle, whom he was finding it hard to stay with, kicked him out of his house over a misunderstanding with his wife. The wife had never really welcomed him to the house. She often leaves him without food or gives him the leftovers from her children's plates or the old spoilt *gari* to make a meal for himself.

He was almost used as a domestic servant in the house by his uncle's wife. He washes and keeps the house clean while her children attend to their studies and homework. While his uncle's children attend private school, his uncle enrolled him in a local public secondary school. The problem heightened when the wife got tired of his presence and decided to do away with him once and for all. She accused him of stealing some money she left in her clothes that she gave him to wash. His uncle got angry, and prodded by his wife sent him packing, away from his house. It was when he was going about dejected and at a lost to what to do with his life, that someone advised him to call motivation dance show and tell his story. When I heard his situation, I invited him to the studio and he relayed his life story to listeners. He was the first listener I ever invited for an in house interview.

It was while he was relaying his pathetic story on air that one of the callers, the contractor he is staying with now, invited him to come to him. I can remember the time he was crying in the studio as he narrates his story. He looked at me and said, "sir, why am I so unlucky in life?" I looked back at him smiling and replied "Yes Julian, you aren't the only one I knew who was also unlucky in life." I looked at him closely, he was staring back at me blankly not sure of what to say.

"I know someone unlucky like you his name was Joseph, just as you are Julian."

I got his attention.

I pushed the microphone nearer as I was sure the listeners would now be arching to get to hear what I had to say after listening to Julian. But I had nothing new for them.

"Joseph was unlucky to lose his mother at an early age like you, Julian. Joseph was unlucky to have brothers that hated him; he was unlucky to be alone with them in the bush where they sold him into slavery. He was unlucky to have a Master whose wife's lustful desire made her to attempt to seduce him. And when he refused, she hated him the most, and got her husband to throw him into prison. You see? Joseph had people all around him who also hated him for no fault of his. But while they thought they were busy hating him, God was preparing him."

I looked at him; he was staring at me attentively.

I continued the talk, "when his bothers sold him into slavery; they thought they were through with him, but God was preparing him. When Joseph was in prison, he thought he was unlucky in life to have brothers that hated him, and then he was unlucky to have a master's wife who lied against him, but in all, God was preparing him. As you know, Julian, God raised Joseph to be the second in command in a country where he was sold as a slave."

I now turned my attention to my millions of listeners.

"So I say to you all out there, when they devil brings challenges of life to you, God is preparing you. When he throws frustrations and disappointments at you, just know that God is preparing you! When people lie against you, God is laying something for you! Do not be distraught; God is preparing you in the midst of all the hatred, frustrations and disappointments. And one day, He will bring you out to your victory like Joseph." It was after I have finished with saying that, that a caller called offering to meet and take Julian in and ensures he continues with his education that was interrupted when his uncle sent him away. That was the last time I saw Julian in person but he had called my personal line on few occasions to let me know how he was doing. And he was doing well.

"So how are you doing in school, Julian?" I asked.

"School is fine sir. I just called to let you know I'm fine and to give thanks to God for using you in my life." He said.

"Thanks, Julian, good luck to you and please continue to keep in touch." I said as I end the conversation.

"And to my listeners, I'm ever grateful for all those that assisted Julian in whatever way you could since the day you heard him tell his story on the motivation dance club. Your assistance will not only see Julian through school successfully but create in him a great person! There are many Julians in our streets, in our working places, and amongst us who just want us to hear their stories! Doctor Terry wont have been the successful cardiac surgeon he is today if someone had not taken care to know his story and come to his help at the critical point of his life." I hope, I have enough time to go through another narrative.

"My listeners, in the few minutes remaining please let me take you on a narrative on the importance of listening to someone's story before judging the person." I looked into my small archive and quickly brought out a piece of paper.

"Terry was a difficult child at school. The teachers didn't particularly like him. He was always withdrawn, and hard to learn amidst the order kids. Miss Jones tried to bring him out but after sometimes, she gave up on him. She saw him as a problem and Terry withdrew into himself the more. When it was time to give gifts to the teachers at the end of the year, every kid brought a very well neatly beautiful wrapped gift, prepared for them by their mothers and given to the teacher. Terry only had a small gift wrapped in a brown grocery bag that he seemed to have himself.

Miss Jones collected Terry's gift reluctantly but seeing the tears in the little 10 year old boy's eyes, she decided to open it. Inside was a small perfume bottle. She took and sprayed a little of the perfume on her blouse and hugged little Terry. Terry looked at her and forced a smile trying to stop the tears from his small eyes and said, "Miss Jones, you smell just like my mother did." And he left! Miss Jones was puzzled and so she decided to know Terry's story. She went through his past reports; grade one . . . . Terry showed a good promise, but mother was sick at home. Grade two, Terry is losing concentration at school—mother just died. Grade three, Terry is doing badly, and father didn't care!

Miss Jones went on her knees and asked God to forgive her for all the ways she treated little Terry, she never knew the background he was coming from. From that day, she took interest in Terry and assisted him all the way and Terry's life and performance in school changed.

Terry successfully graduated to college.

Terry sent Miss Jones a message from college in his first year "Miss Jones thank you, I'm now doing well at College." The following year; "Miss Jones, Thank you, I'm on top of my class, yours Terry." Fifth year," Miss Jones I have just graduated from college, yours Dr Terry!"

Five years later, Miss Jones got another message from Terry. "Miss Jones I am getting married. I want you to be there to sit by my right, where my mom would have sat if she was alive, yours Doctor Terry!"

Sometimes we judge people by our background, life, by our good decisions, by our fortunate circumstances and by our lucks, and we see them as being below what they should have been! . . . Oh, I can't be divorced like her, oh, I can't stay unmarried for that long like her, oh, and I can't live in that neighbourhood like her! Oh, I can't follow men for money like her! Oh, I can't work as a waitress like her, oh, I can't be a mechanic like him and so on . . . . and so we end up treating them badly! But most people that are down don't need our judgment, they need our love, and we can't love them when we don't take time to understand their story! We have many Terrys' in our streets, in our neighbourhood, in our schools, in our workplaces that would end up badly instead of reaching their potentials, because nobody cared to know their stories . . . ." I quickly put the piece of paper back into my bag.

No time for receiving compliments now!

I looked up at the studio wall clock, the time for the show was almost over, and I needed to get ready to go to Covenant University to represent Chief at the symposium. I pressed the button on the receiver to block all incoming calls so that I could give the normal end of show valedictory speech.

"My darling listeners, I enjoyed your company in the past one hour or thereabout. I appreciate all those that called in with their issues, and those that commented on my show this morning. I love your dancing steps! And to those that were unable to get on the dancing floor, I say, next time I will make a big room for you to show your moves in the motivation dance club with DJ SST! And to all I say, if water encourages you, stay near water, if friends encourage you, stay near friends and if motivation dance club show encourages you, stay near our show! The produce of life's farm is too much—the time to harvest is too short. Do not rest on your oars, stand up and find something to do today! Have a wonderful day and God bless you all! I love you all!" I said.

And I closed the show for the day.

I quickly removed the headphones, bid a farewell to Mark and the rest of the crew as I hurriedly gather my few narratives and put them in my bag. It was time to be on my way to Covenant University to represent the chairman of my company at the students' end of academic year symposium!

The Motivation Dance Club
The Tide Always Returns

The Covenant University Ota, was established in the year 2000, by the Living Faith Church International. The Church has its headquarters in Ota, a small town near the city of Lagos where the University is also located. The Covenant University is amongst Nigeria's most advanced and progressive private universities. The town of Sango Ota, where it is located, is at a distance of about 50 kilometres from my studio located in Lagos. Normally, it would have taken me just an hour to get there, but taking into cognisance the heavy traffic experienced on the road, I decided to budget two hours for the journey.

By the time I arrived at the University, the lecture theatre where the symposium was to take place, was already full with lecturers, students, visitors, and other guests all seated. A member of the protocol committee went with me round the hall to meet the university dignitaries and other invited guests, including representatives of the media from two other radio stations that were also invited to the symposium. I went round to greet the invited guests seated at the high table, and the guests from media houses that were also represented there.

It was when I greeted the next two people seated away from me that I got to where he was seated! It was a big shock seeing him for the first time since the episode when he had me practically thrown out of his office.

I stood there looking into the face of Mr Dan Paul, the head of production of Star FM 123. He shook my hand warmly and greeted back nicely. There was no sign of recognition on his face. I knew why. Mr Dan Paul could never remember or expect it to be the same young man that was in his office, seven months ago, begging for an airtime in a radio show.

Seven months ago, when I decided that it was my calling to run a motivation programme on radio, I went about in search of a radio station that would be interested in airing my show. I went to about three FM radio stations on my first day of search without success. I was confronted with the usual excuses; *sorry we are booked up . . . we will call you when we are ready . . .* and all the polite excuses people give to get rid of someone they don't want.

It was even worse when I got to Star FM!

Star FM at the time was the number one FM station in Lagos. The current rating has however placed Static FM ahead of Star FM in listeners' coverage. I don't need to say how Static FM rose to first position so fast.

When I got to Star FM headquarters; a big modern building located in the highbrow areas of Ikoyi, I passed through one or two officials while asking for whom to meet regarding my desire to present a show on their radio station. I was later directed to the office of the production manager, Mr Dan Paul. He wasn't in the office when I got there. His secretary had me wait in the visitor's waiting room, which was connected to where she had her own office before reaching the manager's office.

Mr Dan Paul was back before long.

As he passed through the visitor's waiting room to his office, I stood to greet him, but he didn't as much as looked at my direction than acknowledge my presence. I sat back at the reception room waiting for Mr Dan Paul to call me into his office two hours after the secretary had informed him of my presence and the reason for my coming. After what looked like eternity, the secretary told me; I could enter and see the boss, as she called him. I met Mr Dan Paul in a large beautiful and exquisite office seated behind a long glass table. He was writing impatiently on a pad of paper.

"Yes, what brought you?" He said loudly without taking his attention from the paper in front of him or from what he was doing.

He did not offer me a seat or returned my greetings when I greeted him. I stood there like an accused in a dock.

Smelling the hostility in the air, I abandoned all pleasantries and went straight to the issue that brought me. I told him of my vision of presenting a motivation show on the radio station. He didn't have the patience to even hear me out.

"Look here my friend," he said harshly, taking his attention from the pad in his hands for the first time since I entered.

"I don't have time for all that childish stuff! If you are looking for where to pluck alms, this is not the place. We are a serious media house; you can try your play elsewhere, please, don't intrude on me next time, I'm a busy man!" He picked up the TV remote control from the table and turned his attention to the flat screen television on the wall. I stood there humiliated and ashamed. I offered a short apology for intruding on him which he didn't bother to reply, and as I quietly turned to leave, he added to my back with a sneer, "maybe you can go to Static FM, they are the type that might need that kind of stuff, that is if they are still on air and not out of circulation by now." He said it carelessly.

I calmly turned back and thanked him. I also thanked the secretary on my way out and vowed within me not to have anything to do with the place again. I was despaired by the experience and felt discouraged to continue with my search.

It was two days later that I gave serious thought to what he said about carrying my vision to Static FM. I started thinking of going to the place. I told myself I had nothing to lose anyway, it definitely would not be worse than what I went through at Star FM. After all life is a journey that one must meet obstacles. When you meet a brick wall don't waste your time trying to force your way through or sitting down and wishing it vanishes away—just take a detour and look for a new opening to continue your journey.

I tried to encouraged myself!

However, it was when I overheard the discussion in the bus, about Static FM, that I was able to summon the courage to pay a visit to the place. The rest of the story is where it has gotten me now.

I shook Mr Dan Paul as he stretched his hand to me. I noticed that as soon as I introduced myself as SST, of Static FM, he became very cordial and nice. That came to me as a surprise because all the while I thought he had a low opinion of Static FM. I left him and took my seat some few seats from the master of ceremonies.

The symposium started with the normal ritual exchange of courtesies and academic short talks by the senior academic staff of the institution. After which there was a short talk by students and lecturers before the guest lecturers were called in. I was to speak last amongst the invited guest speakers, and immediately before me would be the guest speaker from Star FM, in the person of Mr Dan Paul.

I took the stage after Dan Paul finished his speech. Three guests' speakers had already finished their talks and the hall was looking bored with many already falling asleep. I do not blame them. I would have fallen asleep myself if it wasn't that I was sitting on the high table. I realised that to get my lecture going I must find a way to awaken the audience.

I was prepared for that!

"My dear hosts, I am highly honoured to be invited for such an interesting programme in a very respectably and reputable institution."

I started with the normal customary pleasantries.

"I can see around me a very diverse, and enlightened audience of students and lecturers, guests and family, male and female, married and single, and all the other social diversities of our being, present here. And nothing can be more befitting for such an audience than the theme given to this end of the year symposium "Overcoming the challenges in an ever changing world" I said.

I could see some students and guests starting to yawn again. I knew what must be going through their minds 'here comes another boring speaker.' I ignored their initial reactions and continued building up on my statements expanding the scope as I move forward along just as I always in my shows.

"I have listened to the last speakers. I must confess that I have benefitted a lot from their insight on changes brought about by the nuclear age, global warming, free trade zones and all of that. I am not an academic speaker, I am a motivational public speaker, so forgive me if I see change in a less grandiose form."

I could see some excitement being stirred amongst the audience; maybe this one is different from the rest!

"I, at a low level, love to see change more in terms of how the world affects our ordinary life, as in our careers, marriages, businesses and in our jobs! We human beings are always seeing change in terms of how things are going well and how they are going bad with us when the tide is low and when the tide is high in our lives."

I looked around the hall; I could see I was arousing their interest.

"While coming in, I saw one of the young men outside by the gate selling photo portraits. He was carrying a nice picture of a canoe stuck in the mud by the waterside. It wasn't the picture of the canoe that interested me but the caption under it—'the tide always returns." The tide withdraws leaving the canoe stuck in the mud, but anytime the tide returns, the canoe will once more float and be of use! I then realised in our everyday living, sometimes, we get stuck when the tide withdraws! But I know it will be well with us because the tide always returns!

I should know about canoes. I was in the army and I was once deployed in the creeks of the Bakassi Peninsula.

The Bakassi Peninsula is a water tributary area, where the rivers make entries into the sea; it has a lot of creeks and waterways! We lived in raffia houses in the creeks by the muddy watersides. Our mode of transportation was by wooden canoes, only our big bosses use the speed boats to move around! As we anchor our canoes by the waterside, every time the water rescinds from the riverbanks, the canoes get stuck in the mud, and we get stuck in the creeks too, as we couldn't go anywhere without the canoes! And we had to start waiting for the tide to return to get our canoes back into the waters and start paddling again!"

I have now gotten the full attention of the audience.

"I don't know what is stuck in the mud in your marriage, in your business, in your career and in your life! I don't know how long you have been waiting to get the canoe of your life out of the mud, and into the waters to start paddling again! But I know, it is not over with you! Just as we knew it was not over with us in the creeks, because the tide always returns! And I also know, it is not over with you in your marriage! It is not over with you in your career! It is not over with you in your business! When you are facing your darkest hour, know that God makes everything in the world to move around to face darkness and light intermittently, and soon your world will be facing light! In life the tide always returns!"

I took a sip from the cup of water on the table as I always do when talking to an audience, taking time to peep at my audience. I could see the students getting excited as they whisper to one another.

"As soon as the tide returns, our canoes became active and floatable once again, and we only needed to enter and start paddling smoothly, as the tide also comes back with a change in the direction of the wind. We didn't need much energy to paddle, or get moving, as the wind assisted us by moving the canoes along! I also want you to know that as soon as the tide returns to your marriage, to your business, and to your life, you will realise you do not need to put much effort for all things to work in your favour, as God will bring everything to work for your good!"

I had completed the first page of my lecture and that gave me some time to recover my breath. I had been raising my voice for some time.

"While we were waiting for the tide to return, and with our boats stuck in the mud, we were not worried, as we sat down patiently watching the waters. We were waiting in expectation, because we know God has made the Earth to move the winds, and the waters in our favour, and soon they will all gather together to bring back the tide to our side of the creek and move our canoes back into the waters once again! And just as it is, as you watch that stuck marriages, as you pray for that stuck business, and that stuck career that is not moving! I want you to know that the tide will surely return! And I want you to also know that as you are waiting, God is making a lot of things to work in your favour to bring back the tide to your side once again, and get your life back to moving smoothly again!"

The hall was now glued to what I was saying. I could see some students and lecturers in the hall feverishly jotting in their notebooks.

"Whenever our commanding officer called for a meeting at the headquarters that was located on the island of Abana, he would have to wait for when the tide will turn to our favour before he starts anything! And not only him but also the businesspersons at the other side of the river that we do business with would also have to wait for when the tide returns to our favour! So, we had no fear of losing anything while we wait peacefully stuck at our location in the creeks, and having no anxiety to missing anything, because we know all that we needed are there waiting for us; waiting for when the tide will return to us, and we come out to have them!"

I raised my voice. I have a lot of young people in the audience and I have come to the area of most of their dominant concern in life.

"That husband God has for you, he will be there waiting for you! That great appointment God has for you, will be there waiting for you! That business God has for you, will be there waiting for you! That great life God has for you, will be there waiting for you! They will all be waiting for when the tide will return to you, and you'll come out to meet them!" I could see many of them raising their fists, with their eyes squeezed and their mouths shouting—amen, amen repeatedly. I had to wait a bit for the hall to be calm before I continue.

"The times we sat in the creeks waiting for the tide to return, we saw fishermen that the turn of the tide met in the middle of the waters struggling against the wind as they paddled along. But we were not bothered, as we sat waiting in the creeks with our stuck canoes but we know that the waters will take us out to meet them in the sea, and moving with the wind, we might even pass them along the way, as they must have lose strength, from struggling against the tide for long!

I want you to know that those you see today paddling in success as you get stuck in frustration, when God brings back the tide to your favour, and takes you out there with them, you might surpass

219

them as they have exhaust the momentum of their success. Wherever in your life you might have been left behind, please know that being behind does not imply you are coming last! Starting late does not mean being last! When God brings back your tide, He will restore all you have lost in time!" I paused.

"And on that day, we were never worried as we waited in the creeks, waiting for the tide to return! Because we knew in us, that as long as there is a change of morning and night in the earth, it is a sign that the earth is still revolving around the sun, and the tide will surely return. Because that is what God has promised in His words! Our Lord says; as long as there is change of morning and night, His words remain forever on the earth! Therefore, you shouldn't worry, He will bring back the tide to you in your marriage, in your business, in your academics and in all areas of your life!"

I could see the Dean of students affairs that I was earlier introduced to, shaking in his seat. There was nobody yawning or looking sleepy in the hall anymore. It was now a lively audience.

"Anytime you see your business grounded and not moving, remind yourself the tide will return! Anytime you see your marriage that was so blissful losing its steam, just know that the tide always returns! Anytime you see your career or your future seemingly stuck in frustration, just know that the tide always returns, and soon you will start making progress once again! And whatever the devil has stuck in the mud in your life, to deny you movement; I want you to know that the tide will return to your life soon! I don't know what frustrations the devil has brought to your life, I don't know in which area of your life the devil is tormenting you, I do not know how many years he has kept the canoe of your life stuck in the mud, but I know the tide will soon return to you! And Just as it did for us in Bakassi Peninsula, when we entered back to our canoes and started moving, so shall it return to you in your marriage, career, business, and to your life! And you will start making progress once again! Just as the tide returned, and picked our canoes back to the waters, and God brought all things to work in our favour, giving us a smooth sail, so shall it be, when God brings back the tide to pick your life out of the mud, and put it back in the waters! And all things will work for your good and give you a smooth sail again in life! And I say to you today, the tide is returning to all areas stuck in your life! And there is a good lesson about the return of the tide; you should never allow yourself to fall in despair when the tide leaves your side, because the truth is it will surely return!

My friend, are you are facing disappointments and problems today? What you need is not to be consoled, but to be told the truth! Are you feeling as if the whole world is against you, and nothing is working for you? What you need is not nice explanations, but to be told the truth! Are you feeling low, defeated and hopeless? What you need is not assistance but to be told the truth!

You need to be told the truth that when God is about to carry a man up, He first allows the devil to bring him down! And when the man survives the tribulations of being down, God will assess him worthy of the glory of being lifted up! So, anytime the devil pushes you down in failure, know that you are going up! When he brings friends or enemies to attack you or ridicule you, know that you are still going up!

When they say you are not going to make it, smile and tell them that they might be seeing you down and dejected today, but you are going up! They may see you defeated, and abandoned but you are going up . . . . you are going up, because God is going to carry you up and make your tide to return! Men may stab you in the back but God will pat you on the back. Man may push you down, but God will push you up! So, don't you worry about where you going because God will always return the tide. Sometimes, because of impatience, we do not wait for the return of the tide and instead go about looking for other means to carry us across the waters, and we end up adding frustrations and sufferings to our lives. If God wants to answer all our prayers at once, we would be getting the right things at the wrong time and that would only lead to more frustration. Effort and skill may take you up but it requires strength and patience to keep you there. And when you wait patiently, the tide will give you the strength you need. I recall an incident when I was training in the army. There was an aspect of our training called the obstacle course. The obstacle course involves various aspects of training that include several set apparatus that resemble various natural obstacles troops might encounter while fighting in the battlefield.

There were tunnels, high walls, and man-made water ditches, all amongst others that a trainee is required to pass through before reaching safety by crossing a simulated minefield at the end of the course.

One day during a training exercise, the best trainee amongst us was in the front when we were crossing the obstacles. He was far ahead of all of us because he had the skills and ability to cross better than all of us. But when he got to the last stage, the simulated minefield, he was able to get over the vertical rope but on trying to hook his legs on the horizontal rope to cross to the other side, his legs slipped and he was left hanging by holding the horizontal rope. There was no way he could lift his legs to hook to the horizontal rope and drag himself across, because he has lost a lot of energy.

The only thing left for him to do was to keep on hanging till help comes or he drops down to the minefield and be counted a casualty. Because he did not only had skill but strength, he was able to hold up till the next man reaches and assisted him in lifting his legs to the ropes, and that was when the tide returned for him. Likewise, in life, we might be able to achieve success as we move fast in life, but along the line, we might find ourselves hanging up there as all seems to go wrong, unforeseen misfortunes threatening to overshadow us, everything about to crash and brings us down and that's when we need strength!

We need strength to hold out against all the frustrations and disappointments that threaten to overshadow us until the tide returns. And I want you to know that you have all the strength you need! Before anybody can say anything bad about you, God has said something good about your future! Before anybody can say you cannot succeed, God has said you will succeed! Before anyone can say your future is bleak, God has declared a bright future for you! It does not matter what anybody says, what matters is what God says because He will always make the tide return to you! Even if you are thrown to prison like Mandela, God is not finished with you yet! Even if your life is a string of losses like Lincoln's, God is not finished with you yet, God is not finished with you as He will always turn the tide to you! Welcome to the time of the return of your tide!" I raise my voice and my hands above my head, to herald the end of my speech.

One of the lecturers stood up and started clapping and in a short while, the whole hall was full of people standing and clapping hard. The high table also joined, first the lecturers, then the Deans, and after that the invited guests. I noticed Dan Paul was the last to stand up and rather reluctantly joined in the clapping.

All of a sudden one of the students shouted "the hub!" and before long other students joined in the shouting of the "the hub!" I looked around at those with me on the high table, surprised at what was going on. I noticed they too, were as surprised as I was.

Then I remembered where the word, hub, came from! Oh mine! The newspaper clip, the one I got from Mark, yeah! The hub! I then knew where they got the name, the hub! I closed my folder, took a little bow, and went back to my seat. It was then the hall was brought under control. The whole event left me sitting there pleased but embarrassed.

At the end of the event, I took some photos with students, staff and their families, grouped into various snap shots, because of the large number of those present and those who want to be in the photo. I was moved around from one person to the other, and all that want to have a photograph with me.

The heads of department and some members of the teaching staff wanted a copy of my lecture notes. I promised to make one available to each and every one of them. I could always send a soft copy to the university website. Before leaving I had a short close session conversation with the Dean of students affairs; the chief host, who congratulated me on the success of my radio show, the motivation dance club and he confessed he had not being following but agreed he was now a converted fan of mine and will not miss another edition. He asked me to convey his gratitude to Chief Dokubo for honouring the university's invitation by sending me to represent him. I then took my leave, thanking him for the invitation, and promising to convey his message to Chief Dokubo.

I was on my way to the car park at the main administrative parking lot when I heard someone shouting my name as he hurried to catch up with me. I turned to see who was calling me.

It was Dan Paul!

"SST, please can I see you for a minute?" He said.

"Yes sir, what can I do for you?" I asked. He pulled my hands dragging me away from the car, in a way that would make one think we were well acquainted with one another.

"Let us go to the cafeteria at the corner, and discuss over a few drinks. I won't take much of your time, I promise." He said.

He did not even bother to seek for my opinion as to if I would accept his invitation. He was behaving as if we were old friends.

We were soon in the large student cafeteria, and he ordered drinks for the two of us at the counter. We moved to an empty table in the far corner. After some few unimportant conversations, Dan Paul moved on to what he really wanted to discuss with me.

"SST, I must admit I have been closely watching the change of fortunes at Static FM. I knew you are behind that achievement, and today I was more than convinced you are a great asset to any media house." He was talking so seriously and passionately about the whole matter, that I was convinced he had something more personal than wishing me well. I thank him for the compliments.

"Star FM was number one before you came on at Static FM. I must confess, it had not only affected our fortunes in loss of advertisement alone, but also our rating amongst the media houses." He said sourly. I smiled. I could see he was more concern about being number one. It was an ego thing.

"That is not our main concern. It goes more than that. Our problem has to do with the ambition of our chairperson who is going to contest for senatorial office in the next coming elections." He said. *What! Another media boss going into politics? It seemed every media mogul in Lagos was eyeing an elective office.*

Dan Paul was still talking.

"The FM station is not the financier of our elections, so the loss of revenue is not the issue. We are more concerned with the loss of audience because the radio station is the main mouthpiece of our campaign. The more people turn away from listening to our station the more it will affect our electoral opportunity." He said it as if he was the one running his chairman's campaign team! Maybe he was, but I cared less really!

"I am sorry to hear that." I said.

Dan Paul burst out laughing.

"I was not asking for that! I am here to ask for something more. I am asking that you move over to us." He said, extending his hands to touch mine on the table in a friendly way.

"Move over to you?" I repeated his question.

"I want you to come work for us, we are ready to pay you more than Static FM is paying you now, and we are ready for whatever more you might want as an incentive." He was openly pleading now. I realised how painful it had been for Star FM losing the number one position to Static FM.

"Dan, I will think about it. Please give me a call tomorrow, sorry, I got to me going, I'm late, and thanks for the drinks." I said extending to him my complimentary card. I stood up, bid him well, and walked away briskly. I could feel his eyes on my back as I go out of the cafeteria. Dan Paul's proposition took me by great surprise. I guess I do not really know my new value.

You can't blame me for that! It was all happening too fast . . . . ! I needed time to give him a reply. I believe I will be ready when next he calls.

I entered my car and started the journey back to Lagos. It was late already; I would have gone back to the studio before Mark closes for the day. But I decided to go home instead and brief him the next day on the outcome of my visit to the Covenant University. And that was for him to relay it to chief Dokubo whom I represented at the function.

I believed in adhering to protocol, what we call when I was in the army, following the channel of communication. It merely means you report to your immediate boss first and wait for further instructions. I tuned on the radio in the car and listened to the music being played at the studio as I hurried along the traffic back home to have a shower and long rest after the hectic day's activities.

The Motivation Dance Club
The Hub

The next morning when I got to the studio, I could see my colleagues stopped what they were doing as soon as I entered the small hall. They all rushed to my side, the men shaking my hands and the women hugging me as I struggled to set myself free from their grips. They were congratulating me on my performance at the symposium held at Covenant University the previous day. But it was in Mark's office that I got to know other new things that were added to me.

"Good morning, the hub." He said.

The hub? Is that what everybody will be calling me now?

"You started it, Mark; they must have picked it from you. But really, they were referring to the studio as the centre of attraction, the hub of radio broadcasting, and not to me." I tried to disentangled myself.

"You made it the centre of attraction with your show, so it was right all the same that you are the hub." He was obviously happy with the increasing publicity by the way he was patting my back commendably.

"Thank you, sir, but I am here to brief you on how it all went so that you can get the message to Chief Dokubo." I said.

"Any need for that? He sent you to represent him. I believe you can do that when he sends for you, beside what he heard about it in the news is usually sufficient for him. The Chief hardly has time for after mission assessment as long as it does not concern his finances." Mark was lecturing me on how things are done in the world of big business moguls. I remember I was no more in the military. I decided to tell Mark all that transpired during the symposium, all the same. When I mentioned my meeting with Dan Paul, he flared up!

"Dan Paul, that pompous rascal?" He was fuming in a way I never knew him before.

"You know him?" I asked, shocked at his reaction. He looked at me sharply. I could see how red his eyes have suddenly turned. He quickly got hold of himself and lowered his head into his hands.

"Yes, I met him once at such type of settings. I never liked him since then." He said softly.

I could understand!

Meeting Dan Paul for the first time, I could understand how he would leave such a bitter taste in another person's mouth. I told Mark I rejected the offer from Dan Paul. I never said anything about meeting Dan again. Mark does not like further discussion about Dan Paul anymore!

I quickly took my leave from his office and headed to the studio for my show. It was time for another motivation dance club show.

I was back in the air once again, as the studio engineer signalled me to start the show. I was five minutes late for the programme for the first time.

I hope my success wasn't getting into me. I remembered what one of my commanders used to say; never allow yourself to get intoxicated by success or defeated by failure! I placed on the headphones and started talking.

"Hello, good people of Lagos; this is your motivation dance cub DJ SST, on your favourite programme motivation dance club! I must apologise for opening the dance floor in your favourite club late this morning. But my people, it is not whether you are early or your late in life that matters the most, what matters is that you make sure you are in the right plane, and don't be like Pastor Jasmine Smith." I brought out the narrative on the pastor Jasmine Smith story and placed it in my front.

"Many of you will be asking who is Pastor Jamine Smith?" I coughed little to alert my listeners a narrative is about to start in the show.

"Pastor Jamine Smith was a great preacher. The one we normally identify as SMOG—Senior Man of God. He was not only known as a fervent preacher, but a miracle worker, and a leader of a great congregation as well. Above all, he was an enthusiastic evangelist, one who was always eager to travel around the world to preach the Good News!

One day, Pastor Smith set out to undertake a journey to Malawi. His flight was scheduled at the JFK International Airport to take off by 8 o'clock in the morning. Smith as a busy man, usually comes late even for a scheduled flight, but being a man of God, he always trusts it shall be well with him.

As he arrived at the Airport counter at a little past 8 a.m, the receptionist told him, his flight had taken off. He was shocked and angry. "Lady, am on the Lord's assignment. I have an appointment at Malawi with the Lord's family, I must be there today!" The lady replied that there was nothing she could do about it. But Smith would have nothing of that.

He continued to complain, visibly agitated. An airport worker saw him and on recognising him to be a preacher by the white collar on his shirt, came over and asked what the problem was.

Smith blurted, "look, young man, I have to be in Malawi today for the Lord's work, and this young lady is telling me my plane has taken off."

The man looked at him surprised "oh? To Malawi? Preacher, there must have been a mix up, the plane to Malawi is yet to take off, look at it over there at the tarmac, it is about to close."

Smith took off in a dash and entered the plane just as they were about to close the door.

He went to seat number 16 as indicated on his ticket. A lady was on the seat. He shouted at her.

"Lady, this is my seat. Am a pastor on a journey for the Lord's work." The lady insisted it was her seat, and a small quarrel ensued between the two.

One of the air hostesses sighted them, and moved over to their side. She asked, what the problem was, and on seeing the man was a preacher, her good manners took over.

"Pastor, there is no problem, we have an empty seat in the first class cabin, you can come over." Pastor Smith smiled and said to the lady sitting, "my dear, you can have the seat, my Heavenly father just got me a seat at the first class cabin! I'm going first class." He smiled following the hostess to the first class cabin.

Pastor Smith sat down and stretched himself in the first class cabin, thanking God; "Lord I have a business class ticket but you reward your servant with a first class seat, you are always faithful to those ready to serve you, I'm in first class now!" He decided to add to the comfort of the journey by taking a short nap.

He was soon awakened by the pilot announcing their arrival. "Ladies and gentlemen in the next twenty minutes we will be arriving at our destination in Rio De Janeiro, Brazil, fasten your seat belts as you observe . . . ." Smith was in a shock, he had an appointment in Africa, but he had travelled hours only to land in a different destination. He shouted for the air hostess. His suspicion was correct, he was in the wrong plane!" I concluded the narrative and shifted the paper aside to start the end of narrative exhortation.

"As I've said before, it doesn't matter how early you start or how successful you have been! Your life might have been moving fine all along, you might have been having a first class job, a first class career, a first class business. Your life might have all along been all first class, and people are always joining you to thank God for your first class achievements early in life. But please stop and ask God if you are really on the right plane! Check the basis of your first class success, and ask God if really, it's the plane that will land you in the right destination with Him!" I concluded.

"Now my listeners lets take a good lesson from that and always know that in life it does not matter if the plane takes off with us early or late, but what matters is if we are in the right plane. But I can assure you all; you are in the right dance club. So, who is going to give us the first dance steps today?" I was calling on my listeners to contribute to the show so as to stimulate more meaningful discussions. I picked the first call.

"Morning, SST, this is Jatau from Maryland, I'm happy to be on the floor this morning sir." He said.

"I'm happy to have you brother." I replied.

"SST, I been listening to you—but you can be in the right plane and not end in the right destination! People were in the right ship and the right direction when they got on the Titanic, but they didn't get to the right destination." He said.

"Yes Jatau, I agree with you, in life is not only getting in the right plane that guarantees our getting to our destination. I want you to understand that sometimes it is an issue of knowing who to call out to when we find ourselves in trouble in our journeys." I said.

"Yeah? What do you mean, SST?" He asked.

"Yeah, Jatau, in all aspects of life, trouble could come unexpectedly. It could be in business, politics, marriage, relationship or whatever. When trouble comes, we will find ourselves running helter shelter looking for help, but who do you actually call out to? Do we call out to the experts or do we call on the Master?" I asked.

"The Master? Who is that, SST?" He was curious.

"Jatau and all my listeners this morning, I want you to know how to go about the Titanic in your life, when it gets in trouble on your journey, and why knowing how to call on the Master will save your Titanic from destruction." I said.

I brought out a motivational narrative I wrote on the Titanic and started reading. This morning it looks like I was going to have lots of narratives to read.

"The Titanic was the greatest wonder of its time. When it was launched in 1912, it was the biggest man-made object, measuring 900 metres long and 175 metres high. It was the best act of engineering. On the day of its maiden voyage, it attracted the highest fanfare ever seen. The best engineers designed it. With full confidence in their ability and expertise, and even before the ship sailed, the engineers, relying on their wisdom, declared the Titanic unsinkable!

Likewise looking into the lives of many of us; maybe because your marriage was the talk of the town, or your spouse was the best of men you could find, and so relying on your wisdom, you enter into what you saw as an unsinkable relationship. Or maybe because you sit on the throne of a business empire that has a turnover in millions, and relying on your wisdom you were sure nothing could sink that your ship. Maybe because you possess intimidating credentials and relying on that, you believe your career is unsinkable! Or you had great godfathers who are in—charge of the system and relying on that, you believe that job or appointment must come to you as nothing could stop you from getting it. Maybe you place so much confidence in your own wisdom and knowledge, that you already see yourself victorious in what you are about to do, even before you start it, and you are sure there was no need to worry as nothing could sink your plans!

As the Titanic sailed, the ship captain received warnings of approaching icebergs. But he was not perturbed, because the ship was the best of its kind ever, it was unsinkable! He still maintained speed, he believed in the power of the ship and that he would still be able to steer it out of harm come what may.

Maybe you too believe so much in the power of your love, that when you start receiving rumours of the other woman or seeing changes in your spouse, you refuse to take it seriously and find out what was going wrong. Maybe you believe so much in the power of your friends or your godfathers! Or maybe it was your intelligence and skills that you relied on, such that despite clear signs that things were not moving right in your business, job, or with your career, you refuse to be concerned and do what you were supposed to do. Instead you took it lightly and continue the way you have been doing.

When the Titanic hit the iceberg, the crew gathered together and started deliberating on the next course of action. They however, thought themselves lucky, as they had the best engineers with them, even amongst those that design the ship. Those were the ones expected to bring a solution to the problem!

As your marriage, or your career, or your job or even your political campaign hit a big setback, you still remain assured, because you believe you have the best of experts, friends, and colleagues to advice you on the problem. You are confident in their wisdom and expertise!" I paused as I reached the point to give myself some rest.

"Looking at the Titanic as many did years past, it might be the way you also look at affairs of your life! But I want you to know that nearly 2000 years before the Titanic, a small wooden boat sailed from an obscured small port. But unlike the Titanic, there was no fanfare as it had only a few ordinary fishermen in it.

Maybe when you had that your marriage ceremony there was no fanfare, it was an obscure event because you were just an ordinary couple! When you started that career there was no fanfare because no one even knew you. When you decided to start that business, or that campaign, there was no fanfare because no one gave you a chance to reach your destination. And as the small boat sailed, the 12 fishermen saw signs of a gathering storm and became afraid, because they knew their boat was weak. And as your business starts moving on, you hear reports of inflation and you are afraid because you are aware that your capital is small. As you start on that job, you suddenly hear reports of retrenchments, and you are afraid because you know you had no high connections to save you at the office or maybe your credentials were weak.

When the small boat entered the storm, the fishermen started running helter-skelter in fear because they believe their boat could not withstood the power of the storm. When your business hit a crisis you started running helter-skelter because you believe your small business could not withstand the pressure. The fishermen were afraid as they saw the storm gather, they had no navigational experts to call on, like the Titanic, and so they were afraid. They had no experts to cry out to! But then, they remembered they had carried the Master along and he was not far from them! He was sleeping in the cabin below.

They decided to call on the Master! But they were still having some doubts! They had seen the Master perform miracles as he healed the leper, gave sight to the blind and faced many other challenges! But that was on land and they were now at sea! And that was just healing ordinary men, and this was a great disaster about to happen! They forgot to call Him because they thought He might not really tackle this challenge!

When your marriage hit the storm, when your business hit the storm, or your career hit the storm, you start running helter-skelter from pillar to pillar looking for help. You forget that God is not far from you and that He is always near and waiting for you to wake Him

232

to your call! You have seen God perform when out of thousands, you were chosen for that job, or that appointment! You have seen God perform when out of many you became the spouse! Or out of many more qualified applicants, you were given that contract. But now there is a problem in the marriage, in the job, or in the career, you are running helter-skelter, you are no longer sure if the God that choose you for all these, is also able to perform!

The Master came up and faced the storm! He did not address the storm. He had no time for that. He did not beg the storm; he is too big for that, he did not negotiate with the storm because it was not his method. The Master rebuked the storm! The Master knows the storm was supposed to bow and not to roar when he was around, because the storm had a name but a hidden face! Whatever names the devil has chosen to call the storm in your life; career failure, marriage crisis, financial crisis, health problems, failure, and disappointment! The face of the storm is known and the Master says they must bow! Sickness must bow, failure must bow, disappointment must bow, poverty must bow, and whatever forms the devil chooses to hide behind the storm to attack your life or to attack your life, he must bow before you!

The small boat that left without a fanfare reached its destination safely! The big applauded Titanic never did. The small boat that started without anyone paying attention over 2000 years ago is today celebrated as a success—and I want you to know that the business you started without a big capital or any chance of success will years from now be the talk of millions and generations! That marriage that you started without a fanfare and as an obscured ceremony shall set the off springs that will move generations! That career that you started without anyone paying attention will in many years from today, celebrated around the world.

The great Titanic that started with a big fanfare 100 years ago is today rued by many people! But the small fishermen boat of 2000 years is celebrated by millions! Because the Titanic carried experts and the small boat carried the Master! Because as the Titanic encountered a problem, the passengers relied on the wisdom of their experts and the strength of their ship! But as the small boat encountered a problem, the fishermen had no confidence on their knowledge or the strength of their boat, and they relied only on the Master! Because as the Titanic was sinking the passengers were calling for the experts, but as the small boat was about to sink, the fishermen were shouting for the Master." I stopped to take a small sip from my cup of water.

"My dear listeners, who do you see near you in time of trouble? Do you only see that storm gathering and forget that the Master is always near you, and will not abandon you? Who do you call to in times of crisis? Do you go about in fear and confusion looking for friends, godfathers or do you call for experts as the Titanic passengers did? Or do you, like the poor fishermen call upon the Master for help? Always remember the end of a matter is better than the beginning! A big fanfare at the beginning doesn't necessarily herald a happy fanfare at the end! And the end can only end well when you carry the Master along in your life boat. Cry to Him when the storms of life try to overshadow your marriage, job, business, ambition or happiness! The experts did not save the Titanic! And I want you to know that experts can't save your business, marriage, career, or life from disaster, only the Master can; just as He saved the poor fishermen!"

I concluded the narrative on that note.

"Now, my listeners, I'm sure you all know why we must learn to call on the Master at all time" I said.

Another caller came in.

"SST, this is Caroline from Victoria Island, I'm happy for the encouragement on the Titanic. It reminded me once again to know that in life, we have no one to trust or rely on but God! In my life, I have learnt to trust no one but God, because friends have failed me when I called on them in time of my affliction." She said.

"Yes, Caroline, Jesus wants us to know that only God is infallible, He is the Master and also a true friend and He wants us to be true friends too! But even if we can't save a friend from destruction, we shouldn't abandon them. Even when the experts could not save the Titanic, it did not make friends to abandon each other in the ship. The love of friends can survive the disasters brought about by the foolishness of the experts of our lives! Do you remember, the love of Jack and Rose? And how he gave his life for her when the Titanic was sinking?" I was referring her to the academy winning film, the Titanic.

"Please leave that, SST, that was just a film, who will want to die for a friend?" She asked rhetorically.

"Only a true friend would, my dear!" I answered her.

"And where will you find a true friend, SST?" I could feel the mocking laughter in her voice.

"Jones did!" I told her.

"Who is Jones?" She was sounding curious, like all my other listeners, she knows when I'm drawing to a narrative. I know that's what most of them love the most about my show.

"Jones was a British soldier during the Second World War who preferred to die with his friend than abandon him to perish alone." I told her. I brought out the narrative on the story and started reading.

"Jones and Jim (*real names withheld, my friends*) joined the army about the same time. It also happens that they were posted to the same regiment, where they got to know each other, and became very good friends. When the war broke out, they found themselves with their battalion at the warfront facing a heavy German formation. The battle was very heavy and the situation very bad, but not for Jones and Jim, who found solace in each other's company, occupying the same two man foxhole! One day, as Jones went to the rear logistic dump to get some supplies, the German army launched a heavy attack on their location, and within a short time the German force was overrunning their forward locations! Jones and Jim's deployment was at the forward location! The platoon commander ordered what remained of his men to retreat further backwards, but Jones bolted out, and made a quick attempt to run back to where Jim was! The commander shouted for him to come back to safety, but he could hear none of that as he ran back in frenzy in an attempt to go and save his friend. When their force was able to beat back the German offensive, the commander moved forward to check his men at the forward lines, he met Jim dead, and Jones bleeding by his side, 'you idiot' he shouted at Jack, 'I told you not to go back! Now see, I'm going to lose the both of you, instead of just losing one man!"

"Jones opened his eyes filled with tears and looked at his commander, struggling to speak, he uttered the words with difficulty 'I'm sorry for disobeying your orders sir, but it was worth it, before Jim died, he opened his eyes and saw me and said, Jones, I knew you will come back for me! Sir, I can't live knowing I abandoned Jim, knowing I never tried to help him." With those words he closed his eyes for the last time, the smile of contention still hanging on his face! The platoon commander realised that one can never know his strength or that of his relationship until both are tested by adversities."

I had finished when Caroline came back on the line.

"I was almost shedding tears, SST, how I wish I could have a true friend like that." She said.

"You can, my sister, you can be one yourself." I told her.

"Thanks SST" She said.

"Thanks for calling too Caroline"

The next caller was a lady with a personal problem. She had been out of job for a while.

"SST, I have been unable to get another job since the mass retrenchments."

There had been a mass lay off in the banking sector since the reforms brought in by the government to prevent a total collapse of the banking sector.

"I have been to many corporations but nobody seem to be employing these days, SST. I can't stay like that without a job, how am I going to pay my bills?" She lamented.

"My sister, you don't need to run from one big office to another, let them come to you."

"What do you mean, SST?"

"We all carry seeds that the world needs, great seeds that need a breeding ground. It may be small because it is a seed, but when planted it brings great fruits" I said.

"SST, I don't have any skill, I don't have capital, I have tried my hands on several businesses without luck. I only have to get a job in an office. SST, what else can I do?" She asked.

"There is always something you can do aside from working in an office. You only need to search for the seed in you. We all carry seeds of greatness, we all have great stars embedded in us that is waiting to be released to rise to its rightful place for all to see, whatever you need to succeed is in you, you don't need to go anywhere just look in your garage" I told her.

"my garage?" She asked.

"Yes! Whatever you need to succeed in life is all around you, for God has made all that a person needs to succeed to be available around him. But you need to recognize where it is first . . . you need to be humble enough to look in your garage. Steve Jobs started Apples incorporated not from running for an office space or from one corporation to another; he just started from his garage. Bill Gates started Microsoft not from seeking a partnership or desk job in any big firm, but he just started from his garage, Mark Zuckerberg didn't look far once he got the idea in his bedroom to start FACEBOOK, he simply went to his garage.

My friend, you are going up and down early morning from town to city looking for a job but God is saying come back, your success it is all in your garage. You are traveling far looking for a job when you have jobs to create lying in your garage! You are waiting in people's offices to pick a job when you have jobs waiting to be release to the world in your garage. You are looking forward to shuffling files on someone's table, but God is saying come back home and shift the junk in your garage and see the great things that I have for you.

You are running after the big bosses from office to office bowing from toe to knee but God is saying come back home to your garage and bow a little in your efforts and they will all be running after you. You think your success is lying in a big cool office somewhere but God is saying your success lies in the heat in your garage. You are looking all about the places for success, but God is saying just look around you and see the great success that He has for you hidden in your garage. King Saul was looking all about for what to fight

Goliath with, but David just looked around him and picked up the stones lying around. David looked around because he knew God always puts all that a man needs to success around him! God does not need to take you far to carry you high .... It is all in *your* garage! I want you to know that whatever God has for a person in life, is not in any far place but it is all around him, and He has kept it in his garage because He wants him to be humbled enough to look into his garage. Only humility can seat you in your garage and only humility can take you to where God wants for your life! The Law of recognition says everything you ever need to succeed in life is already within your reach. You just need to recognize it. You need to recognize what is in your garage! Dear friend, I don't know the garage God has given you in life .... maybe it is a small provision shop, maybe it is that small capital in your hands that you are looking down at, maybe it is the small idea that you have now which is looking silly to you, maybe it is that talent you are having that looks so ordinary to you, maybe it is that act that you can do but looks so low for your status to be engaged in, but God is saying look into it, it is what will give harvest to industries soon, it is what will lift you high to your destiny, stop narrowing your mind for who to employ you in life, and start opening your mind to whom you are going to be employing soon, be humble enough and start looking with faith into your garage and you will be surprised the great things that God has planted for your life right within" I told her. "Look into garage today!"

"Yes oh yes! Thanks SST; I believe there is something I can do. An idea I had for long, thanks, it has not been easy going about without a job, I'm glad you understand. I am going to look into my garage now" She said generously.

"Yes, I do understand Caroline." I said nothing of the days I walk the streets of Lagos in frustration looking for who wants my services.

She called back to thank me again.

Three more listeners called after Caroline and we had an interesting discussion before I closed the show.

As I was getting off from my seat, I could hear Mark calling me from inside his office. When I entered the office he handed me a card. I looked at it closely; it was another invitation card that was addressed to Chief Dokubo.

"That is an invitation to the convocation ceremony symposium that is organised by the Lagos State University taking place tomorrow. Chief Dokubo and other media moguls were invited as guest speakers. He wants you to represent him there too!" Mark gave me a gorgeous smile.

"What have I become Mark, a double body?" I demanded with a feigned anger.

Mark burst out laughing.

"Of course, SST, it's because Chief and all of us have a great confidence in you, that we feel you are the best man to go there! You are our hub, remember?" He was again referring to the name he had given me.

"I hope this time around there won't be any carnival shouting there too!" I said.

"All that depends on what the hub gives them! But I know what you can do, SST, bet me, they will shout hub too, that's how these students are!" He told me what I feared the most.

"Ok thanks, Mark, I got to be going. I have some shopping to do for Christmas." And with that, I left him to continue with his work.

The Motivation Dance Club
God Will Give You a New Song

The journey to Lagos State University took less than an hour. I would have made it in less time if not for the normal heavy morning traffic. The lecture was billed for 9 am, so I decided to go straight there from home, and not pass through the studio first as I use to.

When I arrived at the University, I met an usher waiting at the gate, who directed me to the hall where the lecture was to take place. I saw the place was filled with students, lecturers and invited guests already. I was led to my seat when one of the guests on the high table called out my name. It was Dan Paul again! I acknowledged his greetings, and shook the hands of the officials on the seats next to mine, before I took my place.

The symposium started in the normal fashion of calling on the guest speakers to deliver their lectures after all was said by the university officials. There was to be only two lectures, I was to deliver one, and one Mr Charles Chukwu from the Lagos State Television was to give the other. On the programme of events, my lecture was to come first, but to some last minute changes, I was shifted to be the second speaker.

Mr Charles Chukwu's lectures dealt on the need for preparation to emerging challenges which covered the theme of the symposium which was "Facing the challenges of life in an evolving world."

I took the stand to start my lectures. I could see the hall was very quiet and attentive; there was no sign of boredom in the crowd.

"The representative of the vice chancellor, president of the governing council, the board of overseers, members of faculty staff, lecturers, students and graduates. I want to congratulate the university authorities for such an inspiring theme which covers the contemporary issues that the graduates will face in the present world as they leave the university. I was once like the students here also undergoing training for a future endeavour. Though I was not in a civil institution like this, but the challenges were all the same.

The challenges you face under training is similar to the ones you will come across in other areas of your lives as you graduate and move to the outside world.

Some years ago, we all reported for training at the Defence Academy and today my colleagues are decorated as commanders in the Navy, commanders in the Air Force and Colonels in the Army! When my friends and I reported to the Defence Academy, as "raw civilians." We also had a desire we wanted to attain; a desire that we all committed to God!

When we arrived as young freshers at the Defence Academy, the senior cadets we met at the gates were all there waiting eagerly to torment us! Those of them that were above us, our seniors, were calling us with several derogative and demoralising names! Some said we were bloody civilians, others called us unfortunate human beings, some said we were armed robbers, a few spat on us. The rest just pass by without even giving the slightest regards to seeing us as fellow human beings. I was shocked as I was immediately discouraged.

I was suddenly losing hope in all that brought me there! My initial excitement has vanished. We hadn't done anything to them, why were they treating us so badly? I was told it was because we were at the lowest stage, the first termers! We were 'a nobody'! The fact that we were 'a nobody' was our only offence!

In life, those that life and circumstances had placed above you; your bosses, rich people, employers, leaders, in—laws, spouse or people that life had given them advantage above you, might attack you at times for no reason! They might attack you at the time of your greatest afflictions. They might attack you at the time of your greatest sufferings. They might attack you at the time of your failures; they might even attack you at the time of your trials, and all adding to your injury. Some might accuse you of what you don't know, some might just sneer you, giving you no regards because you are at the lowest ebb of your life! Some might call you with insulting names. You might feel discouraged, and lose your spirit, you might feel bitter that God has no plan for you and has abandoned you! And you might try to give up on Him, looking for success elsewhere. But don't you worry, God has not forsaken you! As long as you remain in His presence, His plans will soon unfold for you.

We were then made to sing so many songs by the senior cadets, containing names that were meant to dehumanised us, such as "I am a clown, I am a stone" and with terms that were meant to discouraged us, such as "I am a puttee material." All that made some of us to feel all hope was lost. But when the senior cadet, known as a cadet sergeant, who was to train us for our first bush camp came, he had a new word that he gave us, a song that he always wanted us to sing. He called it, "little tender cus cus, do not cry, you will be a senior, day by day." He said the song was to restore our hope in what had brought us there.

Because you are at the lowest ebb of your life, people will taunt you with so many names, they might call you barren, they might call you wretched, they might call you a failure, and they might call you names of what you are innocent of. And all other names that the devil wants to use to discourage you from attaining what God had prepared for you. But God will bring a new word, a new song of hope to your life, and when you sing it, and when you hear it; your hope in Him will be restored!

The cadet sergeant then handed us to the class above us, the second termers, many of them had names they love to be called with; some called themselves 'evil' some of them said they were 'devils' others just said we should know they were 'useless'. These second termers, that called themselves evil or devils, went about tormenting us day and night. But just at the time we were about to break down and run away, the cadet sergeant will appear and stop them, giving us a respite. But anytime he leaves, they will come back again and continue tormenting us, and just when it was getting too much for us to bear, he will reappear again and stopped them! I again asked why he allowed all the torture to happen to us! I was told he allowed the second termers to torment us, so as to train us for what we were about to attain. But he was never far away, and will not allow them to torment us beyond our will!

God might have destined you to attain a great marriage, a great business, or a great job. But He might still allow the devil to put you to a test, like He allowed the devil to test Job. It could be in the form of a calamity, a business or a career setback, or the death of a loved one. And while it looks as if the devil was about to destroy you finally, God will be there to rescue you. The trials of the devil might not end there, but God will not be far from your area of test, He is always there watching over you!

The cadet sergeant later told us that we should not mind the hardships in the training, and we should instead focus on the promise, the promise of a brighter future as contained in the song. The song said, as long as we continued to persevere and remained faithful in the face of the hardships, "We will be a senior day by day." Being a senior is what will take us to the gate of our ambition!

God is saying you should not focus on that length of barrenness; you should instead focus on the promise in His words for your future that you will go to the world and multiply! He said you should not focus on that financial problem; you should instead focus on His promise that He will always supply all your needs according to His riches. He said you should not focus on that persecution you are undergoing; you should instead focus on His promise that He will never forsake you. He said you should not focus on that threat to sack you from your job, to condemn you for what you do not know, or to forsake you by your spouse; you should instead focus on the promise in His word for you that all shall be well with you! And as long as you do not give up on God or run way from His presence, you shall reap His promises!

As long as you continue to persevere in that marriage despite the problems, as long as you continue to persevere in that business despite the setbacks, as long as you continue to persevere in that office despite the persecutions, as long as you continue to persevere in prayers despite the long wait in expectations! You will be a senior to that problem, a senior to that setback, a senior to that sickness, a senior to all persecutions, a senior to financial difficulty, a senior to barrenness day by day.

And so day by day, as we sang the song, we were becoming seniors to the problems that were tormenting us, and seniors to the humiliations that we were facing, without even consciously realising it, till one day we woke up and saw we had become the seniors in the academy, and we were therefore above all humiliations of the 'evils' and the 'useless' ones! I was so surprised when our salvation finally came! Though I knew we were persevering day by day and becoming seniors little by little and in four years, we will reach the top class in the Academy and be the most seniors. Nevertheless, the day all the persecution disappeared, all the humiliations disappeared, and we were like them that dreamt . . . four years looked like four days!

And I want you to know that the day God will lift away the humiliation of barrenness, the humiliation of spinsterhood, the humiliation of financial difficulty, the humiliation of career setbacks and all other difficulties that had kept you in captivity of the devil for so long, you will be like one that dreamt. Though, you know that you are getting over that marriage problem, day by day! Though, you know that you are getting over that career setback, day by day! Though you know you are getting over that business failure, day by day! Though you know you are getting over that sickness day by day, it will still come as a surprise the day they will all disappear! And you will finally enter the blissfully realm God has prepared for you. It would all look like a dream when it finally happens!

And so, one day, we woke up and saw ourselves at the top of the system, all those that we feared, all those that tormented us were all gone, we were on top, Halleluyah!

And I want you to know that one day all the business problems you are facing today, you will wake up and see that they are no more there and you are the one on top. All the sicknesses tormenting you today, you will wake up and see they are no more there—you are the one in control. The girls trying to steal your husband from you, you will wake one day and see they are no more there—you are the one on top! The people in the office that are persecuting you, one day you will wake you and they are no more there—you are the one in charge! And now when I see those tormentors, I fear them no more, they have no power to torment me anymore. I only laugh!

One day, the sickness that is tormenting you today, you will see it and laugh, because it cannot torment you anymore! One day, the commercial motorcycle rides that are always giving you a fright, you will see them from the windows of your bright new jeep and laugh, because they cannot frighten you anymore! One day, the long barrenness, or spinsterhood, that has kept you in sadness and humiliation for long, you will see it with your large family and laugh, because it has no power over you anymore! One day, the joblessness that was talking you from office to office, you will sit in your big office and laugh, because it cannot frighten you again!

And when I sit down today, I only tell the stories of the days of humiliation, the days of torments in the hands of the 'evils', in the hands of the 'devils', in the hands of the 'useless ones'! And so likewise, one day, you will sit down and only tell the stories of the days you could not have been able to buy that your car. You will tell the stories of the days; you could not have been able to build that your house. You'll tell the stories of the days you thought you could never get a husband. You'll tell the stories of those days that you thought that the sickness was going to kill you! You'll tell the stories of days you thought you could never reach that position or that rank. You'll tell the stories of the days you thought you could never find happiness in life, and the stories of the days you thought you could never be somebody that anybody would give any regard. You'll tell the stories of the days the devils tried to frustrate you in many ways from attaining what God had prepared for you when you were at the lowest ebb of your life, and the devil was persecuting you with all kinds of afflictions!

God did not forsake you, because you are His "little tender cuscus." And because you refused to run away from His presence, or give in to the struggle you were going through, God made sure you become a senior to those problems of failures, of humiliations, of disregards, and of bitter attacks day by day. And because you focused on His promises, and not on what you were going through, He will carry you to the top of that barrenness, joblessness, hopelessness, sadness and the loss of a loved one day by day! And one day, you can only see it, and laugh, and tell stories about it, because it cannot persecute you anymore, it cannot humiliate or torment you anymore!

So, whatever you are going through my friend, my brother, my sister; it is just a temporary trial, to prepare you for what God has for you. If you are able to persevere day by day in His promises, having faith in Him, and refuse to give up and run from His presence, you will be a senior to all that you are going through today! So, I say, please do not cry, God's 'little tender cuscus!' You will be a senior to spinsterhood, financial difficulty, failures, sicknesses, barrenness; a senior to hopelessness, and a senior to all humiliations of the devil over your life day by day!"

I had stopped as the hall was wrapped with a rapturous clapping. After a few minutes, the audience finished their clapping; I decided to end the lecture on a last note.

"In conclusion, life as I said, is all but a process of trying to attain a desire. And so, when we start whatever we set out to achieve in life, we must call on God to see us smoothly through. When you enter a marriage, you entered with the desire of having a great family, when you enter the university to study engineering; you entered with the desire of leaving with the title of an engineer. Or when you were born, and growing up, there was a desire that you will attain great heights, but in between, trials come to challenge you from achieving that position or achieving that status in life, and you find yourself at the lowest ebb of your life.   .

And you might be tempted to want to lose hope in God, or believe because it was not smooth, He was not there, or He was not able. And you would want to run away from pursuing your ambition—and by so doing, you unwittingly run away from what God has prepared for you! At the end, you cannot have a great career when you run away from the job or have a great marriage when you run away from the marriage. I say to you, whoever you might be, today, please persevere; God is never far from you in your time of trials. He will not allow trials to destroy you; your happiness, your career, your marriage, your family, your ambition or your business. Rather He will use the trials to unfold His promises in your life. And the trials will at the end, make you to realise that life is complicated, and beyond anyone's control.

It's only God you need to see you through the challenges of life in an evolving world as contained in the wonderful theme of our gathering today! And the humility you would acquire from this realisation will enable you survive whatever comes to you." I looked up towards the high dignitaries as I closed my lecture notes.

"As I come to the end of my lectures, I would like to once more express the gratitude of my Chairman, Chief Dokubo, whom I am representing today, to the authorities of this great institution and also extend his best wishes and prayers that you attain greater strides in the future. And to the graduates, I pray you carry the lessons you have learnt here that will assist you in future struggles as you enter the real world. Thank you and God bless you all." I had finished.

I took my bow and returned to my seat. The whole hall stood up and gave a long resounding applause to a speaker for the first time since the event started. I felt elated and honoured, there was no shouts of 'hub' as in Covenant university, it's either they didn't want to or have been cautioned against it. It all ended as I wanted all the same.

At the close of the ceremony, I saw Dan Paul exchanging views with some of the staff as I took my leave. I was walking down the hall corridor when I heard steps hurrying behind me.

It was Dan Paul once again.

"SST, I must once more congratulate you for another insightful speech." He was trying to get his breath as he caught up with me on the corridor.

"Thanks Dan." I replied.

"Your conduct once more convince me on the need of having such a great asset as you with us at Star FM." He was holding me by the elbows in a friendly and familiar pattern as we walked down the corridor to the car park.

"I thought I have given you my answer on that, Dan." I said with a smile.

"No, you have not, SST! I tried your personal number twice and it was always busy. I considered myself lucky to meet you again." He said.

"No, Dan, I want to make it clear, I can't come over to work with you. Static FM gave me a chance when all have rejected me including you." I could see he was surprised at my words. "Maybe you can't remember me from the time I came to your office and you turned me away. I don't want to remember the experience, but aside from that, I'm committed to Static FM and nothing is going to make me move to another radio house." I said with a clear final note.

"SST, I'm sorry about what might have happened before, but I can't remember as you said" He shook his head apologetically "but I'll still advice you not to turn your back on us, Chief Chekwas won't like that, it will affect him more than you can think and that won't be good for you." He said in a very cold voice.

"Dan, please do not get desperate and give me that silly threat. I own myself, and will determine where to work, and not you or your Chief, period!" I could see he was very unhappy with my response.

Who cares? He had his chance!

I turned to go "Dan thank you and I wish you the best. I'm always available as a friend but not a co-worker, good bye." I left him standing and staring at me.

It seemed I had annoyed him with the manner of my reply. I didn't really wanted to do that, but as the elders say, a person can't walk without his head shaking; you cannot go through this world without annoying someone!

When I got back to the studio I told Mark of another unexpected meeting with Dan Paul.

"You mean that swine threatened you?" He asked furiously.

"No, I don't see it like that, he was just trying to tell me that they were serious about their offer." I tried to assure him. I regretted telling him of my meeting with Dan Paul, seeing the hard way he was taking it.

"Well, next time he does that again, I will drop a complaint with the police. I can't have anybody harassing my staff." He said angrily.

"Ok Mark, thanks. I hope it won't come to that! Hey, how about that game of snooker you promise me?" I said, trying to digress away from the Dan Paul discussion that was getting sad. We took some minutes talking about the snooker game, and the usual latest events in the English Premier League before I quietly slipped away and headed back home at the close of the day's work.

The Motivation Dance Club
The Devil Came in the Flesh

The next day I was early at the studio, giving me enough time to put in good preparation for the show. I had put the episode with Dan Paul behind me, after my discussion with Mark. It wasn't that I was really giving it any serious consideration anyway. I can't work with someone I do not like, and the pompous oaf, Dan Paul, was certainly one of such. I like Mark and the rest of the crew at Static FM. It would take more than money to take me away from their side. I intend to remain static at Static FM.

This day, was New Year's Eve and I started my programme with varied load of encouragement and motivational tit bits for my listeners.

"Good morning all, this is your friend, DJ SST! I am here once again on your favourite show, the motivation dance club! And we have a lot of interesting music to play, so get your dancing shoes on this New Year's Eve and groove on!"

I hope that would stir up their interests as usual.

"Whatever you are facing today, the hard economic situation, the rising insecurity in Lagos, or your partner is threatening to abandon you, please put all fears behind, because fear will only carry you to the rear! When you are pushed against the wall, and there is no way out—then it's time to go against whatever is pushing you! It's time to face your fears! And the moment you are ready to face your fears it's the moment your fears would not be ready to face you!

You cannot find a river that is straight and wide, because rivers meander to avoid their fears! But the oceans are straight and wide because an Ocean removes all fears by facing up to its oppositions!

And it is only in the ocean that you have the great things in the water—the sharks, the whales and many others!

Whenever God is about to take you to a new level, you would confront greater oppositions! On your way to a new level there will be a new devil. There will be new battles to fight, new obstacles to overcome. Most a times, God uses your adversaries to promote you! Joseph's father loved him so much that he did not want him to leave his side for a moment, but it was the hatred of his brothers that carried him to his great destiny in Egypt! David's brothers wanted him to be safe by avoiding fighting Goliath, but it was in confronting the great opposition posed by Goliath that the seed to his greatness was found! My friend, in that hatred, opposition, misfortune that you are facing in your life lies the seed of your greatness; confront it! The lion came against David, it ended as a testimony, the bear came against David, it ended a testimony, the great Goliath came against David, and it ended as a great testimony of the achievements God has given David! Whatever is coming against you today will end as a testimony tomorrow!

Do not be discouraged by what you are lacking now. It's not what you have at hand that will get you what you want, but what God is ready to do for you! Moses went to Egypt with only the rod in his hands, and he left with over three million people and the riches of the land! Joseph went to Egypt with only the clothes on his back and he ended up with the control of the riches of the land! I don't know what little thing you are holding in your hand today that is making you feel inadequate, but I want you to know God can turn it to a substance of wonder! It's not goods you need but God! It's not drinks you need but dreams! It's not fear you need but faith. It's not struggle you need but strength! And God is able to give you all that you need. The fact that you are not seeing it doesn't mean it is not coming to you! You are not seeing it because you are looking for it the way you know—God is bringing it the way only He knows!

Whatever you might think you have lost in your life before is nothing compare to what you are about to gain when it's your time! Abraham Lincoln lost four elections but when it was his time, he won the presidential elections! Barack Obama could not get a seat at the democratic convention in 2000, but when his time came, he got a seat at the White House! Jacob Zuma was dragged before the court as a vice president, but when his time came, he was taken with honour to the presidency! A knockdown is not a knockout, all great men have received a knock down in their lives but they all came back on their feet, because a knockdown is not a knockout! Whatever you lose in life, never try to regain it with tears; use hard work!

Victory will always be yours because God is cancelling all the appointments of the devil in your life! The appointment with failure, disappointment, death etcetera, in order to bring you into an appointment with success and greatness!

You are a precious being, created by God Almighty. And God is not short-sighted that He would create you without planning for you! He has picked the right partner, right career, and all the right breaks you need in your life! You only need to be patient and wait for the unfolding of His plans in your life. I don't mean sit down and wait! I mean do your part in unfolding your destiny! And when you do your part, God will add more to you! And you will continue to have more because to them that have, more shall be added to them!

Failure is a crawling python, if you do not know how to run fast, it will swallow you! And also, my friend be careful when you are successful, because success is a raging beast, if you do not know how to tame it, it will tear you! Success has a way of making an achiever the victim of misguidance!"

I came to the end of my introductorily speech in the style my listeners were well getting used to!

"Now who is ready to come to the dancing floor and show us his or her steps this morning? DJ SST is ready with the best music in town for the dancers." I said.

The phone was already ringing. I took up the receiver from the hook and pressed the receiver button. "Hello this is DJ SST, on Motivation Dance Club. What have you got for us this morning?" I said.

"Hello, SST, I just want you to know I have been enjoying and following your programmes." It was a lady caller. She sounded

252

reluctant to speak, not quite sure of herself, as if not certain whether to continue the call or not! I tried to encourage her to go on.

"Good morning, my dear, you are welcome, are you a dancer in my club, a new arrival, or the usual gate crasher?"

Those that have been calling regularly on the show and I had become familiar with their names and I call them my club dancers, while any first caller is known as a new arrival at the dance club. The gate crasher reference was to introduce some humour.

"But of course, my dear, I know you didn't gate crash. The bouncers would have informed me of your action, or did you knock them out with your dressing? You know what I mean?"

I remember when ladies say they dress to kill! If dressing could kill, knocking out should not be a problem to it. I could hear her laughing at her end.

"Noooh, SST, I didn't do anything of such; maybe I'm so drab and ordinary that they didn't notice when I slipped in! Anyway SST, just want you to know I enjoy your show, you're good man!"

I blushed whenever my callers compliment me. I appreciated it, but really, I wish they wouldn't go about it so often.

"Thanks, my dear, you have any steps for me, or you just want to sing for our idol show?" I said.

Everywhere you go there is idol this, idol that, why not have one in my show? It's supposed to be a dance club, isn't it?

"Mmmhhh," she was just laughing.

I knew I should move on to other callers, but something just kept me going with this lady! I was not really like that, taking time discussing frivolities with a caller when other callers with problems that needed attention were waiting. But something kept me with her!

"Well, SST I don't know how to start." She said softly.

"Of course you know how to start! You can just start from the beginning!" I answered her.

It was then I recalled she didn't tell me her name. I always like talking to my callers on first name level, not minding if it is their real names or not. I can understand some people don't want to mention their real names on radio, considering the kind of secrets they reveal about themselves.

"SST, really I feel I'm not worthy to be here." She spoke softly again, displaying a reluctance to speak out. I immediately got interested! From experience, such people have interesting stories that will make my day.

"My sister, don't worry, you have come where your problems will be attended to." I was cajoling her to speak out! "And please I didn't get your name or you don't feel like telling me?" I said.

"It's not like that SST! It's just that I don't think I should say what I want to say." She was shying away. I was right, she didn't want her name to be mentioned, there's a story alright!

She came back reluctantly.

"Ok, SST, my name is Joan." She said.

Joan like hell!

No problem, I can use that name, names are like ages, they really don't count on my show, because you hardly get the true dose, all the same I just needed it for the reference.

"Ok Joan, what's the issue, let me see your steps, the floor is all yours now." I decided to spur her, I haven't got all day even if she was my only caller.

"Joan, let's hear you before our show time is up, and we might just miss you for life!" I was pushing her.

That seemed to wake her and from then she started coming out like a canary. When something is bottled up for long inside someone, and it wants to spurt out, a small nod will collapse the whole balloon.

"SST, you see I never knew my life will drain to this level. I was not brought up to be like this. I had a good family upbringing, nice parents that wanted the best for me; it was not meant to be like this for me. I bet I was led astray by the company I made in school."

That's it, she is talking now!

"I went to an all girl's school. I came from a religious home with a very strict father. I guess when I was at home, the restriction was too much, and we don't watch films or go out or do what other kids of our ages do. My father sees it as a bad influence on us. But when

I entered boarding school, I was away from his direct influence and that's when my life started to derail" She took a small pause. I guess she had reached an important junction and wanted to organise.

I brought out my biro to take note, not necessarily to ask her questions but to form an idea of which narrative I will use that will serve her purpose.

"At first, I got lured by the adult magazines the students bring and hide in the hostels under their mattresses only to bring them out secretly at night." She said.

I know the typical things that happen in girls boarding school, her case wasn't really something revealing—or maybe not yet!

"You know, all that awaken feelings in me that I never knew existed. It was the senior girls that lured us, the junior ones, into all that. At first I thought I could still be able to resist because of my hard upbringing. I should have run away from the beginning! I now know that until you learn to run, you cannot outrun the devil!

We had what we called school mothers, you know, a senior student that takes a junior girl under her personal care for protection and guidance? That's what it was supposed to be really, but in my case it was a different story. My school mother turned me into something else! She introduced me to lesbianism. I was practically her sex slave, to please her when and how she wished. You won't want graphic details, SST." She laughed. Of course not! Surely not what I need here! I quickly answered.

"No, my sister, this is a respectable dance floor, you must go on the stage with your clothes on, it's not a nude club you know!" I laughed back. But I noticed she was silent for a little long before continuing and with a little hard edge in her voice.

It must be something I said.

"Oh, SST, as I was saying about my school mother, she later got me to join her in sneaking out of school, jumping over the fence to go to parties at town where she hands me over to different men. I was no longer the innocent angel my parents raised. I did my best to hide my new self from my parents. Whenever I go home on holiday from school, I did my best to act the good girl! You know the regulations,

SST? Go to church, say morning prayers, dress the nun! My parents never suspected anything. They were still thinking all was well.

Well, maybe what they were seeing was normal, but my soul was way gone, SST, gone from God where my parents once led me to." She was sobbing quietly now.

There was no way I can give her a handkerchief across the radio, so I tried to console Joan, as best as I could.

"Sorry, dear I'm so sorry. It's all right; it's all going to be fine" I said. Of course I wasn't going to tell her to continue. It's always better to allow the person feel you care more about the situation than the story, which normally keeps them going the more with their talks. She continued with her story after a while.

"Thanks! The school authorities soon found out when one of the girls fell sick and was discovered to be pregnant! She revealed our secret. I didn't tell you, SST, it was a missionary school, yes, a missionary school, where we were all expected to say prayers daily and do all the religious stuff. The school authorities was scandalised, we were all interrogated, and what do you expect? We all denied it. The school authorities weren't fooled, they are very strict on such matters, and we were supposed to be virgins till we graduate from the school.

We were all tested on admission, just one of their rules to keep us chaste and maintain the reputation of the school. They decided to carry out a pregnancy test on all of us. When the pregnancy test results came out, I and my friends failed, of course. But mine was even worse. SST, you know I told you I was young and naive? Well, that explained how I was certified 3 weeks pregnant! What you force down will one day force you out." She laughed ruefully as she continued with her story.

"The school was supposed to send for our parents before sending us away, as it was in the regulations, but out of anger, you see SST? It had never happened in the school before . . . we were all expelled that day. My school mother, her friends and I. But expelled to where? I wasn't going back home! I would rather die than face my parents, especially, my dad!" She said.

She speaks like somebody really scared when she mentioned her father!

"My father was the perfect example of a pious man in the community and he always wanted his family to be seen as the model of a Christian home. So you can understand how he must have felt when that happened." She said.

Yes, I can understand how it is! When a man starts seeing himself as an example, the devil will start holding him for an examination. His life and his work will come under attack of the devil. Sometimes, it's better we allow some room for shortcomings in our lives.

"We were kept under the care of the school matron before our parents come for us, we couldn't bear being taken home so we escaped at night; we were adept at jumping fences anyway! And so I followed my school mother to Lagos. She and her friends were much older than me. She was expelled in her final year and I in year two." She said.

Wow just two years in college and she got herself into all that?

As if she was reading my thoughts, she said' "It sounds so fast to mess one's life, don't you think, SST? Well, it's always hard to get to learn and live the right life. But the influence of evil is so powerful; if you aren't strong, it can sweep you in a day and land you trouble for years! Just Imagine, what my parents build for fourteen years was completely wiped out in two years. I have learnt that when you give the devil a little chance he will take over your life, and if you open a little chance God will leave your life!" She exclaimed.

I agreed with her totally!

"It was in Lagos that my story really started. I became a full time commercial sex worker here, I'm sure you will permit me to use that term." She laughed loudly.

Yeah, I knew two or three names to call it too! But I agreed with her commercial sex worker will be just fine for the show!

"We were moving from one place to another satisfying the rich men, politicians, military top brass, just anybody with money, SST, even religious figures" She laughed loudly. "They prefer we meet them in the secret of their homes, they have families, you know? And moreover, we were so young, and so they preferred we meet in secret houses than in hotels. We get handsomely paid at the end of the day. These days more money is kept at homes than in banks and more prostitution is done in homes than in hotels." She lowered her voice to a tone that sounds conspiratorial.

Yes, I know how it is with the corrupt elite in the society . . . The decay in our society is a collective statement on how far we have moved away from God . . . . and how far God is moving from us!

"I won't mention names, my people out there." Her voice came out loudly on the radio. "But we really live in a funny world. No wonder my parents were fooled for so long. We are all being fooled one way or the other, my people." She was speaking firmly now, and loudly too, like a teacher admonishing her pupils. I suspected she was speaking directly to the audience, so I let her be.

"The commercial sex business, was not that easy going and lucrative for long. These men won't want you once they have had you! There are younger girls, young teenagers joining every day, once they had a taste of you, they lose interest and go looking for some new girls out there. And these men prefer little girls the more, something about it being a good elixir for aged men! So, the more you get lubricated, the less lucrative the business becomes for you! You understand me, SST?" She said slyly!

Of course I do! But it's not my place to answer that on a radio programme!

I just laughed, and urged her to continue.

"Well, SST we soon lost our important customers, you know? When you call their lines, it's always busy? Meaning you are out from their lists? The money coming to us started reducing. Our friends when we had money started leaving us. Money doesn't leave you without a warning, SST!—People start leaving you first! So we had to change our style, in order to survive in the only thing we knew how to do! We thought about going to the streets, but we were too proud to stand by the roadsides, it's for the low class worn out workers, we were young and classy." She said.

Yeah, I know every job has its pride base. I have long given up on receiving calls from other listeners now, this girl has taken over the floor, maybe when she is through others will start calling in—she was back talking.

"Soon we were attracted to the various nude clubs that sprung up in town; you see SST, I know how to dance on the floor, with or without, you know what I mean? Depending on which dance floor I got myself in, sir." She said, laughing out loudly.

This *girl has a sense of humour* I thought.

I can remember when the nude clubs first came to our relatively conservative society. It was started by some bold youths that brought the idea from their stay in America. At first, they faced serious opposition from religious groups and the government. But the moment one or two people are bold enough to come out and do openly what everybody is ashamed of, (but what some secretly loved) the danger of it being a societal norm is just a matter of time!

I refused to comment on that and instead prodded her to continue with her story.

"We were arrested once, and the club closed. We had powerful friends or should I say clients? Before you know it, we were back to business big time! SST, I knew my life had gone down the drain; my body became an object of dirt, for any man from anywhere to touch and play with. Sometimes those touches are not as human as they seemed!" *Her voice was now going low and scary.*

"There was this rich, big and very dark in complexion man that use to come to the club and spray us with big money. He took an immediate interest in my school mother and one of her friends, and seeing how protective she became towards him, all the girls, including me, kept off, though he had shown he never wanted me anyway! We use to give lap dance on our bare butt to the men while they sit down and enjoy the view and their drinks. It doesn't matter who gives to who as long as he pays, but my friend got so possessive towards this man and so most girls kept off." She said.

I guess this girl's story has carried the day; when you add my narrative and exhortation at the end of it, of course. I was sure other listeners have glued their ears to their radios; Lagos people love such lurid gossip!

259

"The customers were not supposed to touch our bodies, when we dance naked on their laps or use their hands and tongues on our private parts! But this man got so absorbed with my friends that they allowed him to break all the rules openly. The house chairperson that was to impose the rules didn't care in his case as the man tips him well. He put his hands and tongue into everything, you know what I mean, SST?" She asked.

Was I supposed to know? Yeah I'm over 18, but we have all kinds of listeners out there, the radio is not a secured line! There are some things you are expected to learn in life and there are some things you are expected to know!

I told her to continue with her story and stop interrupting to ask what I do or do not understand!

"Well, this man just one day stopped coming, of course none of us knew his address or where the man came from! Men go to nude clubs for a moment of madness; they are not there to build long acquaintance or discover love!" She was taking a deep breath before continuing with her talk. She was so eloquent and flowing and I know the listeners would have no problem following her story.

"And as if by arrangement my friends started falling sick from that day! We tried all we could, from spending our small fortune on medical treatment to going to spiritualist for help, before long their bodies started oozing pus from all openings! SST, the club had long sent us away. They said what happened to my friends was not good for their business! But I suspected they wanted to get rid of us long before, anyway. Their customers wanted to see new faces, they have messed us up enough and don't want a taste of us anymore." *She* said in a sad voice.

After what seemed like a long silence of sad reflection, she got herself together and continued her story.

"It was a day to my friend's death, that we were directed to a man of God who revealed everything to us! You know, SST, the Bible said we should be kind to those we associate with as we might one day entertain angels that took on human skin!" She said boldly. *This girl had not completely lost her pious roots. I could detect a revered tongue when she talked of what the Bible said on angels. Well no matter how the tree withers, the roots even when dry remain attached. But I believed she was just saying out what she got from the man of God, I just kept listening to her, I'm an audience now, no more a moderator.*

She was talking firmly and intelligently.

"It's not only angels that do take on human skin, SST, the devil does it too! The devil was created an angle too remember? It's not always that the devil deceives us to do what is wrong, sometimes he gets enticed to come down and take a part in it too!" She said forcefully what was in her mind.

"For years, we had slept with men we knew and those we don't even know, those the devil deceived us to deceive, and those that came out to deceived us to his acts. But never had we slept with the devil himself, all the time we were moving from one bed to another. And it was like that, till I met him in the flesh in the confines of that nude club. And as no man sees God and live, likewise no one who touches the devil can survive. He will first destroy your life completely, mess up your destiny, nothing will work in your life; before leading you to a miserable painful death. I guess in our case there was not much of a life to destroy, anyway! What remained for the devil was to lead us to the horrible end that beholds all those who relate with him in flesh. The sin you cannot end today is the sin that will end your tomorrow, and with most of us it is our lifestyle that limits our lifespan. The things that would finally destroy us the most are not the big things of life, but the little things we just can't stop ourselves doing them!" She admonished quietly as she observed a brief break.

I must admit I was overwhelmed with sad feelings to the point of shedding tears for her.

That was very unusual in my case.

I never knew this girl was going to say such a powerful life-teaching lesson. If I had known earlier, I would have placed her on a special programme, and alert our listeners the day before, to be on a watch out! It was a story many would love to draw some lessons from, not only ladies. She was back again on the air talking confidently as ever.

"It's all over now, SST; I can't do it no more! God is giving me a last chance to escape from hell and I can't miss it now. It's been

261

four years since I had a direct relationship with my parents or even a contact. My father had forbidden any of my siblings to have anything to do with me since the day he was told of my expulsion from school! I later got to know that my mother had been crying her eyes out for me all these years. She had been on fasting and prayer session for me, SST! She was once in the hospital for denying her body food for long in fasting for me. My dad threatened to send her out if she tried to come look for me." She was sobbing silently on the phone.

It took a while before I could get her back on air again.

"SST, I was told by a neighbour's friend whom I met at Ikeja, that when my father heard I was pregnant and cursed me! My siblings also joined! Do I need to say what my church people say about me when they also got to hear about my case, but my mother has been crying and singing praises for God's favour over my life." She burst out crying loudly, I had to cut off the connection and put a musical interlude, apologising to listeners, while I wait for her to get hold of herself.

She was back in a few minutes, but her voice was still shaking.

"For the first time in their over twenty years of marriage, my dad slapped my mum. But she never was bitter about it, never once talked back, but kept on praising, fasting and praying, and never lose heart whenever a curse was released on me." She was sobbing quietly.

Yeah, I know how soft mothers love their children! I believe her father was just being a natural man; hard and highly reactive. But can you blame such a man, after all he has been through? I was left ruminating silently.

Her voice was very clear when she came back on the radio "Please, I'm not accusing my dad." She said.

This girl must be a mind reader, as her next reply answered my thoughts. Well, it's normal with an intelligent mind, she sure was an intelligent person from my assessment of her.

She was very considerate of her father's behaviour towards her.

"Who am I to accuse him?" She said of her father "He is a deacon in the church, a pious and hardworking man who gave the best he could afford to his family, only to be disgraced in the eyes of the world! It is too much for any man to bear! I am the first child he used to love so much but now he hates me so bad!" She narrates her story with great pains in her voice as she talked of her father.

Love breeds the worst kind of hatred. Nobody would hate you with intensity if he never loved you with same intensity.

"From the day I ran away, my two younger sisters found themselves sitting on hot iron pins in the house. They dare not even talk in my dad's presence, because he became very hard and bitter towards everyone in the house. It was not surprising they hated me too! But despite all, mum kept believing and praying for me even as I have destroyed the joy of her once blissful marriage!" She was gaining control of herself now.

I guess in every story there is a high point where our emotions has to rise. But as soon as we passed that point, we would be able to get hold of ourselves once again. She was soon back because she continued with her story

"I now understand why the huge black man was so hostile to me whenever he comes to the club. My late friend, my school mother, once invited me to the seat where she was giving the man, the devil, a lap dance. As soon as I move in, he moved away as if touched by fire, and warned her strongly not to ever invite me near him. And whenever he enters the club and sees me, he moves away from where I am sitting. I just thought he had an issue against me and generally avoided him too, especially as he was a good friend to my mentor. I didn't want her thinking I was making her best client uncomfortable. She would beat me up! You see, I was still her slave, just as it was when we first met in college!" She stopped talking and paused.

I knew she was trying to get her breath back; it had been a long story. Such things are normally hard to come out. People, once reluctant to speak about the dark secrets of their lives, will open up once they start and wouldn't know when to stop.

"SST, I now realise it was the prayers of my mother that was hedging around me in the confines of my miserable life! I thought the big dark looking man was just uninterested in having me entertain him like the other girls! I didn't know the devil himself was scared of me! My mum was sending a power that was so strong, that he

263

could not handle!" She said with the confidence of someone that has authority!

She was back sobbing again! *Women!*

"SST, I want to go back home pleaseee!"

She was still sobbing quietly again as if pleading with me to do what was in my power. Who, me? Carry her home? How? I don't even know her! She was just a statistic digit amongst the hundreds of people in Lagos that call in my programme and relay their problems daily! This is a radio call in or talk show if you like to call it that, not a family reunion forum! I was holding a motivational talk to direct people on how to handle and solve their problems, and not to carry them back home! Yes, I accept that by the loving grace of God, the show has been achieving good success in helping people with their lives. But it has a limit!

She got control of herself and came back on air.

"I'm eager to be with my family and seek their forgiveness! But will my dad accept me? After all these years, can he find a place in his heart to accept me and take me back in his house? I don't mind being a servant at home if only they will accept me back! Anything is alright with me, I just want to leave Lagos and go back to Ibadan and leave my former live completely. I was on a good path to being something in life before the devil deceived me. Sometimes, the devil will tempt us with peanuts when he sees God preparing us a great dish! I don't want to be reminded of what happened! I just want to go back home!" She was sobbing and repeating herself continually.

Ibadan town? Good! I now know where she came from! Unfortunately, whatever I have to say will matter not to her family in Ibadan. Our FM station is still struggling to cover the length of the ever-expanding Lagos not to talk of reaching Ibadan. FM stations have shorter range, than the AM or SW stations. I just hope my listeners were aware of that!

"Joan, please take heart, take heart, my dear. God is faithful when we come to Him. He rewards to the least all we did for Him and forgives to the last all we did against Him." I said softly into the microphone. "God arranges your life as you arrange your new steps. What is in the past is gone and has no bearing to God's plans for your future! When David was told his son was dead, he stopped crying and washed up and was merry because he knew his past has nothing to do with his future. Your past failures have nothing to do with God's plans for your future successes! Comeback to God, He is looking to establish your glory and not to hear your story!" I was trying the best way I know to console her. I'm a motivator not a consoler, anyway, I'm beginning to learn they all go together.

She had stopped sobbing and her voice came very clearly on the air.

"SST, sometimes when I look back I get angry at all those people that exploited my naivety, I feel so . . ." She started.

I quickly cut in! I can't have her getting angry on my show, just when the listener's sympathy had built towards her situation. It was better she continued sobbing than getting angry, sympathy could bring her result—anger will not!

"No my dear, don't be angry! God does not want us to be angry. When we smile God smiles with us, when we laugh God laughs with us and when we cry God comforts us. But when we get angry God leaves us. For the anger of man does not work the righteousness of God. Whatever your situation may be always learn to smile and laugh over it, count it all joy for God has overcome your trials and He has forgiven you." I hope she was listening and stopped getting angry.

"The prodigal son was forgiven by his father, I see no reason why your father, a man of God as you said, will not also forgive you when you go back to him in repentance. Some things are too late to be mended, but they are never too late to be forgiven. And there is no true forgiveness that comes without some amendment. Anyone can feel for himself but for one to feel for another, you must have a feeling for God. I'm sure your father, as you claim is a man of God and will still have feelings for you!" I said coolly drawing reference to the parable of the prodigal son in the Bible. The prodigal son returned home after a sojourn of riotous living abroad, and was receive warmly by his father. I thought it an appropriate reference, as I believe I was dealing with another prodigal child here. I started talking directly to my large listening audience to pass across my message.

"Ok, before I allow in any calls from listeners to tell us what you have to say about Joan's story, let me read a narrative to Joan. And also, to her family if they are listening on the need for forgiveness."

I knew my listeners within Lagos will now be glued to their radio sets to hear another story, especially after the excitement of Joan's touching story! Some of them must be itching to call. You know how it is with people; eager to give a sanctimonious sermon, typical of what people do when someone has fallen! But now that I have a story to tell, they will not mind waiting till I'm through. People love stories.

I gave my trademark small cough whenever I'm about to start reading a narrative.

"Joan, Clinton James was a young man that left home like you did, and found himself in terrible situation while roaming around in sin. Clinton was brought up in a God fearing home by very good Baptist parents in a small town in Oklahoma, the United States. His parents were good church members who brought up their two sons in the way of the lord. But as the kids grow up, their youngest son, Clinton, started mingling with bad company and picking bad habits that were strange to the teachings that Mr and Mrs Mathew James gave their children.

He left home and joined a bad company in the city of Los Angeles. His mum broke down physically from the anguish of his behaviour that she was confined to a wheel chair. With five years past and Clinton was nowhere to be found, because he had stopped communicating with his parents since he left home after a fight that led him to slap his mother. But his parents had not ceased praying for him, unknown to Clinton.

In Los Angeles, Clinton got himself involved with drugs and pornography and all the social vices the city could afford. One day, there was a fight between the drug gangs, Clinton's two friends were shot dead and he was left lying on the street with a bullet in his leg. In the hospital, there was nobody to cater for him or pay his bills, he was left in anguish and pains when a missionary organisation on evangelism heard about him and took over his care and bills and also kept on coming on visitation to his hospital bed. Clinton became highly remorseful over his behaviours and realised God spared him in the drug fights because God still loves him. Clinton decided to come back home after 12 years of no communication with his parents.

He wrote a letter to his parents asking for forgiveness and added, "Mummy, daddy, I'm coming back home. If you are ready to accept me back please put a white handkerchief on top of one of the trees behind our home so that if the train passes and I see it I will know you have forgiven me." Clinton's home was near and adjacent to the railway station.

On that day, Clinton was returning home, he sat solemnly in the train praying and asking God that his parents find it in their hearts to forgive him. As the train approaches his home, he looked out of the window and saw not one handkerchief hanging on the tree behind his home, but dozens! And not only white handkerchiefs but white bed sheets, white pillow cases and anything white that his parents could find! No matter what someone has done, no matter how much they messed themselves up, there is always something to admire about someone when you love he!"

I was sure that will give a message to anybody related to Joan to know that forgiveness is always possible where there is love.

"So, my listeners on Static FM 111, I'm calling on you all, parents, brothers, sisters, husbands, wives and whatever we are! Let us always remember forgiveness is the key to soul cleansing! God has forgiven us all our sins, is now left for us to also forgive and accept back those who erred!

Joan, please go back to your parents, your past is gone, you are now a new creature and I'm certain God will touch their hearts to welcome you back with a thousand white handkerchiefs." I concluded.

Joan came up again she sounded still disturbed. "But SST, who would want me now? You know I'm a lady. I'll get to marry one day and raise a family but my life has a story, you know." She said.

"Yes, Joan," I said to her. "Our lives all have stories too! I always say there is nothing like a bad person, maybe somebody less fortunate than you, maybe less loved or less guided but certainly not a bad person. If all abandon you, God will bring someone that will lift you up, someone with a story like Jimmy." I said. Joan burst out laughing. "Who is Jimmy, SST? You've got another story?" She was still laughing!

"Yes Joan, Jimmy had a story too! Jimmy was in second grade when he met a story like his. He was to have a dog show at school. The kids were told to go to the local dog station and pick a dog each. When Jimmy reached the local dog husbandry, he saw the other kids running to pick the dogs, but one little dog was left alone in the corner. Jimmy was attracted to it so he went to the dog. The headman met him and said, "oh you won't want that dog if you know its story." He said. Jimmy replied, "I want to hear it." The man replied disapprovingly. "You see my boy, little Billy was hit by car as a puppy, it's no good, it can't run like the rest, you won't want it."

Jimmy picked little Billy up and held it to his chest, he then dragged up his left trousers. He had iron fixed to his legs too! The headman was shocked. Jimmy said, "I'll run with little Billy, it needs someone that understands." He said quietly holding little Billy that nobody ever wanted because it had a story. Jimmy had a story too! Jimmy lost a leg in an accident when he was just 2 years old. He never got to run fast in his life. Just like little Billy! And Joan, you will always meet someone that would want you too."

Joan came up on air to express her gratitude for my exhortation. She said she was now sure God had forgiven her and her dad will accept her back. She also wanted other young girls to take a lesson from her story, and be weary of bad companions, and never disdain parental strict rules.

I decided to give her more encouragement.

"Joan, do not be discouraged, do not be disillusioned with life; a knock down is not a knock out! You can still rise up and make a success of your life! Mohammed Ali was knocked down by Joe Frazier, but when he came up in the same round, in the same ring, in the same match, nobody needed to ask who the winner was! Joseph was knockdown in prison by Photiphar's wife, when he came out of the prison, nobody needed to ask who had the last laugh! And I want to tell you today, it doesn't matter what disappointments and frustrations the devil have knocked you down with! Today, I'm telling you, Joan, when God brings you back, in the same town, and before the same people nobody will need to ask who the winner is!

It does not matter in which prison the devil knocks you down, when you come out you; will have the last laugh! Many people are down to nothing when they lose loved ones, job, and investment or get involved in an accident and down when they find themselves in a situation like yours, but know that anytime you are down to nothing; God is up to something for you! God is not looking for a solution to your problems; He had them even before you had the problems. He is just waiting for you to come to Him! Stop wasting time for a way out, look to God to show you a way out." I told her.

"I remember when I was in Liberia during the war. I was invited by a peasant to his home. When I got there, I was repulsed with the environment; the area was a ghetto, typically of what you would expect in a poor country enmeshed in war. The house looked like an abandoned building from the outside; it was lacking paint and care, and did not look like a place anyone lives in. My heart was down even in the situation at hand.

But when I entered inside; I was taken by surprise. Inside was one of the most beautiful and neat settings I have ever come across even with the elite homes I had visited. The peasant was able to fix clean comfortable furnishings inside with flowers for the comfort of his family. All what I felt about the house from the outside, immediately left me as I entered inside. Then I know, it doesn't matter how life has treated us from the outside, or what kind of environment we found ourselves from the outside, God wants us to maintain a clean setting in our inside. Because He is knocking at our doors, He does not expect to remain outside; He is waiting for us to open the door to our inside so that He will come in! And as long as our inside is clean, He will not be put off by our outside and will find a comfortable abode inside us! So, if your outside says you are poor, let your inside say you are rich! If your outside says you are defeated, let your inside say you are victorious! If your outside says you are worthless, let your inside say you are precious, and when God comes to your inside, He will sort out your outside!

So, Joan and all my listeners out there facing similar challenges in life please continue to maintain a positive attitude inside and it will overcome your challenges outside! Joan, please rejoice, victory is yours and thanks for calling and letting us share in your story." I said.

"Thanks SST, I will forever be grateful. There are many wrong things I did that I do not want to remember or talk about it."

"Please don't talk about them, Joan, God has forgiven you and when God forgives He also wipes away the evidence, so don't talk about it, it is gone!" I said.

"I believe you, SST."

"Yes, Joan, God always wipes away the evidence! And I want all our listeners to know that too! Whatever crime you might have committed before, please know that God always forgives when you repent and would also wipe away the evidence! When King David repented of the adulterous relationship he had with the wife of his soldier, Uriah, God forgave him. But God knew that forgiveness alone would not restore David in the eyes of the people, as long as the evidence was there! So God wiped away the evidence.

Peter, a disciple of Christ, out of a moment of indiscretion removed the ear of one of the king's messengers. Jesus knew that cautioning Peter was not enough for Peter to be fully restored, so He wiped off the evidence. Whenever you come to God in penance, He will not only forgive you but will also wipe away the evidence. Because when God forgives, He washes away your sins! But when man forgives, he watches out for it!

There are many wrong things you might have done before that, if God did not wipe away the evidence when He forgave you, you won't be having that great marriage you are enjoying now, you won't be holding that great appointment you are holding now, you won't be that close to your friends when you reconcile with them as you are now! Because some wrongs do not only need to be forgiven but the evidence need to be wiped out.

Whenever you repent of your wrong deeds, God sees only the new you, but men prefer to remember the old you. So for God to ensure you enjoy a complete restoration as He forgives you, He also wipes away the evidence. Because whatever turnaround you might achieve in life as you are restored, the evidence can turn you back! No matter how high you might have climbed after a fall, the evidence can bring you down! No matter how much they might have said they have forgiven you, the evidence would make it hard for them to forget! And as long as they are continually reminded by the evidence, they will continually hold you in guilt! And so God wipes away the evidence of your wrongs because God desires that your repentance comes with a complete restoration, and so whatever evidence stands between you and a complete restoration God will wipe it away.

No matter what action might have been concluded against you, God is going to turn it around, for He will wipe away the evidence! So my listeners, rejoice as you come in repentance with God, because God will not only forgive but will also wipe away the evidence! Don't be bothered with the attacks of the devil; the devil won't fight you if you don't have a destiny worth fighting. When a builder wants to build a house he first digs a big hole in the ground. It does not matter what hole the devil is digging in your life; it doesn't matter what name he chooses to call it, hole of disappointment, hole of frustration, because God is going to use the devil's holes to raise your life to a skyscraper."

The next caller was a young man that had something to say on adhering to parental guidance.

"SST, it's Steve. How are you doing, man?" He said in the normal way I have gotten used to being addressed by university undergraduates on this show.

"I'm fine, Steve." I replied.

"SST, I really feel sorry for that young lady. You see most of us young people sometimes err because of the high handedness of our parents! Imagine SST, I'm in the university now and Popsy wants to treat me like a kid, being harsh about my friends, blowing hot anytime for simple things like being out for parties. You see what I'm saying? Sometimes, it's parents' harsh behaviour that pushes us, the youths to astray, you know?" He said with youthful exuberance.

"You are right, Steve. Hard handling could be very discomforting." I said.

"You agree with me, SST?" He sounded as if he did not expect that.

"Yes, I agree with you Steve, hard handling is discomforting and should be avoided. If you ask the formless clay, it will agree with that! But if you ask the beautiful vase, it will say it was discomforting but worth it." I said

"What do you mean, SST?" He sounded curious.

"When I met the beautiful ceramic vase on the counter of the super market, I told it how beautiful it appeared. It replied me that it was not always this beautiful until it decided to overcome discomfort." I paused to alert my listeners that might be interesting in note taking that something is coming up.

"It was once just a formless, dirty clay, on the ground, lacking self esteem and value. Life was just a flurry of activities to it! Children will match on it, picnickers will hold party on it, some will urinate on it, and cars on four wheel drive smash on it! It was always a life of activities but of no good worth. Everybody was interested in playing or matching on it but nobody wanted to mould it into something special like its friend the iron that became a beautiful car and no longer lives in the same neighbourhood but moves around with important people and rests under a garage where its one time friend the clay was not invited. Or its other friend the big tree that was moulded to beautiful furniture and now lies in comfortable offices with air condition and in places where our dear clay dare not visit. Life remained that like that; miserable and forgotten for the clay until one day a potter decided to remove it from its surrounding and mould it into something better. It started by placing it on a potter's wheel, it spins and spins until my dear clay lost its balance. When it was still yet to regain its composure from the dazing of the potter's wheel, the potter carried it and put it in a hot furnace.

The heat was highly discomforting, my dear clay cried out but the potter looked at it from the window with a grin and said it is yet to be refined. Just as the clay thought life was all over because of the heat, the potter brought it out. Thinking that was the end, it was disappointed when it saw the potter coming back with a paint and brush, and the potter started painting it with a sticky and smelly liquid. Our dear clay was left uncomfortable and sweating. When the potter was done with the painting, the clay took a big sigh of relief, maybe now it was all over. But to its discomfort again the potter put it back in the furnace. This time it was worst as the sticky substance made the heat of the furnace even more discomforting than before, once again the clay cried out from the furnace to be released and this time its shout was even louder! However, the potter just looked in smile, and told the clay it was nearing its new form.

After what seemed like an eternity of enduring discomfort, the potters brought it out and placed it before a large mirror, and behold the clay saw a sight so beautiful that it was tempted to ask who it was. And today our dear clay is in a beautiful glass house in a nice shop, fully air-conditioned environment and with a servant to clean it daily! No more will children come and match on it, no more will drunkards come and urinate on it, no more will picnickers come and drop trash and expended tin cans on it, no more will it be treated without respect, because it now has a value! And only those that can afford its value can come near it and forever will it be treated with respect." I said.

I hope the narrative of the formless clay would make him see the importance of instructions in our lives.

"I am sure my friend, Steve, and also other young listeners out there, will understand that as you are in your formative stage in life as youths, you are just like the formless clay! You will need potters in your lives to mould you to a beautiful and valuable form! Parents are potters in your lives. Teachers are potters in your lives. Preachers are potters in your lives, and books are potters in your lives too! And only when you are ready to endure the discomfort that these persons give, would you overcome, like the beautiful vase, and become something of value in life!

When Moses went to Pharaoh, the palace magicians understood how to turn a rod to snake just as Moses did, but Moses snake swallowed all their snakes. They all understood how to do it! But to every understanding, there is a greater understanding! God's understanding is greater than men's understanding. Teachers understanding is greater than students understanding, and parents understanding is greater than children's understanding." I decided to go a little further with the message.

"There are three criss-crosses you are going to pass through in your life. The criss-cross you meet as you enter school, the next is when you decide on a career and the third crisscross is who you marry. How you manage these criss-crosses would have a profound effect on your destiny."

I was doing my best to make him see my view.

It was always hard convincing the youths, especially the boys. They tend to be hot-headed and adventurous, or what one can say to be rebellious. Youths are in the age of radicalism, and knowing that, I always try to approach their discussions more tactfully, always trying to agree to disagree with them.

"Whatever, SST, I got what you're saying. I mean no jibe, but I think someone else needs the advice. I still hold it, we need some little space from parents, you get me, SST?" He said defiantly.

I wanted to advice him to form a habit of speaking to the mirror often; that's where you would meet the man that needs your advice the most. However, I decided to play it safe and move on with the show.

"Yeah, Steve, I can feel you, I can't agree with you less! Thanks for calling brother! And who is next on this show, remember it's New Year's Eve and we got to give some resolutions for the year." I decided to end it there with Steve. I guess he wasn't in the mood to consider beyond his opinion. I decided to keep quiet. The good thing to say is not always the right thing to say when you don't get the timing right. But Steve is not through with me!

"But SST, why doesn't God want us to have a good time? All these laws and what have you! What's wrong with living an exciting and active life?" He asked forcedly. I decided to go on easy with him; I knew he was speaking the hidden views of many youths.

"Steve, God is not against us having a good life. In fact, He planned that we have an exciting and active life but the devil came along with a counterfeit and corrupted all the activities God planned for us to live a good life!" I tried to move away from Steve, he seemed a difficult person. I moved my message to the general audience.

"God is not against us having a good life my friends, He wants to even improve on that, He wants us to have the best life! He is not against you being on the run, sister; He just wants you to apply the right breaks in the right places! He is not against you going on with fast life brother; he just wants you to be on the safe lane! He never said we should stop, He said we should change!

You said you like drinking? Good, God is not against that! That was why He made three quarters full the world of water; He even created our body to need water more than anything! Go on and drink brother! He never said stop, He just said change!

You love going out on Friday nights? God is not against that! He made the nights for you to rest and not for Him. He does not need rest. But He understands you might need to take a walk out on a night like that and that was why He created the night vigil and worship to keep you happy with Him on Friday nights! He never said stop, He just said change!

Sister, you love having the men around you always? No problem, God loves being around too! His spirit revolves all around us. He doesn't care if you have men around you, God loves fellowship, let all the men come around you, but He planned that only one is to formally come into you, and He requires a small formality for it, that's all! He never said stop, He just said change!

You love spending money! Beautiful! God created money for you to spend. He knows money answereth all and that was why He made it for you, because He wants you to solve all your problems! But the devil has a lot of counterfeit that spend your soul! God wants you to spend and not for your soul to be spent! So He put a sign behind the money He wants you to spend, it reads, "legitimate income!" Go on spending! He never said stop, He just said change!

You are in love with music? Oh beautiful! God loves music too; in fact, He lives in an atmosphere of music! He wants you to make a joyful noise to Him with drums? Guitar music, Computer music, it does not matter!? Yes! In fact, with anything! He does not mind what you use or which kind of noise you make, God loves it all! He loves the music, only that He requires you check your lyrics and check His words and ensure there is no conflict and you can continue making the joyful noise. God never says stop . . . He only said change! God never told us to stop most of what we are doing; He just said we should change our attitude to it!

You love giving lift to the young ladies in your beautiful big car, mister? Good, you are doing what is demanded of you! God wants to see his children being assisted. He won't give cars to all His children lest He creates a chaos in the world. But He loves to see those that are always available to help. But brother provided your help does not extend to asking for a date or requesting for a phone number but just restricted to brotherly love. God did not say stop, He just said change!"

I moved away from the topic so as not to get Steve back!

I brought up the issue I knew will take up the remaining time. It was New Year's Eve and resolutions are the traditions of the people. Few keep to it anyway, but many manage for a week or two.

My call for New Year resolutions opened the flood gates! Listeners started calling in to tell me about their new year's resolutions. Some promised to quit smoking and drinking, others tell of their desire to stop lying and be more committed to their duties and many more. And a lot of other queer resolutions, I guess most just wanted to have a good time. It was always like anyway. Just when I was thinking there wasn't much to discuss on the show, a unique call that I least expected came in!

"Good day, my dear SST," the caller said. It sounded serious and business like, I decided to accord it some good respect. I was grateful I did!

"Yes, good day sir. Thanks for calling motivation dance club and who am I talking to?" I said cautiously.

"Thank you, this is Babatunde Fashola." The man said.

My heart skipped! It cannot be him. It must be a namesake!

"Oh! Fashola, you have the same name with his Excellency." I said cautiously.

That was the governor's name, and I also noticed that the voice was sounding good to be him too!

"Yes, you are right, we have the same name and the same office too!" He said with a laugh. There was no mistake about that voice

276

now! I have heard it many times before, except someone, good at it, was playing a Gabo on me by mimicking the governor on my show.

"Wow, your Excellency, I am highly blessed this day! And to what do we owe such a great honour today?" I said profusely kowtowing as I speak and acknowledging the presence of no other person than the chief executive of the state on my show. It was something I was never prepared for!

"SST, it's my pleasure really, I wanted to come on your show, that I have been monitoring for some time. It was my kids that made me a fan." He laughed. It was well known that the governor was a committed family man. "I want to congratulate you on your show which had impacted positively on the lives of millions of our citizens." He paused.

I guess I was expected to come in and say something here. "Thanks your Excellency, I'm grateful." I said cheerfully.

"Yes, SST, I also want to commend the good people of Lagos and thank them for their support over the years and wish them happy New Year." He said. I was afraid this was turning to a political campaign. I don't think I want that for my show. I hope his Excellency was not trying to use my show that had a wide audience to further his political campaign. I quickly added, "I'm sure they are hearing you sir." I said, hoping he will get on to another topic, I was happy when he did!

"SST, I want to say that really, you have been a source of inspiration to us all" He said modestly.

"No, your Excellency, if I had been able to achieve anything at all, it was because of your superior guidance and support." I added quickly.

"Really, SST, I thought I was the one learning from you?" He said in humility—a well known quality of his.

I wasn't going to let that go, especially before a large audience—always give the shine to the boss!

"Yes, your Excellency, you are right as always and I know we all have a lot to learn from you." I was almost bowing in my reply.

"Thanks SST, and have a nice day, it was great talking to you." The governor said, politely dismissing me.

"Thanks sir, it's a pleasure, honour, and blessing to have you on my show. Thank you and May God continue to guide and protect you as you pilot the affairs of the state." I quickly bid him a farewell. I was left ruffled by unexpectedly taking on the governor on my show! There was no warning of his coming! Normally, the state house protocol staff would have arranged such sudden encounter to avoid any unforeseen happening. To make sure you don't unknowingly embarrass the governor. Freedom of speech ends the day you use it to insult those that guarantee you the freedom!

However, this governor was known to be a down to earth person, who always avoid protocol, and had a tendency of being ordinary and natural.

"My listeners, it looks as if we starting the new year on the dance club on a high note, that was his Excellency, the governor on the show for the first time, it was really great!" I said.

Another caller called to pour encomiums on the governor for his good efforts at good governance. Two other people who shared his views also called.

"SST, I love the way you handled the interview with his Excellency." A caller said. I didn't know what to say to that so I replied calmly, carefully choosing my words.

"We are all learning, sir." I said.

"Oh yeah? So was that why you refused to agree with his Excellency that you are a source of inspiration to him?" He asked.

"Never tried to outshine your boss my brother, that is the first lesson. The boss is always the one in charge." I said laughing out loudly.

"You learn that from Robert Greene's book." He said it as a statement.

I knew he was referring to the popular Robert Greene's book the; 48 Laws of power, where the writer warned against outshining the boss.

"Yes, my friend, and I also learn from what I witnessed at the battlefield." I said.

"You were in the war front, SST?" He asked.

"Yes, and that was where I learnt the lesson to avoid taking the shine off those above you, if you can." I said.

I then started reading out another narrative I had written from my personal experience.

"As I said, it is a good lesson to know that you should never outshine your boss. It can spell your doom wherever you find yourself. But when I was in the army this lesson was lost by a young major who led a successful onslaught of West African troops known as ECOMOG forces, against the rebel invasion of Freetown; the capital city of Sierra Leone." I started the narrative with an enticing academic introduction.

"When the Revolutionary United Front rebels invaded Freetown on 6th January 1999 under the cover of darkness and treachery of some Freetown residents, fear graduated into terror and later burst to pandemonium. Freetown, the capital of Sierra Leone became an untenable location for the presidency and ECOMOG top military brass was to command a counter attack; moreover the war room in the presidential villa had already been turned to an enemy armoury. The strategic planners had to relocate to the safety of the island of Lungi off the coast, which offered not only geographical safety, as it is separated by large body of water from Freetown, but also pragmatic safety, as it has a functional airport; should further retreat be necessary.

Destiny the maker of history bestowed the task of organising the disorganized ECOMOG forces in repelling the rebel invasion on the major, who happened to be one of the few officers left behind in Freetown after the hurried retreat of the top brass to Lungi; a feat that ended in favour of the ECOMOG forces. Later stories and pictures of the major started appearing in world magazines with scanty mention of the generals in command. The major adorned the cover of BBC Focus on Africa magazine in well starched and bright camouflage uniform with an extremely pronounced name tag that looked like a sign post. His model-like pose and demeanour betrayed the picture as the work of a well articulated media campaign than paparazzi shot. The caption carried his death sentence, 'the liberator of Freetown', by so doing he had committed the cardinal sin that had brought down greater men; he had taken the shine off the masters. Such action was not compatible with tradition and discipline ... and neither was leniency; the impudence must be punished. The masters had bidden their time knowing that the ambitious when left for a while will supply the noose for the hangman." I said as I came to the end of the narrative and then started a short exhortation.

"Shine is a sensitive area to the boss, in all profession, especially those like the military that hinges on effective command and control. Napoleon Bonaparte once remarked that men fight wars and generals take the credit and so has it remain ever since. The higher the shine, the higher the prestige; no boss worth his salt would allow a subordinate rub the shine off him.

The subordinate must be clever enough to do the work and leave the shine for the boss. To compete to be recognized by all and sundry as the one who does the work is to compete for a position reserved for the boss. The subordinate should only compete to be of good recognition to the boss and leave further recognitions to the boss. Handle the works behind the scene and let the boss handle the press, if you must speak to the press let it be ... the boss said ... the boss did ..." I said. I was now putting in the last talk of the day.

"To my listeners, it's time to close the show this morning so that you will prepare for the coming new year, but first let me wish you the best for the year!

Money is a concern, health is a concern and food is a concern but whatever is a concern will not be a concern to your life in the coming year! Whatever you have, be it money, knowledge or whatever God has given you, give it freely in the coming year! The more you are eager to give, the more God is eager to replenish you! Do not mind the level you are now this year there's no great story without a humble beginning.

Charles son of Queen Elizabeth becoming a king isn't a great story, but Barack Obama, son of an Africa immigrant father becoming President of America is a great story. So, don't despite your humble status. You are the next great story to come out in the coming year. God will make you as He made them.

What is it that's making you less confident of success? Is it lack of education, or is it lack capital, no experience or supporters? God does not require raw materials to make you. He just said you should come with the right attitude to him. Whatever you desire to do in the coming year please first check if you have built the right attitude. Knowledge can carry you far but only attitude can keep you there.

Before you look where your knowledge can carry you, please check if you have the right attitude. A preacher with the knowledge of the scriptures but without the attitude of a preacher can't command a great congregation. No matter how high your intellect carries you; your attitude can bring you down. No matter how romantic your marriage took off, your attitude can turn it sour.

No matter how bright your career looks, your attitude can turn it dim. No matter how promising your business looks, your attitude can break it down. Talent is never enough; most of the talented people are in prison, you need the right attitude. It is your attitude that will determine your altitude. There are many things you can be wrong in life, but you can never be wrong about what you think you can do. If you think you can, you can. If you think you can't, you can't. So build the right attitude. You might be born with greatness, you might have been thrust upon with greatness, or you might have achieved greatness, but if you don't have the right attitude, you would lose it. Often what destroys us are not the big things of life, but the little things we just can't stop ourselves doing, you need to build the right attitude. Attitude must be clear, consistent, and complete. It reminded me of the story of a man whose possession of the right attitude saved his life".

I brought up another narrative to fill in the time for the day seeing I still had some minutes left on the show.

"Mike Jackson was on a journey to the countryside when the heavy downpour met him on the way. It became difficult to drive in the heavy rain, and as he struggle to move along the road, he saw a castle by the roadside. There was a big tree in the garden beside the house. He decided to park under the tree and wait until the rain was over. As he looked outside the window of his Corolla saloon car, he saw an old lady shivering in the rain as she stood alone in the middle

281

of the garden. He was immediately overcome with pity for the old woman in the rain. He decided to come down and assist her back to the house.

It was still raining heavily and Mike was in his best attire. He was on a journey to visit his in—laws at their country home. But that didn't matter when he saw the poor old woman left standing in the rain. Mike went out of the car, covering his head with his designer suits as the rain soaks him; he rushed to where the old woman in the green wool sweater was standing.

But as he reached where she was standing, something strange happened. The old woman disappeared. In fright, Mike turned to run back to his car when he saw the huge tree under which he parked his vehicle falling as it was struck by lightning and totally crushing the car. Mike would have been crushed to death had it been the tree met him still in the car.

He went to the front door of the house and knocked, a little girl appeared. He asked her about the old lady left in the rain.

"There's no old lady here." The little girl said firmly.

"No, there is." Mike was adamant. "I saw her in a green wool sweater, with a pink hat, standing in the rain." The girl looked at him with shock as he described the old lady he saw in the rain.

"That's not true! It is granny." She said, tears filled her eyes "Granny died last year, she is no more."

Mike was full of shock; he had actually seen the little girl's granny who came from the dead to save his life from the thunderstruck. Mike had always been a guy with the right attitude, he had never thought twice to come to anybody's assistance, but never before had he rushed to his own assistance as this. He had the attributes of the right attitude—compassionate, consistent, complete and clear. It doesn't matter who you are being good to, friend or foe. But nothing uplifts you before God than giving where you are denied, blessing where you are cursed, helping where you are sabotaged, and praising where you are condemned. That's the right attitude.

My listeners develop the attributes of the right attitude, like Mike, and one day, it would save or make your life!" I looked at my wrist watch, my time was up.

"God is going to open the doors to your destiny. He will bring the opportunities for your breakthrough, the means to your liberation and the route to your accomplishments. He will bring the persons, the plans, and the motivation that you need to reach to your destination in life. He will bring all things along your way in order to connect you to your path of destiny in life, but only the right attitude would take you through the open doors. Only the right attitude would lead you to connect to the path of your destiny in life.

If you don't have the right attitude to people, you won't know how to use opportunity. Build the right attitude in your work, God planned creation in way that it ends with rest. When you have the right attitude, rest will not be the beginning of your creation! So built the right attitude in all you do in the coming year.

Happy New Year from the motivation dance club to you all. And Happy New Year to you from the club with the right attitude!" I extended my greetings to my listeners excitedly as I close the day's show.

I needed enough time to take a long rest before the next activity at the studio begins!

Mark had planned a late evening New Year party for all the staff at the studio. It was to start late in the evening when all programme had been recorded, hopefully it will finish early enough to afford those that stay in far places good time to go back home. As I left the presenters seat, I checked my handset to see if there were any missed calls or left SMS messages, as expected there were many! But one of the messages drew my attention, it had been coming for the past two days, and carrying a message I didn't understand. It was just a short message telling me to be careful and to be wise.

I had been receiving queer messages from my fans; however, that was to be expected, as most of them were youths, and young people are known to be playful. But this message always got me a little jittery. It looked like a warning, especially since my last encounter with Dan Paul. (I guess that was what was raising my concern.) I tried calling the number, but no one picked. I later discussed it with Mark, whom as expected, pointed the accusing fingers at Dan Paul, threatening to call the police. I advised him against it. What if it was a prank from a fan and we might end up embarrassing ourselves? Dan Paul would gleefully charge me for character deformation. I was doing well at my show; the last thing I needed was a bad publicity.

I went to wait at the common room, which had been refitted with superior Italian leather seats and a large LG flat screen television set connected to the satellite providers. Like other areas of the studio, it has also undergone much refurbishing since the studio started accruing much revenue. I stretched fully on the sofa, watching the news on CNN. Glancing at my wristwatch, I saw I had plenty time to go before the party starts. I was hoping the party finishes earlier so I could reach home in good time and commence my plans for celebrating the New Year with my friend, Segun. I had the day off on New Year day.

CHAPTER THREE

The Kidnap

The tall man with the black leather jacket dragged me forcefully by the shoulders out of the car. I was trying to look up at his face when he hit me on the side of the head with the butt of the pistol. I could see the whole area around me spinning as I gradually lose consciousness. The next thing I knew was the strong feel of boots kicking my side. I tried to move myself but I could not control my body as it seemed to be glued to the cold hard floor. Slowly my eyes started opening to the surrounding. I could see I was in the back of a truck and lying on my side. I tried to bring up my hands to my face, but realised they were tied together behind. I shifted and looked to the side; a man wearing a black leather jacket was sitting on the side bench. My mind quickly recalled what has happened. I looked up at the man again; he was wearing a black hood over his face now.

"You are around now, good boy." He had a deep husky voice. The pistol was still in his hand and he was waving it in my face.

"Behave yourself, and no harm will come to you. Try anything funny and you will go join your female friend!" He gave a short laugh with a sneer. He then brought out a small tin from his pocket and poured a little of a white substance from it on the tip of his index finger and was sniffing it into his wide nostril. He was referring to Sasha. I could see her as she was shouting and trying to cover her face with her hands as the bullets hit her chest, her youthful body hitting hard against the front of the dashboard as she felled forward. I tried to open my mouth, but my lips were heavy as if sown together. I realised they had placed a cellophane over my mouth. The

285

truck came to a stop and the man brought down the rear hatches. He used his legs to push me out of the truck and I fell hard on the ground. The other man, the one driving, came around to my side, and dragged me with force to my feet. It was night but the surrounding was brightened by the clear moonlight.

We had stopped at a place that I saw to be an uncompleted building, a housing project under construction, and scattered around were the usual building materials and equipment left lying around by the workers. I was pushed into one of the rooms in the building that had no doors or windows. The floor was full of sand as it was yet to be plastered with cement. The man that was driving the bus told me to sit down on the floor. He was the one in the green shirt and jeans trousers; he was now wearing a hood too. His friend with the leather jacket was nowhere around. I started observing around my environment. It was a large building. I could see the pillars on the building that showed it to be of a one story building. There were two of such buildings adjacent each other in the compound.

The man in the jacket came back and ordered me to move outside. I found myself again in the middle of the compound. The place seemed deserted aside from the three of us there. I could see near the walls, under the dim moonlight, about two big trees that I knew were mango trees. It is funny how the mind of a man in trouble could work wonders. The whole area appeared clearly in my mind as if I was looking at it in the broad daylight.

We were back in a bus again and as soon as the bus left the compound, the leather jacket man, still with me in the back of the bus, pulled a hood over my face and I was thrown to a world of darkness. The bus once more moved along the road. But after a while I could feel the road becoming bumpy as the bus struggled on what I believe must be a very bad road. My instincts told me we have left the major road now and are travelling on a rough road, going off into the bush.

After travelling for what seemed like hours, the bus suddenly stopped. The man used his two hands to lift me by the shoulders from the floor of the bus. I felt myself being dragged and pushed around again till my feet felt a hard ground and then I heard the sound of a door being opened. The man pushed me from the behind into what I knew now to be a room. I could hear the door closing behind me. I tried moving forward but tripped and fell to the ground. It was a bare hard cemented floor, and with my hands tied behind my back and my face blindfolded, it became difficult for me to get control of my balance. I managed to dragged myself and sat down.

I was sitting like that, in such an awkward and uncomfortable position for what seemed like hours, and was getting uncomfortable and restless when the door opened and I heard someone entering the room. He removed my hood. I could see it was the man with the leather jacket, and he was wearing the same hood I saw him with the other time. He untied my hands and told me I could use the bathroom in the room and take my meal. I saw a small empty plate near the wall. He dropped a black leather bag on the floor. When he left, I ran to the bathroom to ease myself, emptied my bowels that have been screaming for attention for long. I opened the black leather bag. There were two tins of sardines, a medium size loaf of bread and two sachet of water. I knew what the empty plate was left for.

The next time the door opened, the two of them came in. The man in leather jacket was still holding the pistol in his hand. They looked at the empty tins of sardines with satisfaction and smiled. He made a signal that I should turn around. And when I did, he placed the hood over my face and tied my hands behind my back again. I was back to darkness, but I took care to note the position of things in the room to be able to get myself around. There was a small bed and a chair by the wall and nothing more. I slowly felt my way to the chair and sat down. My mind was racing as to the reason for the shooting of Sasha and my abduction. If they had wanted to kill me, then why haven't they done that up till now? Why did they kill Sasha? What have they got to do with her? If it was actually a kidnap, why me? I was not a businessman or a politician, hardly a candidate for kidnap. I had no known family to contact, so what were they after? Ransom? Who will pay on my behalf, whom will they even contact, what will my employers do ... my mind was raising questions, trying to figure out what was responsible for the macabre drama I found myself in.

The door opened after a while, I could hear the familiar sound of broadcast from a radio.

A small object that I felt to be a transistor radio was kept near to me and the door closed. Sounds were coming from the radio, someone was reading news. I recognised Aisha's voice, the Static FM newscaster. She was talking about the reported kidnap of the popular presenter of the Static FM motivation dance club programme. She mentioned my full names but was wise enough to add that I was more known to my listeners by my initials, SST.

There was a report of the police organising a manhunt. She reported that the kidnapping took place, the night before, after the station held an in house New Year party and I was on my way to drop a co-worker at her place. The lady was said to have unfortunately lost her life in the incident. There was also an interview with Mark, it was clear he was close to tears, at a point he burst out crying when he mentioned the brutal killing of Sasha. Mark was full of eulogy for Sasha, describing her as one of the longest serving staff at the studio and a very dedicated and lively person. The station will surely miss her, and the management had taken the responsibility of paying the expenses of moving her corpse to her parents' in Benin immediately so as not to keep them on edge. He said they have received a call from my kidnappers and the police are handling the matter. He didn't talk of any demand for ransom by my kidnappers. Aisha promised to keep the listeners updated on the issue as she moved to the second item on the news. I sat down pondering over all these development. My mind went over what Mark called Dan Paul's threats, and the text messages that Mark insisted I take to the police. Was Dan Paul involved in this? If he was, what was his motive, definitely not to kidnap me to work for his studio? Was he trying to punish me for turning down his offer or was he trying to get back at Static FM by picking their ace presenter? My mind was at a loss. After an hour of what was mostly covered by a musical interlude, Aisha came back on the air again. She mentioned that no further calls where received from the kidnappers and the police didn't know how to contact me as calls to my phone had seized going since the day I was kidnapped. I remembered my handset was left in the car where I used to keep it while driving so that I could easily get to it as I drive. That meant my handset was not found when the car was recovered. She hinted that the police was making progress because some arrests had been made in the ongoing investigations. There was nothing new coming in from the news items for hours.

My captors kept coming into the room to release me to go to the toilet. They ensured I always had something to eat. My diet was improved after a few days. They occasional add fried rice and chicken to the menu, but my meal remained largely bread and tin sardines. From listening to the news items, I was able to keep aware of the days I was spending in captivity.

On 5th January when I had spent 5 days in captivity from the time I was abducted on New Year day, there was an interview with the police public relations officer who informed the public that the police had charged Mr Dan Paul on suspicion of organising my kidnap. They had evidences, from undisclosed witnesses, of the threats he had issued to me days before the kidnapping and also from text messages recovered from my handset. Later in the day, there were reports of riots and demonstrations by various groups in Lagos calling for my release, which included one that was carried out in front of Star FM headquarters.

The chairperson of Star FM, Chief Raymond Chekwas, came on air to clear his name off the rumours going about on the kidnapping. He told the reporters he had never instructed any of his staff to recruit me, and although he was aware I had contributed to the dramatic rise of Static FM, he had not given it more than a passing thought, because Radio was not his main business outfit. And that Star FM had contributed very little to his overall business returns since he entered the radio broadcasting business. His decision to go into radio broadcasting, as he said, was not for money making but one born out of his desire to contribute a little to his community. He also denied the rumours of a political undertone to the rumours going about that it had something with the political rivalry between him and Chief Sylvester Dokubo of Static FM over the Lagos central senatorial seat. He added with anger that no office in the land could push him to kidnapping and he had nothing to gain politically or otherwise in kidnapping a staff of Chief Dokubo.

I fell sick and was vomiting by the second week of my captivity. It must have been caused by the bread and sardines that had become my normal meal, and of course the conditions I was subjected to.

The news broadcast I had been getting from the little transistor radio had not only being encouraging but dramatic. A civil liberty group had held a rally to the Governor's office calling for my release, and pressuring the government to take an urgent action in my case. Several groups have sprout up demanding to foot the bill for my ransom. Mark continued with the motivation dance club, which had become a forum for listeners to express their feelings and spit venom on my kidnappers, especially the prime suspect in my kidnapping, Mr Dan Paul. There were many calls coming in, some prayers, some appeals to my kidnappers, others an appeal for listeners to join effort and raise the ransom. There was a discussion with a caller that I recalled with special feelings. It was a call from a six year old girl that called the studio to ask after me. She sounded so soft and concerned about my situation that I almost shed tears on hearing her.

"Hello is uncle SST back now?" She asked during the show.

"He will soon be back, my dear." Mark was assuring her.

"Please I heard they took uncle SST, please am begging them to release him, my class held prayers for uncle SST, yesterday." She was sobbing now.

"Yes, my dear, we are all praying for him, my wife held a special prayer session for him at the Church and we all know God is in control. My dear, don't worry, uncle SST will be back soon." Mark was handling the role of chief mourner in my case extremely well. I felt encouraged to hear that his wife and her prayer team are on my case. It reassured me more than the prayers I am doing for myself, because I know how pious and dedicated Paul's wife was. The last time we discussed was on her plan to open her own church and I promised to always pay my tithe there.

The little girl came up again with a very touching proposal.

"Please tell those holding uncle to release him, all the children in my school are going to contribute our lunch money to send to them." She said.

That got Mark laughing.

"So, how will you eat if you give all your lunch money?" He asked her. The little girl came back forcefully.

"We don't care about our lunch, we just want to see uncle SST back." She was sobbing out loudly now. That night I couldn't sleep. I kept thinking of the love of that small girl and the thought kept me crying throughout the night.

The following week, the governor came on air to assure the people that his administration was doing everything possible to secure my release. The police had still not made any significant progress in their investigations about the case. They were still detaining Mr Dan Paul, as the court had remanded him in police custody, for his own protection, after two people were caught attempting to burn down Star FM buildings out of the heightened tension in the city against Star FM, and Dan Paul in particular. The premises of Star FM radio station was assigned heavy police protection. Mark had been doing his best to assuage public feelings and continued reassuring them that I would soon be released.

In the fourth week of my captivity, the man with the leather jacket came in while I was finishing a meal and seized the small transistor radio. I was distraught. The radio was my only companion and the only link to the outside world. My spirit would have collapsed long ago if it had not been for the companionship of the small transistor radio. The hood was again placed back over my head. They also taped my mouth and tied my hands again. After some time, I felt hands lifting me off my feet and pushing me out of the room. My mind was racing over all possible options. Were they so scared of the reports on the news of the police being hot on their trail that they were now going to kill me? Or was the ransom paid? I never knew how much they were demanding; there was no mention of it in all the news I have monitored.

Once again, I found myself on the cool floor of a bus and the journey resumed. From the sound of crashing tree branches and the violent shaking of the bus as we moved, I knew we are going further into the bush. After what seemed a long journey, the bus stopped and the man with me at the back of the bus shouted at me to get up. I tried to but fell down on my side. The man pulled me by the collars of my shirt and dragged me out of the vehicle. I started a quiet but deep prayer to God, committing my soul to His care. I was sure they brought me there to kill me and bury my body in the deep jungle. I can hear the bus starting again, the man shouted on me to lie face down. I felt my face against the cold sand on the ground. He placed his heavy boots on my back, pushing me deeper into the ground. I could smell foul odour coming from the ground. Or maybe it was odour from my body; after weeks of not having my bathe?

I didn't know how long I stayed there but I must have fallen asleep because I was woken by the sound of shoes shuffling the dry leaves. The sound was getting louder and nearer as I strained my ears to the ground. Somebody was shaking my body and was turning me over on my back. I could feel hands over my face as the hood was pulled off from my head. Immediately I felt a sharp pain blinding my eyes coming from the lights of the sunlight piercing through the huge trees that covered the area. I heard clearly, somebody asking if I was ok! I squeezed my eyes tightly and then opened them. My heart took a giant leap of relief. I was staring in the face of a man in full police uniform! I tried to get up but the shock of what was happening seized me like an electric shock and I passed out!

I opened my eyes and I saw myself on a hospital bed. Mark and his wife were sitting by the side and my friend Segun was standing by the foot of the bed. When I fully opened my eyes, I saw the signs of relief on their faces. Mark was the first to talk

"Thank God! SST, you are awake!" He was obviously relief at my regaining consciousness.

"What happened?" I turned my head towards them.

"You passed out when the police found you." Segun explained.

"And Sasha?" I asked Mark. I could see his eyes becoming filled with tears at the mention of Sasha. I knew they were very close. He was the one that always drops her at her place on his way home. It was because he was busy and didn't want her to wait for long that he asked me to drop her at home on that fateful night.

"She is dead." He said with his eyes turning aside to hold back the tears. His wife was holding on to his arm to give him support. I realised they might not know I was monitoring all what was being said on the radio when I was kidnapped. What I wanted to know was about the burial plans.

"Has she been buried?" I asked Mark.

"Yes. I ensured she was moved immediately back home for burial" He said. I wondered what the hurry was about. As if he was reading my mind he added

"I didn't want her aged parents hearing about it and rushing down to Lagos. I sent the body the next day to save them the hassle of the journey." He explained. A man in white laboratory coat entered the room. I could see his tag reading, Dr Sam Chukwu. The way he wore the tag reminded me of my military days.

"Good, you are awake, how are you feeling?" Dr Sam asked.

"I am fine, sir." I said.

"You need to rest to be really fine." He looked around the room and requested my visitors to give me some time to rest. They all left. Mark squeezed my hands as he went out to assure me it was alright. A beautiful young nurse came in and gave me an injection. I lapsed into a long sleep.

I stayed only two days in the hospital. Throughout the period I was on admission at the hospital, Mark and his wife catered for all my needs and were always visiting and staying by my bed. I believe it was the first time in his life that Mark abandoned the studio when he was not sick. My Segun was also around for the periods he could take time off from his office. I was placed under police protection at the hospital. The commissioner of police who was basking in the success of my rescue, had his men taken a written account of what happened and I was interrogated on the second day when the doctor certified I was fit enough. I stated all I knew from the time we left the studio with Sasha, to when I was kidnapped, carried to a secret hideout, to my released and rescue from the jungle. The investigative police officer, Superintendent Timothy Jones, of the State Criminal

Investigation Department, the CID, asked me some questions, which included what I could remember of the hideout I was taken to. Of course, I could only say something about the first place I was taken to because they had not started blindfolding me by then. He was very particular about my relationship with Mr Dan Paul, I told him everything. From the first day I met Dan Paul, when I was looking for a studio to broadcast my show, to our next meeting at Covenant University end of the year symposium, and later the discussions I had with him when he brought a proposal that I should work at Star FM. I told Superintendent Timothy Jones that I never took what Dan Paul said to me to be a threat and so never thought of reporting it to the police; maybe I was being naive! And to the texts messages I received, I didn't know who sent them, though it had something to do with our discussion with Dan Paul, but it came from a number I didn't know him with. And with that Superintendent Jones took his notes and left.

A large number of my faithful fans kept watch over the hospital throughout the days I was on admission. Many sent in hundreds of get well cards and even flowers, which was not a part of our culture. On the day I was to be discharged from the hospital, the governor was informed and he decided to personally come and see me. He was one of my guests on the New Year day show the day I was abducted. He was a very popular and nice governor. The people loved him for the good works he was doing, and what a better way to improve his score sheet than showing his more humane side, especially when the people's idol was involved!

When I came out of the hospital, I took a photograph with the large number of people waiting outside for me. And also with the governor, and the commissioner of police who had been moving up and down since the arrival of the governor, making himself very visible to the press. He went about a long narrative on how the police carried out the search. He refused to admit that a ransom was paid for my release. He said it was not part of the police tradition to give ransom to criminals. I could see the governor beaming a huge smile throughout the photo session, it was not all about my safe rescue of course, it was an election year, and the pictures were to run for days in the major newspapers. It was when I returned home that I learned from Segun the full story of all that took place during the three week abduction.

The day I was abducted, the kidnappers contacted my producer through the studio line, the same line I use for my show. Mark immediately moved to action calling the police and relaying to Segun what has happened to me. Mark assisted the police with useful information on the threats that Dan Paul issued to me, and the anonymous text messages. That led to the police arresting Dan Paul. But when the search was running into weeks without any success of finding me, Mark went a step further to galvanised public support and forced the governor to make available a ransom of twenty million naira. All the talks of the police being on the tail of the kidnappers, that led to my recue was balderdash, a ransom was paid to the kidnappers, and that was what saved my life! I wonder where I would have been if I wasn't fortunate to have an effective and brotherly producer called Mark.

Barely a day after leaving the hospital I received a telephone call from the commissioner of police.

"Hello, SST, how are you feeling?" He had earlier given me his phone number when he visited me at the hospital. His number was amongst the few I had stored in my new handset as I lost my former one in the incident. The day I came out of the hospital Mark gave me a new handset.

"I'm fine, sir. And thank you for all your efforts in rescuing me. I will remember to mention the gallant actions of your men in my next show." He was giggling happily on hearing that like a child in a toy shop. I knew how hungry public officers are for publicity. I could hear him chuckling at the other end.

"Oh, SST, there is no need for all that. I was just doing my job." He said with a touch of modesty. But something in his voice made me believe he really meant there was a need.

"Much thanks all the same, sir." I repeated. I didn't want him to know that I knew that it was a recovery and not a rescue that took place; as a huge ransom was paid. But I knew the police didn't care what I got to know, or how I chose to call it—to them it will always be that I was rescued by their special anti-terrorism squad.

"We are making progress with the investigation. We have received more evidences on the case from the text messages we recovered from your handset, and the one we saw in Mr Dan Paul's handset. There was some communication between him and the kidnappers, though coded, but we have the best detectives here." The commissioner seemed very proud of winding up the case because it has become a high profile case. The people of Lagos were largely interested because of who was involved. The rumour peddled in town was the rivalry in the media houses that led to the kidnapping of a popular presenter and death of one of the staff of an FM station. The more the commissioner talked about the progress being made on the case of my kidnapping, the more uneasy I became. I never expected Dan Paul to go to the extent of kidnapping. I saw him as an egoist but never expected he would stoop that low. What was his motive for getting involved in such a crime, I can't say. Was it jealousy, hatred, or just being vindictive of my response to his proposal?

The commissioner informed me, that Dan Paul was to be arraigned in court on charge of kidnapping and he wants me to be a prosecution witness.

"Tomorrow in the court, I want you to be very clear on the case especially on how he threatened you and the threatening text massages you received just before you were kidnapped. We can't allow such criminals to tarnish the name of the media in Lagos." He was fuming badly.

The next day, I was in court sitting on the second row when they brought Dan Paul handcuffed into the courtroom. He was looking blindly at the half-filled courtroom as if he was in a dream as he was marched to the dock. I can see he has lost some weight and has become a shadow of himself. His head moved around and our eyes met, he appeared startled and confused. I turned my face, I couldn't bear it. The prosecution lawyer read the charges before the court. Dan Paul's lawyer pleaded not guilty. I can see the investigating police officer smiling. The police believed they had a watertight case against Dan Paul, and only needed witnesses and evidences to close the case.

The defence lawyer asked for an adjournment to enable him to be ready with his witnesses. The presiding judge agreed to adjourn the case to the first week of the following month. Mr Dan Paul was again denied bail, and remanded back to prison custody. As I left the court my phone rang. It was the police commissioner.

"SST, I just heard the case was adjourned. Those lawyers are wasting their time, we have more than we need to send that man to jail for life." He laughed loudly. "This is not the first case am handling. I've never lost a case. When I say this person is a criminal, no judge can set him free because I talk as a seasoned police officer." The commissioner started a small lecture on the history of his successful exploits as an investigative police officer and how he had a natural flair for criminal investigation.

I didn't know what to make of his self adulations so I just kept replying back "yes sir," "you are right sir," "that's great sir," throughout.

When he was sure he had exhausted a recount of his achievements, he stopped and invited me to the Police Headquarters.

"SST, please come and see me at the headquarters now, something just came in about the case, I'm handling it personally, you know? I don't want anybody to spoil the case for me, please if you can come right away I will be grateful." He said. I told him I was on my way to the Police Headquarters.

When I entered the police commissioner's office, I realised I still have some walk to do, because the place resembled a large conference hall. I saw in the far end, the bulky dark complexion man sitting behind a large table that was covered with books and papers like a university dean's table. He showed me to a seat near him with a wave of his left hand.

"SST, I have something to show you." He threw a large size photograph across the table at my front. I looked at it briefly and raised my head to stare at him.

"Look at it." He ordered. I looked at it more closely; it was a picture of two uncompleted one storey buildings adjacent each other.

The commissioner asked me to examine it closely. When I did, I saw building implements littered around the area. It was a building that work was still going on.

"Does it resemble the hideout you told us in your statement?" He asked. I was still looking at the picture intensely and couldn't answer him. "Look at it very closely, especially the building implements." He was helping me with the scrutiny.

"I hope am right, but this very much resembles the first place I was taken to by the kidnappers." I said, taking my eyes off the picture and looking up at him.

"Ah ha!" exclaimed the commissioner. He was rubbing his palms together joyfully and shaking his head in the manner of a student about to answer a question in a quiz he knew he had the answer right. "This, my dear SST, is the new but uncompleted building of Star FM. And we were reliably told by the management that our dear Mr Dan Paul was in charge of the construction." He was throwing it to my face as if to say, 'Didn't I tell you?'

"And this?" He threw another item to my front again. It was two sheets of paper. I read the contents. It was a write up signed by Mr Dan Paul stressing on the need to use all means to ensure that Star FM maintains the lead in FM radio broadcasting in Lagos. I didn't see how it has got anything to do with me. I looked up at the commissioner trying to make sense out of this one.

"And this, sir?" I asked, holding the paper up to signify that I was referring to it. The commissioner burst out laughing, like a teacher who can't believe the extent of ignorance of a student on seeing an answer that was staring in his face.

"And this, sir, my dear presenter." He was mimicking how I asked the question. "It is Mr Dan Paul's plan of action that was discovered in the drawer in his office. You can see the phrase *all means*, in the paper. Can we say, all means include kidnapping and murder?" He asked rhetorically. I didn't know how to answer that but I knew how to keep quiet and avoid appearing the fool before such a knowledgeable crime buster. "My dear friend, very soon your kidnappers will face justice, so please continue to cooperate with us anytime you are called to the court." He had stood up now, I saw it as a sign that the meeting was over. I stood up too.

He extended his hand to me.

"Sorry SST, I have to be going now. I have a security meeting at the government house, and the governor is interested on far we have gone. We need to be thorough, because our investigations about the kidnapping are connected to big political figures in the state. I just want you to know how far we have gone on your case, just in case he calls you to confirm how things are going with you." He said while leading me out of his office. I entered my car and headed home. I was to resume work fully at the studio next day. Mark wanted me to take some days off but I saw no need.

The newspapers have been having a field day reporting on the story of the kidnapping. There was a picture of Dan Paul in the dock when he was arraigned in court in the Daily Sun. The newspaper captioned the story on its front page. It was bad for Dan Paul that the Daily Sun was owned by a political opponent of Chief Raymond Chekwas, the chairman of STAR FM. To the public, Dan Paul was the culprit waiting to be pronounced guilty.

I resumed work at the studio. My colleagues were all glad to have me back. But the atmosphere was still sad over the death of Sasha. I could see Mark was affected the most. They were very close and had worked together for years.

The listeners of my popular radio programme were ecstatic when I started the show again. At first I was unable to do anything else than answer calls from listeners all calling to wish me well and wanting to know how I survived the ordeal. I told them all that it was something that will take some time for me to fully appraise, and when I was ready, I will put it down in a narrative for them. I continued with my normal show as the excitement of the kidnapping started to fade.

A week to the resumption of the court trial, the commissioner of police called me. When I saw his name on my phone, my first thought was that it has something to do with my coming appearance as a witness in the case.

"SST, please meet me in my office right away." He was obviously angry. I wondered what his anger has got to do with me. Did I say anything wrong in my statement in the court? I kept on wondering the reason for his obvious anger as I made my way to his office.

When I entered the office, I met him enraged and pacing up and down his office.

"SST, can you imagine this nonsense? Somebody is trying to rubbish my effort after the pains I took to crack this case in record time!" He was shouting as he shook angrily. I stood there looking at him, still wondering what the new development was all about. Something was obviously agitating his mind as he continued talking, mostly to himself as if I was not around.

"After I have personally taken over the case, and have arrived at findings that would definitely close the case in court, the force headquarters is now sending some blue eyed investigator from Abuja to pick holes in it. Just because the investigations involved some high ranking politicians!" My heart skipped for relief as he said that. Now I know what the whole issue was all about. It had nothing to do with me.

"The detective from Abuja wants to ask you some questions about the case. I don't see what new things he wants to find out about the kidnapping. I don't even see any new thing he can get from you that was not already covered in our investigation. Anyway, just cooperate with him. I don't see him staying with us for long. I have to cooperate too, since he is from the force headquarters. But as I said to you; there is nothing new for him to get about the case!" The commissioner said. He then pressed a button on his table and a police officer came in, "Show Mr Tal ... SST, to the CID section." He ordered the man. And said to me, "SST, please follow my orderly. He will show you to the CID section, Superintendent Clark Stevenson is waiting for you there." I went out of the office with the orderly, leaving the commissioner attending to the files on his table.

I followed the police officer to a room upstairs, on the last floor. The moment he opened the door someone inside ordered him out in a hardly audible voice.

"Thanks officer, you can go back now." The commissioner's orderly went out closing the door behind him and left me standing in a very small half—lighted room. The only furniture in the room was a table and three chairs; two chairs at the other side of the table facing the door and one chair against it. I could see two men sitting in the chairs facing me; their faces were not clearly visible in the room. The table had only a small lamp that was kept on the right side of the table and a medium size notebook beside it.

The voice that ordered the commissioner's orderly out, said to me, "Please move forward and sit down." I moved a little from where I was standing, to the only remaining seat, the one facing them.

"Please feel free, Mr Sawuntungo Sasukito Talungo. My name is Superintendent Clark Stevenson. I am from force headquarters Abuja." His accent was smooth and cool. It sounded very far from that of the other policemen I have gotten used to by now. He was talking like a young doctor to a new patient. I immediately felt at ease with him, because he was one of the few people I have met so far since I came to Lagos that preferred to use my name than using my initials. The way he pronounced my full names with surprising perfection warned me that I was before a stickler.

He was smiling warmly at me, making me to feel as if there was no reason to have been uneasy in the first place.

"This is my associate here in Lagos Superintendent Johnny Okoronkwo, he has been handling the kidnapping case, I'm sure you are acquainted with him." I looked at the bearded fair in complexion man beside, of course I knew him. He was amongst those that interviewed me twice after my released by the kidnappers. Okoronkwo smiled at me showing a touch of familiarity, I smiled back and nodded to Clark Stevenson.

"I'm not here to replaced Mr Okoronkwo on the case but merely to compliment his efforts." He said, turning to look at Okoronkwo, who smiled and lowered his head. Clark then whispered something to Johnny Okoronkwo. I saw Johnny's eyes hardened disapprovingly for a minute. He looked unsure on what to do, as he shifted uncomfortably in his chair a little. He stood up and without a word took the notebook on the table and left. Clark Stevenson might not have come to replaced Johnny Okoronkwo but something told me he did not come to work with him either. Clark brought out a tiny notebook from his pocket and placed it on the table in front of him.

"Mr Talungo, I hope you are comfortable here." He said holding out his hand to shake me.

"I'm fine sir." I said, speaking for the first time.

"That's good; I want you to know this is not a different investigation from what you have been subjected to. I just want to clarify some issues after going through your statement and the investigation report on the case." He said, flipping through the small notebook "I will not waste your time. I don't intend to spend much time here Mr Talungo. I do not stay more than two weeks in a place." He raised his eyebrows at me. I nodded, and smiled uncomfortably.

"First, let me start with the account of your meeting with Mr Dan Paul, you said in your statement that you didn't view his remarks as threat and saw no reason to report it, am I correct?" He said.

"You are right, sir." I answered.

"Did you discuss it with anybody?" He asked.

"Yes I did, with my studio producer."

I then told him of Mark's reaction when I told him Mr Dan had a proposal for me and from Mark's reaction I was further convinced Mr Dan Paul's talk was just supercilious.

"You said your studio producer, Mr Mark Paul, told you he met Mr Dan Paul only once and their encounter was not too pleasant to him?" He asked. I answered in the affirmative.

"I can understand why you were not bothered with what Dan Paul said to you on that day, but why were you not bothered when you started receiving the threatening text messages?" He asked with a concern curiosity.

"Mr Clark, I never associated the text messages I was receiving with Mr Dan Paul, it was not the number I knew him with, and when I tried calling that number there was no reply. I am a very popular presenter in Lagos, Mr Clark. I know a lot of people out there might want to play pranks on me, or might not even like me, and really, like my conversation with Mr Paul, I didn't see anything so serious about those text messages." I said that in a more relaxed manner than when I started. I was now becoming comfortable with

302

Superintendent Clark; his questions were more incisive than the statement writing I was drilled in earlier. I am now a full participant in a discussion with a police investigator and I was enjoying it.

"Mr Talungo, are you telling me you saw nothing wrong in this text message you received?" He brought out some papers and handed out a piece of paper to me. It was a photocopy of what looked like a text message. I was surprised with what I read.

"I don't know anything about this. If I had received something like this I would have been concerned of course. Where did you get this from?" I exclaimed in shock.

"It was recovered from your damaged handset. The text entered your phone about thirty minutes before the time you were believed to have been kidnapped, if we are to take what was recorded in your statement." He was smiling at me, his eyes taunting me to come out with whatever I might have missed or deliberately hid from my statement.

"Mr Clark, I knew very well the time I was kidnapped, because the late 12 o'clock motivation show had just started in the car radio as we took that turn. I might have missed the text message because I never answered a call whenever I am driving. My handset is always kept on the dashboard stand whenever I am in the car, and that was where I left it when I was abducted. I'm sure of that because my eyes went to that place as I thought of picking it and calling for help when I heard those shots, but before I knew it, I was hit on the skull with the butt of a pistol." I said.

Clark Stevenson looked at me thoughtfully for a while and said "Are you sure of the position of your handset?"

"Yes I am." I answered. He then brought out a folded paper from his pocket and unfolded it on the table. I looked at closely. It was a photocopied map of Victoria Island in Lagos.

"This is the road you came from your office . . . . this is where the house of your late friend Sasha is, you were kidnapped along Sam Ogemudia Road, Sasha lived at number 2 Ademola Kunle street.

Why go through Sam Ogemudia Road, which is usually isolated as it is avoided by most people at night because of the reputation of the bad boys living there, and it is like moving along a triangle, when you can take the more accessible Ajasin Adekunle Street and reached her house in no time?" He asked. I looked at the map very well. I understood what he was getting at. I knew how to read maps well. I had a brief stint in the army, remember?

"I didn't know the road very well; it was my first time of going to drop Sasha at home. But that was not even the reason I avoided Ajasin Adekunle road. When I reached the junction, we met a policeman on duty there. It was the policeman that diverted us to Sam Ogemudia Road; he claimed Ajasin Adekunle Road was closed for the night as construction workers were carrying out a survey on that road for a future road rehabilitation work. That was how we got ourselves on Sam Ogemudia Road that fateful night." There was nothing strange about that. It was common knowledge that most road construction works take place at night in Lagos to avoid obstruction by traffic.

"Why didn't you include that in your statement?" He asked.

"I didn't remember to include it, and nobody asked me why I followed which road" I answered.

"You said a police officer diverted you at Ajasin Adekunle junction?" He pointed at the junction on the map.

"Yes" I said. I then added, so as not to raise unusual suggestions. "I identified his police uniform and mannerism, if he was not a true police officer, I wouldn't know." I told him.

"Ok, that's all right, coming to your statement, you said Sasha was shouting before the men fired, and you were unable to reach for your handset or even do anything before you were hit with a pistol?" He said. I believed I had to explain better. I was in the army before so it could seem unusual that I was just looking and doing nothing within those few minutes before I was hit on the head.

"You see, Mr Clark, when the police officer diverted us at that junction towards Sam Ogemudia Road, Sasha was complaining about the road because of its reputation of having all those area boys, you know she lived in the area. I didn't give it a serious thought. I saw it as just female intuition. When we were going we met a car parked on the road, and two men came down towards us. When Sasha saw them she started shouting. I was thinking she was unnecessary scared as they didn't appear hostile to me until they started shooting, and by then things happened so fast." I told him of the accounts of those few unfortunate minutes before I was kidnapped.

"Can you remember what she was saying?" He asked me.

"She didn't really had time to say anything much. At first when she saw them coming towards us, she started screaming in fright, then she turned to pleading and shouting 'please I won't, I won't' before the bullets hit her." I said.

"I won't, what?" He asked.

"I don't know what she was trying to say, she was in great fright, maybe she was trying to plead for mercy or something." I said. I went on to narrate the ordeal I went through after I was abducted; all that I knew from the time the kidnappers started blindfolding me to when I was finally rescued from their grips. Superintendent Clark Stevenson asked me more questions and went through the earlier statement I made for the police to ensure I had my earlier details accurate. After about two hours of strenuous drilling, his face became a bit more brighten than when we first started. It seemed he was satisfied with whatever he was looking for, and has decided to end the meeting.

"Mr Talungo, I must thank you for your cooperation. I really enjoyed our short discussion. I will love to have your phone number please, and if there is anything more I need to clarify, I will try and get across to you." He was being quite warm at the end of the long interrogation, which he chose to call a short discussion.

I thanked him for the nice reception, and quickly left the Police Headquarters before anyone could think of another thing. But more than anything else, I needed to refresh myself urgently. After two hours with Police Superintendent Clark Stevenson, I was sweating and in need of a cool shower. I rushed out of the Police Headquarters feeling like a student who had just left an examination hall.

I went back to the studio but there was nothing much for me to do as the studio was repeating my earlier recorded programmes to guard against the incessant calls that were coming in asking about the case; and also my now seemingly frequent interruptions by summons from the police headquarters. The moment Mark saw me back in the studio he called me into his office.

"SST, what are the police still interested in finding out from you again? Haven't you told them all that they needed to know?" He asked in a voice clouded with worry.

Mark had been concerned with the continuous publicity the investigation into my kidnapping was drawing to the studio. Chief Dokubo, the Chairman of Static FM, was preparing for an election and one of his opponents would be Chief Raymond Chekwas the Chairperson of Star FM! The more the press beams light on the kidnapping saga, the more it would attract negative political insinuations. Mark and Chief Dokubo, like all of us, hope the court will speed up with the trial of Dan Paul so that we can put all behind us and move on with our lives. I saw the worried expression on Mark's face. I decided not to aggrieve my friend the more by telling him a meddlesome detective from Abuja had just arrived to draw more highlights on the case. I wanted him to at least have a peace of mind and continue with his work, hoping as we all do, that everything is now behind us.

"No problem Mark, the commissioner just wanted me to sign some few areas in my statement. I think they are about forwarding it with their final reports to the Force Headquarters Abuja. You know they have concluded their investigations and everything is left for the court now." I said, beaming a wide smile, wanting my boss to know he can put all worries about the issue behind him, at least till when the court case comes up. I can see Mark appearing a little more relaxed. He was a man very dedicated to his duties but of recent, I can see the fallouts of the kidnapping had affected him adversely, especially the death of Sasha. He told me how he and his wife were planning to travel to Benin to see Sasha's parents and offer their condolences. They were unable to attend the burial, because they were busy taking care of me in the hospital. I hoped to be able to go with them.

I went back to my office feeling a little relief. It was three days after, when I went back fully into hosting the motivation show once again. I didn't hear from Detective Clark Stevenson for some time after he interrogated me at the Police Headquarters. His insinuations were almost out of my mind. The only thought I still had of the kidnapping was with my coming appearance in the ongoing trials at the court. It was getting to a week when last we met that I got the first phone call from him. When the phone rang my heart jumped when I saw his name, I wasn't expecting that.

"Hello" I said reluctantly when I picked the call.

"Good day, Mr Talungo, this is Detective Clark Stevenson." He said. How I wish he would call me with my initials like everyone else.

"Yes, I know, I have your number, sir." I drew the word 'sir' making it sound perfunctory.

"Well, that's good, my friend I just want to find out how you were doing?" He said. Detective Clark Stevenson never looked like someone who will just call to find out how I was doing.

"Thanks I appreciate that." said. (*Sorry I couldn't say the same Mr Stevenson!*)

"I was wondering if you won't mind coming to pay me a visit at the headquarters." He said in his usual sleekly way of passing a message.

"I will mind Mr Stevenson, because I'm busy now." I said.

"Well in that case when will you be available or should I come over." He requested. I won't want him to come here of course. It will set Mark's temperature on a roller coaster.

"I will close by 4pm." I said hurried.

"Good, I will be waiting for you here, needless to tell you it is very important." He said and hung up.

When I came to the end of evening show, my inner spirit sank. It was time to go and meet Clark Stevenson. I never really know what he had for me now, but whatever it was, I really was not too eager for another meeting with him. I reluctantly bid my colleagues farewell for the day and entered into my official car headed to the force headquarters. I deliberately chose a road that had a heavy traffic, anything to waste some time on the road. When I reached the police headquarters I met a traffic warden by the gate who directed me to park in an isolated shed away from the car park. I guess there were other visitors expected at the Complex and the available stands at the car park were reserved for them. I quietly locked my car and entered the building, slowly climbing to the last floor, to the office where I was interrogated nearly two week earlier. When I entered, I met a young tall fair lady with Clark Stevenson in the office.

"Ha! My friend Mr Talungo, I am very happy to see you again." He said with a wide grin extending his hands. I didn't know what to say so I just shook his hands and smiled back.

"Mr Talungo, have a seat." He was pointing to the empty seat in the room. I sat down.

"Please let me introduce Miss Chinyere Yusuf, a consultant with the Global Systems Electronics Firm, Miss Chinyere Yusuf this is Mr Talungo from Static FM." The lady smiled broadly, as he introduced us. She extended her hand too. I shook it warmly.

"SST, I am a great fan of your show. I told Clark before you entered that you need no introduction. Your reputation precedes you." She said. I was now feeling more at ease seeing someone who I could at least relate with on a more familiar term. It wasn't that Clark Stevenson was hostile or troublesome, far from it, on the contrary he could be said to be congenial. He just had something about him that warns you to be careful. Clark looked at my face and saw a smug look, he could detect I was not too pleased. He lowered his eyes, tapping the pen on his hands on the table. Miss Yusuf sat there waiting for him to speak.

"My Friend, Mr Talungo, please relax your mind. I can assure you, you are not here today for another long session of interrogation. On the contrary, you are here to assist with a new product we want to have in the market. Miss Yusuf has a product from global systems that she wants you to see." He said. The lady brought out a small packet from her handbag and handed it over to Clark. He opened it and brought out a small metal object with strings of wires attached to it.

"Mr Talungo, for some time now we have observed that most kidnapped victims, once the ransom is paid, and were release, easily once again fall victims as their kidnappers or another group sees them as soft objects. And in most cases is not even reported to the police as their contacts become use to dealing with such cases. We cannot of course, provide armed guard to every of such citizens. But we can monitored their whereabouts and get a signal if they were in danger and moved in quickly." He said turning the object in his hands. I can see it resembled a small handset. He looked at the lady and hand over the object to her. She collected it and turned the inner side to face my direction.

"SST, this is a phoning device that functions exactly like your handset that is connected to the global systems mobile. But this has in addition, an advanced global positioning system that sends out both graphic images and sound sensors to a receiver. Wherever this phone is, it sends a signal to a similar handset to which it has been configured with." She brought out a handset from her bag, "this is my normal handset and it was configured to work with this one. If I press here, I can reach a twelve figured grid reference of where this handset is and using the electronic town map settings, I can locate where exactly, in a city, the signals are coming from." She went on explaining how the device works for about fifteen minutes. When she finished Clark started another of his own explanations.

"Mr Talungo, you are about the only person who has been kidnapped in Lagos in recent time. It's not that we are expecting your kidnappers, or any other group to come for you, it was just that you are about the only person we can test this latest device on." He said and added slyly "for now!"

Miss Yussuf went ahead to give a breakdown on other functions the little handset can be put to, as she went forward explaining like a salesperson. I became very interested.

"Mr Talungo, we will want you to be our first test, you just need to transfer your SIM card to this new device and use it as your handset for some days after which we will have it back after checking the progress of its use." He said. Why not? I really saw no harm in trying the device. It has some interesting usage, after all what was there to lose anyway? I agreed to submit myself as their first guinea pig. I was the only qualified for a guinea pig in Lagos after all!

"There is one thing you should know Mr Talungo." Clark chipped in again. Here it comes!

"This device is not yet in the market and is not known to the public. If it goes out, it will lose its value. It was meant to protect only those whose lives are under threat from kidnappers, publicity on the device will kill its value." He sounded very serious as he talked.

Clark Stevenson stretched and looked straight into my eyes "Mr Talungo, you must keep this strictly confidential between the three of us in this room. You must not let anybody into it, not your friends, not even your co-workers, including your bosses." He said. Did I need to be reminded of that?

Chief Dokubo will fall with a heart attack if he gets to know one of his staff was doubling as a police agent, it will damage his political aspirations. That's the kind of publicity Mark wanted the studio to avoid.

"No problem with that Clark, I won't want that too." I assured him.

Clark stood up to shake my hands, his way of signalling the end of the meeting "Thanks, Mr Talungo, I can see you are not too comfortable with the environment. I hope we meet next time in a more acceptable setting." He said smiling. As if he was reading my mind. I could see he had noticed my discomfort with the interrogation room. I hate the place. The whole place makes me feel, like a criminal accused, anytime I entered there.

I left the Police Headquarters after a quick demonstration of the new device. I removed my SIM card from my handset, and transferred it to the new multi—dimensional handset handed to me. The handset appeared from the outside as ordinary as any that is available from the street vendors. It even bears the popular Nokia trademark. To any unsuspecting person, it was the normal Nokia handset. I went straight back home after leaving the Police Headquarters. I thought about telling Segun about the device and thrilling him with how it works. But I decided against it, there was enough time to do that when the experiment was over. And moreover I had given my word to Clark Stevenson to keep it secret between the three of us.

All went normal in the following days at the office. I went back to fully hosting my popular radio show, which had become more popular since my kidnapping saga. Many people that do not listen before or rather never called were now becoming fans. My regular callers brought up some interesting and educative topics for discussion. Life went back to normal, except that I started noticing some uneasiness in Mark wherever I was around. He also hardly calls me to his office for our usual short talks. Whenever I entered his office, he would pretend to be busy and start turning his files up and down, trying to avoid meeting my eyes. I suspected he held me responsible for the death of Sasha, still feeling guilty for handling her to my care that fateful night. It was apparent he had not come to terms with the death of Sasha. Such feelings are normal to anyone who loses someone special. You keep thinking it was a dream that will soon go away, and you will see the person again, until when the days pass and the true impact of the situation brings you back to reality.

It was four days from the day I met Clark Stevenson and Miss Yusuf at the police headquarters that I arrived the studio to see some changes in my work schedule. My normal 9 pm show was shifted to 12 pm! I have never held a show at that hour of the night, that's the time the studio runs all late night music show for lovers who need to reach out to their partners. It was never a time considered ideal for my type of show, which was more of a family and community programme. I met the stage engineer who was in charge of running such timings. He told me the studio producer effected the change. I went in to discuss it with Mark in his office. As I entered, Mark repeated his action for the past two days whenever I get close to him, he would turn his attention to other matters trying to avoid my eyes.

"Mark I saw that my schedule has been shifted to midnight." I said.

"Yes" replied Mark, not taking his eyes from the paper in his hands.

"Mark that would mean, I will have to leave here by 1 am the next morning, you know I live a far away." My voice was besieging him. He took his eyes off the paper and looked at me for the first time. I didn't like the look I saw in his eyes; it was glassy and absentminded like a drug jockey in a trance. I was shaken. I never saw Mark like this. Never suspected he could be doing drugs. He quickly got hold of himself and smiled.

"Sorry, SST, just do us the favour for today. I promised it won't happen again. There is a programme, an interview that the Chief did, it is close to election time you know and we believe the best time to air it is between 9 and 10 pm, that's when the people that matters are near their radios, please bear with us." He said. I wanted to reply that those that matter in party primaries are the political Masters and they do not listen to radio. Well, anyway, at least I know the reason behind the change and hopefully it won't happen again as he said. I didn't want to be going home in late hours. I was yet to recover from my last kidnapping experience. For the first time I was glad for the device Clark Stevenson gave me. I just hope it was working. I really needed some signs of protection to reassure myself in the lonely night as I drive back home. I left Mark looking dejected and went to the other room that the staff use as the in-house common room. There was nobody there, the presenters have gone home, and only the engineers were left. The engineers operated the machines on shift. Soon the group on night duty will arrive and relieve their colleagues for the night, and all they do was to replay recorded programmes and fill the night with musical sounds until the early hours of daytime when the presenters will report and start with the 6 o'clock news broadcast. I intend to lie briefly on the long settee, but only to realised I had slept off when Ken, one of the stage engineers came to woke me up to prepare for my show. It was 11:30pm.

I was drowsy, weak and half coordinated throughout the presentation of the programme. It was the first time I was working that late in the night, but surprising some of my good listeners still followed the earlier notification of the shift in timing of my show and stayed into the night. Together, we did our best to put up a good show, but it just didn't go like it used to be. After only 45 minutes, I decided to end the show, promising them it will be the last time I will hold the show at that time of the night. Feeling drowsy and tired, I still managed to get myself out from the seat and bid the two engineers and the relief shifts that had just arrived to take over from them, good night. The studio was very quiet; Mark had closed at 11pm before I even went on air. The other presenters have long left too, only the engineers were around, and soon the two will leave their replacements behind as they too close for the day.

I made my way to the parking lot and entered my car lazily. At this time of the night, the usual busy streets of Lagos are normally clear of traffic but less safe. It was good that I would take the major expressway that will see me straight to my place, avoiding the dark lonely connecting roads that are mostly unsafe at this time of the night. When I drove out and reached the highway I saw a wide open road that would soon, when the day breaks, turn to an unappeasable sea of people and vehicle.

As I moved on the road, I heard the sound of movement inside the car. At first I thought it was coming from the music, but when I strained my eyes I realised the sound was coming from the back. I was seized with shock. I was the only one in the car, and maybe a cat or something had entered when I packed the car. I tried turning to see what was behind when I felt the cold sensation of an iron on the back of neck. I nearly jumped out in fright and swerved off the road when I heard someone said, "Just keep on moving, don't stop or I pull the trigger." I was moved in shock, the voice was familiar. I couldn't turn my head for fear of startling the man with the gun! The voice talk again, "take the next turn" he said.

I knew that voice.

I turned my head slightly still keeping my eyes on the road.

"Mark?" I inquired.

"Yes, SST, keep on driving." He said

"Mark what are . . ." I was trying to make something out of my mind! What joke was he up to? What is happening to me again? He shut me up fast, pushing the barrel of the pistol; harder against my neck.

"Shut up, and keep moving or I blast your head off!" He snapped with a force I had never known him with. The hostility and seriousness in the voice convinced me this was not a joke or some kind of play, this was serious. I was being abducted again! And what more, by my mentor, friend, studio producer; Deacon Mark Paul!

Mark directed me to go off the road and take one of the numerous bush paths that led deep into the bush and far away from the major

313

road. After driving for some time into the bush, swerving the low bottomed saloon as it go about hitting stones and stumps, Mark pointed to an open space and told me to pack the car there and move out. It was very dark in the early hours of the morning but the bright moonlight was able to make the place a bit visible.

"Move to the right!" Mark said as he nervously looked over his shoulders, the gun still pointing at me. He looked as if he was expecting someone to come and join us.

"Mark what is the meaning of all this?" I asked. I was getting my voice back now, the shock of seeing Mark with the gun overshadowed all.

"SST, shut up!" He was visibly angry now. I decided to keep quiet. I know better than argue with a man holding a gun. Mark managed to look directly at me for the first time but quickly turned his face away. He was finding it hard to stare at me directly.

"SST, I didn't want to do this but you forced me to it. Why can't you shut up and let things be? What is wrong with all of you? First Sasha, and now you! All of you pushing me to the wall!" He was angrily shaking now and almost shouting in the night. Sasha? What did Mark had to do with her? It was now getting clear to me there were still things I didn't understand.

"Mark, you got anything to do with Sasha's death and my kidnapping?" I asked calmly. He looked at me and shrugged with a smug, smiling as if talking to a child.

"SST, there is no need anyway; it will all be over soon! Yes, I arranged it all." He confessed looking at me straight in the face. I could see how his face has hardened.

"Sasha was blackmailing me; trying to destroy my life, my marriage, and everything I have worked for. My wife is a big preacher, SST! I can't allow that to happen. It was not about you SST, it was later I realised I can get you kidnapped, get the money I needed to set up my business and my wife's church, and at the same time get rid of Sasha. It was too good to be true when the idea came up in my mind!" He said. I stood there, frozen with shock by his revelation. But why? What was all this about?

"Mark, what do you mean get rid of Sasha? Mark, what is all this about? Sasha was like a sister to you? What is happening to you, Mark?" I just couldn't figure out what this was all about. I don't know if I was dreaming or what!

"SST, shut up, I am not the one to kill you, but you might force me to, if you don't shut up." He snapped angrily at me. "I didn't dig a hole for you SST, you just fell into one that I didn't cover up properly." He was pointing the pistol menacingly at me, looking as if at any moment he won't mind pulling the trigger. I could see the light of an approaching vehicle. I saw Mark turning to the direction of the coming vehicle with a sign of relief. Whoever was coming, certainly was someone he was waiting for. The vehicle stopped at a distance from where we were, the headlights were focused on where we were standing, lightening the area around us. I could now see Mark's face clearly, it was a mask of desperation, and large drops of sweat were dripping down his forehead.

A man came down from what looked like a police van from the distance and walked to where we were standing. I looked at the person closely. It was a police officer. I was getting more confused with what was taking place around me. What is this all about? I looked closely again at the man as he moved closer, there was something familiar about the police officer. I was trained in the army to always look out for special identifiable features in a person, and my mind drew my attention to the long tribal mark that went down the man's left cheek to his mouth. He turned and smiled at me. That smile again! Yes, I have recognised him now. I should have guessed from how things were unfolding. It was the police officer, the same one that diverted me at the junction on the day I was kidnapped.

"Well done Mark, you can go now, let me have the gun." He said. Mark looked around hesitatingly and turned to whisper something to the man, and then looked at me briefly. Our eyes met and I saw his expression changed to that of a man that knew very clearly what he was doing. He then shrugged and turned away, and then said with his back on me "Goodbye, SST, I never thought it will reach to this stage, but there is nothing I can do, good bye." And with that he turned to enter his car.

The police officer smiled deviously at me, I knew what was to come. He was there to kill and discard my body. And would return later to claim he discovered my maimed body on a routine search. Whatever, it was clear to me as bright sunlight. I'm about to be killed. There was nothing to be afraid of again.

However, what happened next took me by great surprise. The police officer swung with his might and hit Mark on the shoulder, bringing him hard to the ground, Mark was rolling and writhing in pains, when he pointed the pistol at him and said softly "Sorry, Mark, this game has been over long ago!" He then put two fingers in his mouth and whistled. I saw two people coming out of the dark and moving towards us. They must have alighted from the police vehicle as this was all happening. The one at the front moved nearer to me and tapped my shoulders lightly.

"Good morning, Mr Talungo, as I said before, I hope the next time we meet would be in a more acceptable place." He was smiling. I looked into his face under the dim moonlight and gasped in shock! It was Detective Clark Stevenson, and beside him was Miss Yussuf. I never thought I would be so glad to see this two.

CHAPTER FOUR

The Revelation
"as I told you, I don't stay in a place more than two weeks!"

Mark was handcuffed, and bundled into the police van, by the two police officers that joined us at the scene. Clark Stevenson and Miss Yusuf decided to ride with me to the police headquarters. It was already far into the early morning and nearing daybreak when we got to the police headquarters. Clark took me straight back to the interrogation room and this time around I met a small conference going on. There were two other police officers whom Clark introduced as special investigators that have just arrived from the force headquarters in Abuja to continue with the case.

"Mr Talungo, I've finished with my work here, and I'm handing your case over to them. They are to go on with all issues of the prosecution." He said. I was staring blindly at him, at a lost to all that was happening to me. I couldn't understand what was happening to me. Clark Stevenson looked at me pitifully. He understood what I was going through.

"Ok SST," he said calmly, using my initials for the first time!

"Let me bring you to date on what has been happening." He said. And with that he started what I called the revelation of the truth.

It was clear that Dan Paul didn't stand a chance in the trial for your kidnapping and the murder of Sasha. The police investigation reports together with the evidences fully indicted him. And this was corroborated by my account of our meeting where he was seen to have threatened you. However, Chief Raymond Chekwas is a chieftain of the ruling party and a close friend of the president. The Chief refused to accept that his bureau manager had anything to do with the kidnapping, or the whole thing had anything linked to his radio station. The Chief went to see the president directly to lodge a complaint and the president ordered the inspector general of police, known as the IG, to look closely at the case. The IG sent for the investigative report of his commissioner in Lagos. It was clear the commissioner had done a good job at unravelling the case at his level. But that was at his level. The IG decided to send in one of his top investigators, one of those that were only released to a high profile case, and that was how Detective Clark Stevenson, whom his friends loved to call Sherlock Holmes got into the case.

When Clark Stevenson arrived in Lagos, he first went through the investigation reports and the statement I made to the police with an eye glass. As he told me, something always draws his suspicion when he sees evidences in a case deliberately falling into place like a game of cards. He first started on the statements of witnesses, choosing to believe all he was seeing until he sort it out—you don't start getting at the truth by doubting a lie. You believe to the point it stretches itself out of its shell. Clark decided to stretch the lie out of the shell.

Clark became suspicious over the circumstances surrounding the killing of Sasha. If it was merely a kidnapping that was intended, then why complicate it with a murder? Kidnappers are known to be only interested in collecting the ransom, after which they will vanish, hoping all will be forgotten when they release the victim. When Clark checked more on Sasha he found out that her employers hurriedly moved her body to her hometown for burial after the shooting, even before the police had a chance to conduct a post mortem on her body. This was however explained by the commissioner of police who never saw a need for a post mortem because it was a clear case of death from gunshot wounds.

Clark started digging into Sasha's most recent activities before she was murdered. He found out two months before her death she was certified 3 weeks pregnant by her doctor. Sasha was not known to be dating any man, nobody even knew if she had a boyfriend. Her flat mates said they never saw her going out for a date, and no man ever came to see her at home as she leaves for office early and returns late in the night, save for Sundays when she spends her time in the church. No man was seen entering her house before, except of course her boss, Mark Paul. He normally brings her home from office at night in his car, and sometimes stays in for up to an hour with her.

Clark Stevenson visited her church where he was able to get from the pastor that Sasha confided in him about her pregnancy and also of her plans for an abortion that she said was suggested by her partner. He had strongly advised her against accepting an abortion. She never said who her partner was, and he didn't pressurize her to reveal the person's identity. He saw his task stopping at counselling her on how to handle the pregnancy and not to prying into her personal affairs. Clark became suspicious if she had anything more than the ordinary to do with Mark, the studio producer, but all other witnesses pointed to the fact that they seemed to have no more than an intimate professional relationship.

Clark became more circumspect on Mark when I told him that Mark said he met Dan Paul only once. That seemed hard to believe as both of them work in the same media house for years. He decided to dig into Mark's background. It was easy for him to find out at Star FM that Mark once worked under Dan Paul, something like 12 years ago when Star FM was among the very few FM stations in Lagos. Dan Paul sacked him for a reason nobody knew and there was nothing to show for it in the company records. And it took Mark two years of roaming the streets before he could land a low paying job at Static FM. When Clark interrogated Dan Paul at the prison cell where he was being detained, he revealed to him what he had not told anybody before.

Mark was his deputy studio producer when he fired him. It all happened one Monday morning, when he decided to come to the studio earlier than usual. He had a bad day during the weekend with his live-in lover, now his wife, and decided to abandon home and come to the studio earlier than usual, he arrived the office at about 5 am. He usually arrives at about 7:30 am to relief Mark who does the late evening show. It was when he entered his office, unannounced of course; you don't expect him to knock in his own office, that he met Mark on the office table with one of the studio assistants, a young female youth corps member, on intern with the studio, having sex.

The young lady was a niece of a station director who handed her to the care of Dan Paul for her one year compulsory national youth service programme. Dan Paul was livid, aside from the fact that the young lady was his protégé; the behaviour fell far below the expectations of the fastidious man. He decided to keep it a secret so as not to damage his relationship with her father, but more than anything, because that will greatly damage the reputation of the organisation in which he works. He too couldn't work in an organisation where people suspect the staff of having sex on office tables with young female interns. And no organisation will bear to employ Mark with a ten foot pole if he reveals that. So he decided to fire him but keep it quiet. Of course, Mark knew him; he worked directly under him for two years!

Clark focussed the searchlight heavily on Mark. He discovered that Mark was heavily indebted and his wife was making plans to open her own ministry ever since she was ordained, and Mark had been talking to people on where to build her a big church. Where he expected to get money and pay off his debts, as well as finance his wife's ministry, nobody knew? Certainly not from his salary, at even with the recent increases from the successes recorded by STATIC FM, there wasn't much he could gather.

Clark Stevenson was drawn to the last words Sasha said before she was shot. Why was she afraid when she saw the two men coming towards the car even when they were yet to pose a threat? Why was she shouting, please I won't? I won't what? What was she promising she won't do? Was anybody threatening her life? Well, if there was a threat she never seemed to have mentioned it to any one that Clark contacted. But it was clear she knew her life was in danger even before she was attacked. Clark became concerned on how Mark was able to plan the kidnapping.

The kidnapping enable him to get 20 million naira of ransom money as well as to eliminate a potential threat to his personality. If Sasha had revealed she was pregnant for him, the scandal will have led to his sacking from Static FM and also destroyed whatever plans he had for his wife's church that is if the pious woman decides to go with the marriage. Her reputation as a preacher and his, as a deacon would have been damaged.

Mark was determined to get rid of the threat posed by Sasha, and also get the money he desperately needed. His mind seemed to have been made up as soon as I came into the picture. Here I was, the popular presenter, SST, known to the governor and the high and mighty in Lagos, everybody will agree that I was a potential kidnapping asset. And as soon as I told him of my meeting with Dan Paul, he couldn't believe his luck, it was an opportunity not only to quickly close the case but also to settle old scores. That was how he got me to agree to drop Sasha at home; after the late night New Year party that he planned at the office. He ensured we left late in the night by keeping us longer after the party with long speeches of appreciation for a well accomplished year. He was also the one that was sending the SMS messages to my handset with a new hidden SIM that tried to raise my suspicion about Dan Paul. It was when I left the office that night with Sasha that he sent the last message which Clark Stevenson showed me.

Mark was not in the underworld; how was he able to recruit such hardened criminals to do the kidnapping? Mark had a go between. He was police Sergeant Sani Audu. Police Sergeant Sani Audu once worked as a security guard at Star FM where Mark also worked. Clark found out he was fired too, and by Dan Paul. Sani Audu, like the other staff at the studio, disliked the pompous Dan Paul. He was more attuned with the easy going assistant producer, Mark Paul. The day Mark was caught on top of the young girl in the office; Sani Audu was desperate to warn him as soon as he opened the gate for Dan to enter the premises. He was aware of all what Mark does after working hours at the office and aided his escapades with the girls.

When Dan Paul was climbing the stairs of the building complex to his office, the day he caught Mark and the lady, it was Sani that threw stones at the office windows to alert Mark inside. However, Mark and the girl were too engrossed to notice or even to care. Dan

Paul got to know about that and fired him too! Sani was lucky to get himself into the police force through the assistance of a highly placed relation a few months after, but he never forgot.

Later he was to meet Mark again when the police authorities posted him from Kaduna in the north to the Lagos Police Command. When the idea to work out the kidnapping came up, Mark sought his assistance, and promoted his interest by promising him a good share from the ransom. Sani Audu had good reasons to trust Mark. When the two of them were working at Star FM, Mark always kept his promise of a small tip whenever he helps him in his numerous escapades. It became clear that it was Sani Audu that recruited the two kidnappers, and alone. Mark was not that stupid to allow the two wanted men to know he was a part of it. Sani Audu told the two boys, whom he brought into the country from the neighbouring Benin Republic to execute the kidnapping, that it was solely his scheme. He got to know the two hardened criminals when he once arrested them for armed robbery within Marina in Lagos, and their gang later paid him to arrange their escape to Benin Republic. They owe him a debt for that, and more, he promised they will be handsomely paid for this job.

It was Sani that broke into Dan Paul's office, after he was arrested, to plant the incriminating write-ups that the police later found. It was easy as he was very familiar with the place. After the kidnappers, on payment of the ransom, released me, Sani followed them across the border to Benin Republic and collected his share of the loot, which he shared for himself and Mark.

How did Detective Clark Stevenson got to know Sergeant Sani Audu was the link man in the scheme? That was the question I, too, eagerly asked him!

Detective Clark Stevenson said that when I told him about the police officer who diverted us at the junction, he became curious. At first, he suspected it could be one of the kidnappers in police uniform that acted the part. But he decided to look deeper. At first, as we all rightly suspected, there was no construction work taking place on the road that night. It was a hoax. The police officer must have waited for some time for us to appear at the junction, even if he was alerted of our coming. And the way Lagos police command maintains constant and effectively patrols within the highbrow areas of the city it will be a very hard task to deploy a fake police man on such a prominent junction without him being accosted within minutes by a police patrol team. The most probable bet was that it was genuine police personnel.

And how to go about fishing out a face out of over 25, 000 police officers deployed within the Lagos metropolis? Even with little descriptions of the person I met that night, it would still be a herculean task to fish out that individual in that big ocean. The police in Lagos were deployed around the city into different commands that were each assigned specific areas of responsibility in the city. Clark Stevenson started rowing into the profile of the police officer that serve in the area, removing those that didn't fit my description, and eliminating those that were sick, those that were known to maintain only a desk job and not to go on patrols and so forth, until he was left with a small clique. One person in that group attracted his attention.

The police officer was moved to the Victoria Island Command, a week before the kidnapping. He was transferred from the Apapa Port Command, where many police officers loved to serve for the little tips that changes hands at the Port, to the Victoria Island Command, where many hate to serve, for the sole reason that the area is the resident of many highly placed government officers who could be a pain in the ass. And Clark Stevenson found out it was a transferred that was carried out on the request of the police officer and not a routine administrative action.

Checking further on his prime suspect, Clark discovered that on the night of the kidnapping, he was with a patrol team that was covering the area I passed through that night. He was on night patrol duty on that day. How I accosted only him at the junction on that fateful night and not the whole patrol team was something that was hard to understand. This was because a police night patrol team was supposed to consist of not less than 10 armed men at a time. He must have found a way to slip from the rest of the squad and positioned himself where I met him. If he was the person, it meant he was not for duty at the Victoria Island Command prior to the planning of the act. He only had himself transferred to that area for that purpose. It made more sense to Clark. And from there, Detective Clark Stevenson's searchlight was focus fully on Sergeant Sani Audu.

Clark got information that within the period after my released by the kidnappers, Sergeant Sani Audu had bought two new houses for his brother in Lagos. There was nothing strange in that as one would expect someone to do that for a sibling. Afterall as a police officer he stood a better chance of closing a good deal in Lagos than his business brother who was based far away in the northern part of the country. There won't have been any reason for Clark Stevenson to raise any eyebrows on that, save that the said brother was until then a small kiosk owner in the popular Sabon Gari Market of Kano. A man hardly in the league of people to buy four or two bedroom flats in Lagos. Information that would normally have taken a long period to unravel, if at all, was coming to Detective Clark Stevenson

in a matter of minutes from the extensive contacts he had built over the years, he wasn't the Force Top Detective for nothing.

What finally convinced Detective Clark Stevenson that he had the right man was when he found out that Sergeant Sani Audu once worked at Star FM. He was fired too! And at about the period Mark was sacked. The case against Sergeant Sani Audu was sealed when Dan Paul confirmed that he did not only sacked Mark but also the gateman for collaboration, though he actually had problem recognising the picture of Sani Audu as the gateman he fired years ago. It was hardly to be expected that after all these years, Sani Audu would look the same. It was indeed a long journey in prosperity for him. From the lowly life of a poor gateman, barely able to make ends meet, to the affluent life of a police sergeant opened to the numerous financial benefits that accrue from a well-established corruption chain. It was safe to expect that his composure, outlook and confidence would surely change.

First, Clark had to build incontrovertible evidence against Sergeant Sani Audu, if there was any hope of getting to the root of the case. Detective Clark Stevenson requested the police commissioner to arrange a meeting between him and police officers on patrol teams from the highbrow districts of Ikoyi and Victoria Island. He was to appear for the meeting ostensibly as a police expert on anti-terrorism that was around to lecture them on anti kidnapping drills, now that the menace of kidnapping had started to rear its ugly head in the city.

The meeting first took place with the police team from Ikoyi, saving the targeted team from Victoria Island, for the last. On the day he was to hold a meeting with the teams from Victoria Island, he requested that the attendance be pruned by limiting entrance to only police officers of the ranks of sergeants and inspectors, the rank groups actually in command of the patrol teams. That brought the number of police officers of the ranks of sergeants and inspectors from Victoria Island to attend the meeting to a mere gathering of 45 police officers.

The room where the meeting was to take place was wired to hidden high definition cameras that revolved round the room filming the occupants at a very close range. During the meeting, Clark Stevenson threw in the bet, embedded his talk, by bringing up the issue of the ransom paid for the release of Mr Talungo, popularly known as SST, of the Static FM. It was not strange that such should come up in his speech, in fact, it was to be expected. My kidnapping was not only the latest of such happenings, but the only one experienced in Lagos for as long as any of them could remember.

"I'm sure all of you are aware of the details of the kidnapping of Mr Takungo, or should I say, SST, of Static FM, as you all know him." He started as a passing note and then moved to the crux of the matter. "When Mr Talungo was kidnapped, a ransom of 20 million naira was paid by the victim, with the assistance of the State Government. However, a day after his release, a separate ransom of 10 million naira was again paid to the kidnappers in exchange for secret tapes said to have been taken of the captive in a bare state of nature. The governor acting without wise counsel, acceded to the kidnappers demand by releasing the huge sum of money to them without liaising with the security forces, and after finding it was another dupe, the case was silently closed. I'm bringing it to your knowledge, as a teaching point of the high danger portend by crafty criminals in the country, and I also know that as professional police officers the issue will of course, remain here, we won't want to embarrass the governor of course!" He said.

He then proceeded to other areas of the lecture covering personnel security, vigilance and the normal rudiments of security work. The bait had been thrown; it waits to see the fish that will swallow it! After the meeting was dispersed, Clark Stevenson went through the video tapes of the meeting in the video studio. He noted when the issue of ransom was brought up, Sergeant Sani Audu nearly jumped out of his seat when he heard an additional 10 million naira was paid to the kidnappers, and from then he appeared highly uneasy and disturbed throughout the remaining part of the meeting. When the film was focus on his face, his expression was seen to change from a normal appearance, to apparent shock, and then becoming completely angry throughout. The machine connected to the television device noted a dramatic rise in his body temperature too. There was no doubt left he had something to do with the kidnapping. As Detective Clark Stevenson was about to send in a team to arrest Sergeant Sani Audu for questioning, his phone rang. It was coming from one of the Global Mobile Communication service providers. The phone numbers of the police officers from the Victoria Island Area Command that attended the meeting were forwarded to the various mobile communication providers to note who will make a call to Mark's handset.

It seemed Sergeant Sani Audu could not wait for too long as he left the meeting before making a move. The anger in him must have been too heavy to bear, as he quickly put a call to Mark. Clark could clearly recognise the voices on the recorded telephone conversation put to him by the communication firm.

"There is something important we need to discuss now." It was Sergeant Sani Audu speaking. "O.k, please not over the phone, why don't we see by 6 at the eatery in Maryland that we met the last time?"

Mark said. And the conversation ended. The order was immediately issued to quietly bring in Sergeant Sani Audu for interrogation. He was tricked to believing he was send for to bring in his patrol report to the police headquarters before the end of the day, a routine call for all patrol commanders. Sergeant sani Audu reported to the investigation office upstairs, only for him to meet Clark Stevenson and two armed police officers waiting for him. He was immediately relieved of all his possessions, taking away his handset and police pistol.

"Please sit down, Sergeant." Clark said. Sergeant Sani Audu stood there with his eyes wide open, his face full of surprise.

"Sir, I don't understand what is happening here, I was sent to bring in my report. What is happening?" He was protesting vehemently in smattering English until Clark shouted on him to shut up and to sit down. When he calmed down, Clark laid the evidence of his culpability before him. When Sergeant Sani Audu heard the recorded telephone conversation, he knew the game was over. He burst out in tears, begging and holding Clark's hands tightly until his hands were yanked away by the two guards.

"Please sir, I'm sorry, I don't know what got me into this, he never told me they will kill anybody, I swear, I don't know about what they wanted to do." He kept repeating himself and begging. Clark was relieved. It was good he was dealing with a man whose will could easily be broken. Not that resisting and denying will have made any difference anyway, save to waste precious time. Sergeant Sani Audu, was a police officer, he knew the procedures of interrogation at the headquarters. After seeing the evidence against him, he knew any resistance will only lead to unpleasant consequences and he will eventually be cracked. It was then Clark got him to cooperate in the trap to expose Mark's involvement in the killing of Sasha and in my kidnapping, in exchange for excluding him from prosecution for the murder of Sasha.

Sergeant Sani Audu went that day to meet Mark in the meeting place as arranged. However, he was no more there to complain about being denied a share from an additional ransom that was collected without his knowledge. He was there to do what Clark Stevenson sent him to do.

Sergeant Sani Audu went to meet Mark looking alarmed; he informed Mark that there was a new development to the investigation with the arrival of a team of five crack investigators from the Police Headquarters, Abuja. He told him that I had, during additional interrogation informed the new team of investigators that I could easily recognise the police officer that diverted me on the day I was kidnapped, if the person was brought before me. And because of that, there was to be an identification parade of all police officers serving at the Victoria Island Police Command. Sergeant Sani Audu told Mark in panic that he was sure he would be picked out if there was a parade, and if that happens, he knew he could not survive the torture without spilling the beans.

The only solution, as Sani Audu tried to encourage Mark, was for me to be eliminated. Mark categorically replied that he wouldn't have anything to do with it. Killing Sasha was already too heavy for him. Sani Audu assured him that he had no direct part to play in the killing. He just had to lure me to a hideout and hand over to him to do the job and later he will use his position to cover all traces. Mark didn't fully agree to the plan till they ended the meeting. However, Sergeant Sani Audu kept pressurizing him for the coming two days until he agreed to abduct me and hand me to him at a place they chose. Those were the days Mark's behaviour started to change towards me. The days he couldn't look at me in the eyes whenever we meet.

Clark wanted to close the investigations the day he listened to Mark's voice on the tape conversation admitting to the kidnapping (Sergeant Audu had a tape secretly hidden on his body the day he met Mark at the eatery. It was the same handset radio recorder that Clark gave me) but changed his mind when he later heard Mark being reluctant to kill me but agreeing to go along with the plan if his part was to only abduct and hand me over to be executed. It was then he saw no danger to my life, and a better opportunity to build a strong watertight case against Mark.

"The rest you are aware of Mr . . . I mean, SST." He smiled shyly; he was trying to get use to calling me with my popular initials. It was already dusk and he could see I was drowsy. I had not slept since the drama of my second abduction started.

"SST, I will have one of the drivers take you home. Your car will remain here for the time being. There are some devices we connected to it the day you came here. We want to have them removed. It was to help us effectively track you, should Mark decide on another line of action." He said. I was too tired to worry or care of what more secret devices they had on me.

"I have finished my report, and handed it over to the commissioner to carry on with the prosecution." Clark said.

He then looked at his wristwatch and added quickly; "my flight is expected in the next four hours, I have to get ready." He stood up and in the manner I was now used to, he extended his hand to me to shake, signalling the end of the meeting.

I was jolted by his remarks. I have come to see him in more light than before. He was now the person I could trust to really unravel all that was going on around me. "Why, can't you wait a little longer and see if there is anything more?" I asked.

"No, SST, as I told you the first time we met, I don't stay in a place more than two weeks." With that he gave me a wink. I followed the man he assigned to drop me at home to a waiting car outside.

Epilogue

The Motivational Speaker

I left the Lagos Police Command Headquarters that morning, depressed and worn out. I didn't know what to make of the events of the last 24 hours, and of the shocking revelations that came out of it. Whatever led Mark to all these must be more than the devil? I remembered what the Bible said about the strange things to understand about life, and one is the way of a man and a maid. Sasha, the shy, homely and pious acting girl; pregnant for Mark, her father's age mate, a church deacon and happily married husband to a preacher wife?

Life is full of mysteries, and who can tell what can come before him when we can't even understand what is going on around us?

In every man's life there would come a time of the ultimate challenge. When your strength, faith, your values and belief will be tested, when that time comes, how you react could make or mar your life forever. You need to be in control of your life. And you are able to get control of your life when you are able to get control of your spirit. Physically, you can have all that life has to offer while internally you are empty. Only God can fill you from the inside.

Mark, like some of us, could not gain control of his spirit.

I resumed work the next day, after taking the day of the incident off. It was surprising how news travels around. I mean bad news of course. The studio was besieged the next morning by hundreds of people coming from all nooks and corners of the city. Some were there to offer their congratulations on another of my narrow escapes.

And others of course, coming for one or two stories to pick from the incident. I don't want to talk of the number of phone calls I received on the matter. I had to suspend my broadcast a while because it seemed to centre only on one topic. It appeared listeners had nothing more to talk about than the strange happenings at Static FM. Despite the negative publicity the involvement of Mark in my kidnapping and the murder of a co-worker brought to us, we still moved on!

In fact, our popularity skyrocketed. You know what they say; all publicity is good publicity if you are in show business. We were in the show business!

Mark was arraigned before the courts for the murder of Sasha and staging my kidnapping. Dan Paul was of course released and absolved of all accusations and all the charges against him were dropped. Sergeant Sani Audu agreed to a lesser sentence to appear as a prosecution witness. His evidence landed Mark a life sentence and got him off with 5 years imprisonment. Really, I felt sorry for Mark, I still could not see how he fit the character of the hardened criminal he turned to be. I remembered what a man once said that a man's true character is what he would do if he knew he never would be found. That was the real character that was hidden from all, even from his family. The last time I heard of Mark's wife was that she moved up north to the city of Maiduguri to continue her ministry, and to be close to her husband who was serving his jail term there.

The Lagos State Police Commissioner, John Adams (sorry, for only mentioning his name now) was posted out of the Command immediately after the well-publicised trial. It was reported in the media as a normal administrative shake up. His actions, I mean his initial handling of the investigation, aside from nearly leading to the conviction of an innocent man, greatly embarrassed the Police Force. However, the Inspector General was able to redeem the face of the Force in outlining to the media of the remarkable efforts of his ace investigator, Detective Clark Stevenson in unravelling the mystery surrounding my kidnapping and the murder of the young lady.

What about Detective Clark Stevenson? I never got to meet him again, thank God for that! For I was told one only gets to see him when you are entangled in a high profile case. The last I heard about him, he was off to Bosnia as part of a United Nations international genocide investigation team.

As for me, the memories of what happened at Static FM became too much for me to bear and after sometime, I put in a notice for leave. Chief Dokubo and the management tried all they could to keep me with the studio but I had made up my mind. I was not running away from my calling and neither was I leaving the media, rather I was spreading my wings.

I want to becoming a freelance presenter to the media houses. Both the radio and television studios in Lagos now book for my services. I no longer belong to the employment of a single employer but open to the services of all the media houses, where I propagate my message of motivation to a greater height. I knew all what people need is the right word; they have all they needed in them to fulfil their destinies in life and be champions but someone need to speak positively to their lives.

Lagos presents a hard gamble for anyone that desires to make a positive change. I know it is easy to fix a situation when you can fix the people. However, Nigeria is a hard place for an honest person to survive. From the markets to the schools, from the working places to worship areas, the forces of corruption are devouring the fabrics of the society. But when the foundation is destroyed what then can the righteous do? In any society where hard work does not guarantee food on the table; intellect does not guarantee a place of vocation, reasoning does not guarantee a sit amongst the nobles, truth does not guarantee freedom from persecution, integrity does not guarantee acceptance, then they would all eventually cease to be virtues. And if the trend is not tamed, one day the best we might have around would be the less corrupt man.

A man of virtuous strength is nothing but a man of his environment.

All the same, I tried to continue with what I do best; winning the hearts of my listeners. After all, half of the things we do in life—we just do them; at the end it is result that determines opinions.

Nothing makes a man rich than open hands, nothing makes a man wise than open mind, nothing makes a man welcomed than open smile and nothing makes a man loved than an open heart. I was loved by the people of Lagos. And no longer was I, DJ SST, of the Motivation Dance Club, but rather insists on merely being called the motivational speaker wherever I appear in my shows. And from that time, I became known as the motivational speaker throughout the city. It is my calling, and my passion, and I was prepared to go anywhere with my message of motivation!

My relationship had improved considerably with Dan Paul. I had decided to put all that had happened behind me and move to a new beginning. And so when Dan Paul invited me to Star FM to deliver a motivational talk I didn't think twice of going to the place that I once swore never to set foot again!

I decided to use the occasion to deliver a short talk to millions of youths out there like me who might at one time been carried away by other desires and find themselves engaged in other activities, away from the great destinies God had fashioned for their lives.

"My dear listeners this is SST, the motivational speaker, as most of you have followed by history from Static FM when I was presenting the motivational dance club as DJ SST till now. Many of the youths must have seen it as a vocation, but it was not always like that with me. I was into several other vocations before I discovered my calling in life. And I would not want you to miss your destiny too.

So today, I will like to talk on; "ways of actualizing our destinies in life" I cleared my throat and started.

"God in His words said we are fearfully and wonderfully made. Each one of us carries an attribute that is fearful to our enemy, the devil, and one that is capable of producing wonders. God created all of us with great qualities to be stars; none is ever created empty. But we must prepare ourselves.

Stars are not born they are made, what they have in them is just the seed of greatness which is in every person created by God because we are created in His image. We carry the seed of greatness because we are in covenant with God. But covenants are spiritual contracts; we need to fulfill our part in God's plan for our lives because God's plan is only for those that play their parts.

The world is full of great destinies that are living a life of mediocrity; champions that are living as beggars, billionaires that are scratching to make a living, all because we lack preparation to be ushered into the great destinies God has for us. The best time to prepare for your destinies is at your youthful age. A baby is under the care of its mother, nobody cares to call a baby successful or great but as it grows it follows the path to its greatness which becomes clearer as it moves further.

In the youths in Lagos, I can see the rising stars of great industrialists, preachers, teachers, professionals and political leaders, but if they lack preparation they would end up nonentities with wasted destines! Bad decision and poor choices can lead you to lose all that God has for you. God has created trillions of shining stars and you are one of them, it's not whether you have a great destiny, it's there already; you only need to walk into it.

It doesn't matter if you are in a ghetto, because when your star starts shining, the world would come looking for you. However, for every great destiny there is a great opposition. The devil is not going to sit and watch you enter into the great destiny God has for you. The devil would mount a strong opposition to ensure you don't succeed. And one of such ways is to ensure you do not prepare.

God is a creator of champions; He is always on the lookout to producing champions. He is not constrained by age. David was a teenager when God anointed him. Bill Gates was just nineteen years when he left college to form Microsoft. God is not constrained by your history; many rich men you see today were little men of yesterday. God is not constrained by the circumstances of your birth whether you have rich parents or not. Obama was the son of an immigrant father from Africa whom he hardly knows and a school teacher.

God is not constrained by your qualification; Bill Gates never had a degree, the great inventor who had 1300 patent in his lifetime. Thomas Edison never completed schooling; he dropped out after some weeks. Bill Gates' was a drop out. Harry Ford the founder of Ford motors never went to school. God is not constrained by your disability; Helen Keller was born deaf and blind but ended with degrees and award as a prolific writer. Franklin Roosevelt was crippled by polio but still went on to rule the most powerful nation on earth. God is not constrained by the time you spent on the earth, Churchill and Ronald Reagan won elections when everybody thought they were too old for it. God is not constrained by whether you are good looking or ugly like me. Kennedy and Obama are handsome men but Abraham Lincoln who was greater than them all was not so good looking by most people's standard. God is not constrained by anything to make you a great person. He is only constrained by your belief. And when you lack belief you would lack preparation. You can only prepare for what you believe is possible. No matter how much you try, you can never prepare for what you don't belief in, because your spirit won't be involved.

No matter how powerful is the engine of a car when it starts it won't go anywhere if it has no tires. The car would just be making noise at a spot. No matter how great your destiny is, it won't carry you anywhere if you have no belief. It will just be static on one location; making noise in your mind—you know you can do this and that but you are not moving anywhere. Friends keep saying you can do better than that actress, you are a good mathematician ecetera and it ends there; moving round in small businesses and offices. You have the destiny to make a great manufacturer but you are left in a small business. You have the destiny to be a governor or president but you are left in a small office. When we lack belief in the great destiny planted in us, it can't move us anywhere. When we lack belief, we would also lack preparation, and without preparation we can't be ushered into our divine destiny.

When we lack preparation we would also lack the power to recognize opportunities, and without recognizing our opportunities we can't move into our divine destiny. God brings opportunities our ways whenever it's time for Him to actualize the great plan He has for our lives. But without preparation, we can't recognize our opportunities. Goliath's hostility was an opportunity for David; Potiphars wife's unbridled lust was an opportunity for Joseph, and because they had prepared, they were able to act correctly in the face of the opportunities.

Most times, opportunities come and we don't recognize them because we think opportunities must always portend something nice, easy or free. But most opportunities come in the form of demonic attacks—a desire to commit sin, the loss of a loved one, a disaster and many others. It is how we react to it that would open the path to our great destinies. We won't know how to react well if we don't prepare.

David didn't see Goliath as an opportunity to be king. David saw him as an opportunity to act according to his preparation. The soldiers thought that David was going to his death because they didn't know he had prepared. David prepared when no one was watching, he prepared when no one was there, he prepared when he tested his faith in God several times. And because he prepared, God utilized the little skill of a sling and stone to bring down a giant. David went to Goliath not because he wanted to fight for all to see, he went to Goliath not because he wanted to win awards, but he went to Goliath because his heart burned to stand for God. And God open him to his divine destiny.

Sometimes we fail in the test of our destiny when we fail to stand for God when it matters because we lack preparation. When they bring that bribe in the office you quickly join because you lack preparation. When you see your friends sleeping with their boyfriends, you quickly join because you lack preparation and by so doing you miss an opportunity to stand for God when it matters and be ushered into your destiny. Joseph was prepared to stand for God when he went to Potiphar's house. When the devil brought a test to destroy his destiny he didn't hesitate on what to do. His preparation quickly came forth. The devil led his brothers to sell him to slavery that led to him Potiphar's house and when all was well with him again he was thrown to more sufferings.

Joseph would easily have agreed to Potiphar's wife advances and maintained his privilege position in his master's house, but he had prepared and his preparation led him to take a stand. Many of us are still left in Potiphar's house enjoying the privilege of a head slave instead of being ushered to our grandiose destinies; because when the devil brought a test to us we lack the preparation to take a stand for God. God can't fulfil His part in your destiny when you fail in yours!

Some of us miss our great destinies because we fear a lot. We always fear. We fear to do what we can do. We fear what people would say. We fear what the outcome of our decisions would be. We are clouded by fear and so we allow great opportunities to pass us by. We fear because we lack preparation. Goliath was dead the moment he cursed God. God was waiting for a man that had no fear to bring him down. It doesn't need to be David, God has no favourites. He is not a respecter of man. The soldiers were afraid of Goliath. They were afraid of what they were seeing, because they lacked knowledge of what God has destined for them. They lacked knowledge because they lack preparation.

The soldiers were afraid because Goliath was a giant. They were afraid because he was carrying big weapons, and above all they were afraid because they lacked preparation. If they had prepared, they would have known that in the battle of destiny, weapon and size are not needed!

It doesn't matter whether you are born a giant or midget, from rich or poor parents, in poor neighbourhood or a rich district—it all does not matter! What matters is preparation. David was a teenager and the soldiers were men, they were experienced warriors but David was just a shepherd boy. They were with big weapons but David was with only a sling! But David was not afraid because he had prepared for his destiny.

What is it that is keeping you away from actualizing your great destiny? Are you afraid of facing the challenge because you see more talented people than you, or those you term as richer or greater in the enterprise and so you hide amongst the crowd like David's brothers? Where would Obama be today if he had feared that he was a black man and black men don't go to the White House? Where would Bill Gates be if he had feared that he had no money to start a business against the big corporations and all he could afford was his father's garage? I know there are amongst my listeners' young men and young ladies that could do great wonders like David, great achievements like Obama, and accrued great riches like Bill Gates but you need preparation!

Some miss out on their destinies because they listened to too much good advice! Oh, you can't do that! Oh, you don't have the capital, the brains, the family background, the support etcetera. And by following such advices, they miss out on their great destinies! David also had good advice like most of you are receiving from your family and friends. David's brothers even scolded him for thinking such foolishly. It was not that they hated him; they only thought they were thinking the best for him. They thought they should know better. They thought they were wiser, after all they were men and he was a boy, they had battle experience and he was a novice, he was just a shepherd boy. But David had prepared for his destiny. And because he had prepared the devil could not come in the form of good advice of his brothers to stop him. You alone can prepare for your destiny!

Sometimes your parents and friends good advice destroys your destiny. You are a natural debater, a future Rotimi Williams but when you see friends talking down on those doing arts, you follow them to the science class, you might be destined to be a great artist, but your parents want to see you a doctor, to them studying fine art is a failure! Or being an actress, a mechanic, a writer or whatsoever is not good enough for them. They want to see a doctor and so they drive you away from your destiny.

Pele's mother was against him playing football. She wanted him to be a school teacher and buy her a sewing machine. If you don't have preparation, the good advice of friends and family will drive you off your destiny. David would have gone away because he should obey his brothers. They were his seniors. However, he would have ended a shepherd all his life. Pele would have obeyed his mother and stopped playing football but he would have ended a school teacher called Edson Arantes do Nacimento all his life. He won't have needed the stardom name of Pele.

Many youths are taking the good advice of family and friends that would unfortunately lead them off their great destinies. I'm not against the advice of family and friends, in most cases it is the best for us. But we need preparation to know if it is the best for us.

Pele was not a wayward child; he obeys his mother always. However, he didn't obey her in this instance because he had prepared. David respects and obeys his brothers that senior him but he didn't obey them in this case because he had prepared. If you do not prepare, you will miss your great destiny. Many have lost their destinies from following the good advice of friends and family. And because we see it as a good advice, we don't even know when our destinies are destroyed.

Sometimes the good advice is from within. Because of what we see or what we hear around us we become intimidated and lose confidence in our natural abilities. We end up seeing ourselves as being too small and our abilities as being too inadequate, thereby limiting the power of God in our lives. We sometimes see ourselves as average people thereby bringing our God low. As a man thinketh in his heart so is he. Even God can't take us higher than we see ourselves.

Sometimes, we lose our destinies by thinking we are too smart. We lean on our own understanding. Joseph was a slave but a slave that had favour in the eyes of his master. He was even in a more favourable position when his master's wife cast her eyes on him. It was smart for a slave boy to see the benefit of being a lover to his master's wife and securing his place in the house, and would be foolish for him to refuse her and risk being thrown to the dungeons or even being killed. But Joseph refused to follow the devil's plans because he had prepared.

Many of us would find ourselves in the shoes of Joseph, it would be smart for you to be sleeping with your boss and get promoted than refuse him and be sacked. It would be smart for you to collect bribes on behalf of your boss than to refuse him and be sacked. Not only would it be smart to do so, it would also be beneficial as it comes with some rewards of promotion or monetary gains, but in the end you are selling your destiny unknowing. You will be left enjoying the crumbs of a favoured servant than sitting on the throne of your destiny.

Some of us lose our destiny because we kept looking at where we are coming from than where God is taking us to. Because you had been looking for job for so long and living in poverty, and all of a sudden, you land a job you never believed was possible. You then kept on looking at where you are coming from; you feared the past and so you are ready to do anything to remain where you have arrived. Because you fear losing the job you have now and going back to where you are coming from, you are ready to sleep with the boss, you are ready to alter records to remain where you are. And you succumb to all devilish plans to destroy your destiny because you lack the preparation required. If Joseph had kept his mind on the position he was at Potiphar's house before God lifted him up, he would have succumbed to his master's wife plan to seduce him and so lose his destiny but he had prepared. Many of us see the beginning without imagining the end because we lack preparation!

Sometimes, we sell away our destiny to the devil. We give up the greatness of God, for the corruption of the devil, because we lack preparation. We allow ourselves to sell our future for the pleasures of the flesh. Whenever the devil sees a great destiny about to rise that he can't destroy by death, he will corrupt it.

Adonijah was to be king. He was the first born and the devil knew that, so he corrupted his destiny with the pleasures of the flesh. He was filled with the desire of the flesh; his whole spirit was overcome by a desire to sleep with his sister Tamar. He didn't only lose his destiny to be king but died prematurely too! Many people today are dying prematurely for they had sold their lives to the devil for the desires of the flesh!

Destiny is time bound, when you sell away your destiny; you also bargain the time in it. The devil would exchange the years of your destiny for what he has given you. King Solomon said how sad it is for a man to die before his time. Many are dying before their time for selling away their destiny. God had a great destiny for you but before it would actualize, you shortened your life by sleeping with your neighbour's wife, or with a man that you are not married to, and by so doing miss your divine destiny.

Flesh destroys destiny more than anything in our lives because flesh is an extension of our souls. And our souls contain our years on earth. Sexual immorality affects your soul directly. Sexual immorality brings a curse of death that even God can't save you because He can't go against His words; the curse of the devil, the curse of loss of destiny, the curse of premature death!

With some of us, it's not that we don't prepare but our level of preparation is weak and it easily collapses on the day of adversity. The Bible says if your strength fails in the days of adversity, then your strength is weak! It's not that the adversity is too strong. It's not that the misfortune you are facing is too great. It's not that the loss you are facing is too heavy. It's not that the disappointment is too heavy to bear. It is just that your strength is too weak and so you faint in the days of adversity because you don't prepare. And if you lack preparation, the great destiny God has for you to be a great preacher, a great businessman, a great professional will all crumble in the face of adversities that must come along the way.

Abraham Lincoln before he entered politics said he will prepare and his time would come. And when he vied for elections he started on a string of losses, four at ago, but the disappointment didn't stop him. The adversities of the devil didn't make him faint because he had prepared, and he lived to be the president.

My friends, this is the time for you to start preparations to enter your destiny. David faced disappointment along the way but he didn't faint because his strength was strong, he had prepared himself. Many of us faint and give up in the face of adversities thereby coming short to entering our destinies. Maybe you are facing disappointment today at home, in school, at your working place and I bet you when you graduate from school and enter the world you will face greater disappointment and betrayals. It is the weapon of the devil to keep you away from your destiny. You would easily give up in your business, relationship, marriage in the face of disappointment when your strength is weak. You are weak when you lack preparation. Obama refused to give up! Churchill refused to give up! You too will not give up!

Another thing that would keep you away from your destiny is when you wonder away from your nest. God has prepared a great destiny for all His children, some to be great businessmen, some to be great industrialists, some to be great preachers, but many have wondered away from their nest wasting time where God has not called them.

The world is full of people that have wandered away from their nests, and when you wander from your nest, you wander away from God's plan for your life. The devil keeps people away from their nest because he knows in their nests are their great destinies. It's not that you are not working hard in that job that results are not coming—it is just that you have wandered away from your nest. You have the calling of a doctor but you ventured into law, my friend you could be successful and rich as a lawyer but you will never be great in it. No matter how hard a bird flies it needs a nest to be productive and without the nest it would waste energy hovering about until it drops. It might go and perch in someone else's nest but sooner than later it will be displaced by the owner of the nest. You are being outclassed in what you are doing because you are not in your nest; your business is collapsing because you are not in your nest. In your nest, you will be productive; in your nest you will be great, because your nest is your destiny.

Some of us fail in the test of destiny and that's why we don't actualize our destinies. God can do anything but one; He can't break His words! The devil knows; that's why he is the accuser of the brethren. He goes before God and says, God you want to make a great person out of her but see how she is going about sleeping with her lecturers for marks. Surely she doesn't deserve it and you can't go against your word, God!

Some of us don't prepare because we are busy watching and applauding instead of watching and appraising the success of others. Instead of using the success of great men as a support to our preparation, we are using it as a sport for our relaxation. We tied our destinies to idleness. You are watching that writer, that preacher, that film star and living in awe not knowing that the God that made them great would also make you so, if you prepare, because God has no favourites!

Some of us don't reach our destinies because we don't obey. God's promises of a great life looks too simple to be true. When Naamam the captain of the host of Syria went to the prophet Elisha, he told him to go and bathe in the waters of the Jordan; it looked too simple to be true. We are busy looking for a great task that would commensurate to a great reward. We are looking for a great secret to a great success. But God has no more secret than what He has given us in His words. He said pay your tithes and He will open the gates of Heaven for you, but you see it as too simple to be true. We miss our destiny because we refused to hear God's instructions to us. You can only hear someone when you walk in company of the person.

However, whenever God wants to talk to us we are always doing the wrong things, being at the wrong places or thinking of the wrong things. Thereby we miss the word of God, because He can't be where there's something wrong.

God talks to us through His words, through the mouth of His servants, and when we walk in spirit and in truth He further communicates to us through inspirations, ideas, and decisions, as He guides our steps. But because we fail to dwell in His presence and in His words we miss our steps. Sometimes, you see somebody taking what you feel is a funny action or talking of a funny idea but soon these funny actions or ideas become fantastic wonders! The person is acting on inspiration that brings powerful ideas to his thoughts. He is working with God.

Another reason we fail to prepare is because we fail to realise that the battle of our destinies is not against flesh and blood but against principalities and powers and rulers in the kingdom of darkness. Some places are full of demonic forces working against your destiny; you need to come out of them. Some activities are full of demonic forces working against your destiny; you need to come out of them. Some companionship are full of demonic forces working against your destiny, you need to come out of them. Some music and clothing's are full of demonic influence that would work against your destiny; you need to come out of them. The battle of your destiny is a spiritual battle my friend!

Sometimes, the over whelming influence of alcohol abuse is too much in your neighbourhood, you need to come out of them. Sometimes, the overwhelming influence of immorality is too much amongst your friends, you need to come out of them. Sometimes, the overwhelming influence of failure is too much in your communities, you need to come out of them. Sometimes, the overwhelming influence of premature death that aborts great destinies is too much amongst your people, you need to come out of them—to a new environment, to a new fellowship, to a new vocation! If you don't come out from them, your destiny won't come out because destiny is a divine substance that dwells in a clean environment. You are not yet strong to fight them, you need to come out of them. Walking in the spirit is the key to actualization of your destiny.

Sometimes the devil substitutes our destinies with counterfeits that further his kingdom. You had a great destiny to be a musician but the devil tells you singing for God is not profitable enough. The devil then diverts your gift to further his empire. You had a great destiny for organizational leadership but you use it to organize shows for the devil, you had a great destiny to be a great businessman, but you use it to further the devil's businesses thinking that is where the rewards come the most." I panicky checked my wrist watch, an hour had passed already; I must have overused my time. Maybe it's time to start putting in the last words to close the show.

However I could see the stage engineer and Dan Paul standing near the control panel, happily smiling and signalling to me to continue . . . and so I continued eagerly!

It is my calling! I am the motivational speaker!

Appendixes

Parlance Used in the Text

Wahala . . . . sufferings, problems, inconveniences.

Na today . . . . did it start today? It denotes an activity that is not new.

Shakara . . . . Putting on airs to impress a targetted audience.

Tokunbo . . . . Imported Second Hand Cars.

Na wa . . . . What a surprise!

Know better thing . . . . Conversant with the real things of life.

Ajero . . . . someone looking for a free meal.

Wetin . . . . What?

Okada . . . . Commercial Motorcycle rider.

Yunwa Shege . . . . Hunger is terrible.

Eko Ni Baje . . . . Lagos will be better.

Na so . . . . That's how it is done

Awuf de run belle . . . . Free gifts could lead to greater loss, cheap is expensive

Abeg . . . Please.

Ajegunle . . . Popular Lagos Ghetto Town.

Shine your eyes . . . . Be vigilant!

Gari . . . local cassava flakes.

Party na Lagos Get Am . . . Partying is the favourite activity of Lagos girls

Wetin Lagos People Wan Hear Sef? . . . . what do people of Lagos want to hear?

Oga . . . . used to indicate deference to a superior

Naira . . . . Nigerian currency.

Just de open my eyes . . . . I am getting wiser.

Wetin de . . . . what is happening or available.